WHITE MAGIC

The Origins and Ideas of Black Mental and Cultural Colonialism

By
CHUKWUDI OKEKE MADUNO

EKUMEKU COMMUNICATION SYSTEMS

"Rationalizing the slave trade eventually required Europeans to turn a self-blinded eye toward African life itself…."----John Henrik Clarke

"The book (***White Magic***) reinforces my writing efforts (OUR STORY: African/African American History appearing in newspapers and *Winsome Way* magazine). I read the book from cover to cover overnight due to this extraordinary phenomenon--almost unbelievable to me. Subsequent readings bring to the fore the validity of the theorem of "White Magic". I have followed the outline as given to me by Douglass Williams of the Source Book Store.

1. The images and meanings within the book are very startlingly drawn, explained and delineated for the informed individual. How we got to where we are is made quite clear. There is a poetry about the work, throughout, a rhythm, a crescendo built and achieved due to the fashion in which strains of historical events/social doctrine of the European/plasticity of the African cosmological-sociological reality are shown to be interrelated: cause and effect, so to speak. As defined and described, "*White Magic*" is a reality. One needs to be well read, however, to cope with the content of truths and challenges therein.
2. The author makes clear his arguments through the usage of historical facts and events, which occurred in various parts of the world and had affected Africa so seriously as to cripple, decimate and nearly destroy any vestige of her former self. The art with which the author weaves the historical factors together is really very excellent. There is a challenge to the reader constantly – to review history and thereby find reaffirmation of the theorem of "White Magic". One who is in the act of 'overcoming' is strengthened. One who needs to act, will, I am sure.
3. The outline of the book is straightforward and clear in its development. The detailed format enable the reader to refer to a particular sub-section readily for reference, review or clarification.

MY CONCLUSIONS ON THE BOOK

One who has read extensively of the books footnoted in the text will have no trouble identifying with the author's arguments of the existence of "White Magic". The footnotes are very well written, and are amplified where the author felt this was needed, an excellent technique. The bibliography is quite first rate and deserving of the attention of the bibliophile.

Inasmuch as most African Americans are illiterate concerning the true factual history of our ancestral home as well as the factors which brought about the commercial and industrial revolutions, the book is certainly not for the 'average' African American who is under the spell of "White Magic". It is the task for other writers (like me) to propagate, in easy-to-read and primary-level fashion, the historical facts, beginning with Kemet, wherever and however we can. "White Magic" is a theorem of value and substance for serious thinkers and actors of today and the future"----- Edwina Chavers Johnson, EdD (ABD)
February 16, 1995
Atlanta GA.

SECOND EDITION

Published By Ekumeku Communication Systems
EKUMEKU Universal Foundation Number 001
Second Edition* Second Printing

Second Edition: ISBN 0-9644596-0-4
First Edition: ISBN 1-56411-085-0

Printed in the United States of America

Library of the New Age Mission of Nzoputa Uwa

TABLE OF CONTENT

DEDICATED TO:

The memory of Chancellor Williams
(***Chikwado Nwalimu***)
A true son of **Kemet**
A true fighter of the people

He's one with a vision
One who fought for the People
One who lived his life for the People

The one that practiced what he preached
And died that we may live
A true Ancestor!

The Truth is our Savior!

PREFACE FOR THE SECOND EDITION

When this book was first published in 1994 (of the Christian Calendar), the reaction towards ***White Magic*** was silence; while the book was at the same time in serious demand. Within a year after the book was published, the author began to receive many private letters and review articles published in Newspapers and Magazines with regards to the content of the book from many states in the U.S.A. The most rewarding letters were those written by inmates from different correctional facilities within the country. Amongst the letters being received was a review article written by a senior citizen, and an experienced African American Scholar, Edwina C. Johnson, who later became a member of the Ekumeku Universal Foundation. From the numerous letters written to the author, not one person disagreed not just with the contentions of the book but also with the theory itself. The book, no doubt, has done what was intended for it to do. It is now a document of history that can be used to understand the thought process, the how and why the people we call the *Ekwueme People of Truth* came into existence.

The Theory of *White Magic* is fundamental in understanding why the *Ekwueme* came into existence. But it is what happened after the text was published that had changed the history of the human life. The problem of White Magic has not only affected the ecology of the planet but also has affected human morality and can only be resolved with a new human paradigm. This new human paradigm of the *Ekwueme* is necessary for the neutralization and restoration of the much needed delicate balance for the continuously unfolding of life in the universe.

According to the European definition of white magic, "it is the miraculous force of the imagination through faith and love". This was quoted in the preface of the first edition and was countered immediately to prepare the reader for the apprehension of the new meaning which my work was set out to bring into being. If we study the book very carefully, we will recognize that I had defined the idea of white magic as an extreme materialistic force; whereas the idea of black magic which the European tradition always define generally as "magic in league with the devil" was defined by me as an extreme spiritualistic force. The same approach is applicable to many of the important terms used in the book. Most of those words were carefully chosen after meditation on them to convey the inner vision that is being expressed in the book. For example, it is a common practice for people to use the term "slaves", as at the time when this book was first written, without thinking about the implication of the word. But Africans were not slaves *per se*; rather, they were enslaved by the Europeans and Arabs, among others. I strongly believe that nobody has a right to call fellow human beings "slaves" without qualification. Such derogatory label would imply that slavery is a natural state of the Africans as opposed to it being a socially imposed prescription and of which the condition ought to be qualified with historical facts.

As we can see from the cover of this second edition, the idea of changing the name of our beloved continent has been cultivated for many years now and was championed by the movement of **Nzoputa Uwa**. For we believe that despite the initial conceptual difficulties that this might introduce, the name ***Kemet*** is the most appropriate identity and it would inevitably facilitate a better understanding of our continental heritage, image and history. However, for the purpose of clarity and to be consistent with the intellectual impulse upon which the book was originally written, we shall continue to use the terms Africa, Africans, African Americans, etc., as they were used in the first edition except where we found it necessary to introduce the new name **Kemet**. The name **Kemet** should be identified in history with the emergent New Africa and should be one of the distinguishing features that would separate the New Africans from the Africans that were discussed in this text. But for a detailed understanding of how the name evolved in the consciousness of the mission of *Nzoputa Uwa*, we encourage all that are interested to study the text, ***NZOPUTA UWA: The Holy Ankhuwa Abstracts Vol. 2***. Our intention in this second edition is not to produce a text that is fundamentally different from the first edition, except where it is necessary to separate the New Africans who are now known as the Kemites from the conceptual understanding of the generality of Africans.

Therefore, White Magic is a phenomenon that is diametrically opposed to the interdependent order of the universe. This is because it exists in a state of imbalance and tension. White Magic is evil. It is the practice of hypocrisy, inequality and white supremacy. It is deception in the true sense of the word. It is extreme materialism. White Magic is an illusion; but it has a temporal power. The temporary nature of the power of White Magic also underlies its ability to dehumanize, degrade or deform human potentials and possibilities. White Magic is the weapon used to enslave and colonize Africans. White Magic is the weapon used to create a master-servant relationship between the oppressed and the oppressor. It is through White Magic that the patterns of relationship between the haves and have-nots were created and are being perpetuated. White Magic underlies the governing principles of the modern world which have permeated the internal fabrics of human society and its institutions. Thus, White Magic is the dominant ideology of the modern world. White Magic is everything that discourages human freedom because it is predicated on limiting the expression of what it truly means to be human within the confines of extreme materialism. White Magic is disorder because it allows preaching to exist without practice.

The guiding principle of White Magic is self-hatred. Those who are actively affected by White Magic suffer from inferiority complex which makes them to be ashamed of their heritage, phenotype, language and way of life. They suffer from identity crisis and are unwittingly anti-African. In their anti-African hysteria, many seek to be more European than the European. Victims of White Magic have less value for the African phenotype. Some even would go to the extent of surgically altering their appearances in order to conform to the ideological premises of what it means to be human in the world of White Magic. This may include certain surgical procedures to thin their noses, lips, etc.

The idea of white supremacy is an outgrowth of White Magic. The notion that one group within the human family was created to dominate humanity and to rule the assumed "lesser breed" forever because of the whiteness of the skin underlies this idea of white supremacy. But it goes further because the idea of white supremacy hinges on the alleged black inferiority. The notion of white supremacy cannot be functional without the propaganda that promotes the false theories of black inferiority. Through the agency of White Magic, everything that is assumed to be good is whitened. This projects an inflated view of a world which is not only defined by European or Western civilization but also a world which makes the European culture the standard or frame of reference for judging other cultures. When comparing the contributions of the ancient cultures and civilizations, the Greek and Roman civilizations become the true glory and grandeur of the past.

White Magic whitens everything through television and print media; while at the same time, it is used to create negative images of the African people and about Africa. The Europeans are constantly being projected as the model of excellence; while the people of the African descent are portrayed as undesirable, as buffoon, as ignorant and as backward. Through White Magic there is this tendency by the Europeans to distort the facts of world history and the narratives of human civilization in order to falsely exalt themselves as they make claims of being the original cultivating progeny of all the good things in human civilization.

The educational systems in the modern world are the mirror images of White Magic. The prevailing tendency is always to discount the contribution of the people of African descent in human development and this is achieved through the manipulation and control of the false African image that had been created by the Europeans. It is through White Magic that everything meaningful in the continent of Kemet has been stolen under the false imposed African image. Even the ancient civilization of Kemet was almost stolen by the Europeans because of White Magic. According to the prescription of White Magic, the inferiority of the African people is a foregone conclusion which justifies why there can never be any serious development in Africa without outside influence. The so-called Africans have been humiliated, abused, and degraded because of White Magic. They were made to be nothing. This has made the African the laughing stock of the world. Even decent people laugh at the African in his or her face as a fool. Even the African himself or herself has lost faith in his ability to be human. This is why the continent of Africa is conceived as nothing but a waste land that is yet to be blessed with the glory and grandeur of human civilization and yet the Truth is that human civilization began from the continent of Kemet. The Truth of world history was whitened under the banner of the religions of Faith and we the people of Kemet were made to assume the false image of an Africa that never was. But we are not Africans, instead, we are the Kemites. White Magic is the enemy and our beloved continent must no longer be identified from the point of view of foreigners and invaders. The African image of our beloved continent has been false from its origins and we now have totally rejected it. We must reject the false African image and embrace the emergent Kemetic self-definition. Those who follow in the footsteps of the Chosen One of Nzoputa Uwa have since transcended the false African image and have realized the self-definition of the Kemetic World Identity.

Without any doubt, White Magic has no real power because it is an illusion. We all should know that what is destroying human morality and the ecology of the planet is White Magic. *It is extreme materialism* that is now the problem of all humanity. Our enemy is White Magic and not white skin and we are determined to neutralize White Magic by spreading the Spirit of EKUMEKU to all humanity. This underlies the basic mission of the Ekumeku Universal Foundation. White Magic is a phenomenon that would pass away through the advent of EKUMEKU. But it is almost impossible to overcome White Magic unless the human spirit understands how it works and what it represents. There is no human spirit who can escape the demoralizing effect of White Magic without attaining a devotion of purpose to the supreme principle of EKUMEKU.

This Theory of White Magic rejects idle superstitions or dogmas regarding the African humanity or culture and denounces the uncritical acceptance of *anti-Africanism* by introducing a new human paradigm in the project of restoring harmony and balance on the planet. The basic thesis of White Magic is the idea that the problem of the African humanity is White Magic which has created the many patterns of black mental and cultural colonialism. The argument in the book implicitly beckons every so-called African person to justify his or her humanity. It can be stated this way: If the Africans insist that they are human, what are the values upon which their humanity can be justified? It is easy to blame others for your African condition, but reality shows that you have neglected the fundamental principles necessary for you to justify your humanity. Now that we have changed the name of our beloved continent from Africa to Kemet, we shall control and defend its image and must be ready to challenge whosoever shall oppose this important justification of our humanity. The lesson of the past five hundred years has shown that anyone can abuse and exploit Africans because the so-called Africans are divided into different little kingdoms of little minds. Indeed, White Magic is a spell of doom which has altered the thought patterns of the African people. No doubt, the Africans are their own worst enemy because of the spell of White Magic.

In conclusion, what is the future of humanity if the people of African descent become extinct? What is the divine challenge for the future of humanity? We the ***Kemites*** are awoke to the destructive forces of White Magic and have answered the call to serve humanity in Truth and Justice.

PREFACE

The primary purpose of this book is neither to condemn nor to condone. Its goal is to expose readers to the conditions of Africans both in the continent and in the Diaspora, to the historical, cultural, and psychological realities upon which they were born, to infuse meaning to the factors underlying their contemporary conditions and to create an awareness of forces that have affected their present existence. It is my view that the present mental and cultural conditions of Africans cannot be adequately interpreted, if close attention is not given to the historical factors that gave birth to the modern world--and the role Africa and Africans have played in its evolution.

In this historical epoch, it is arguable that the average African's frame of reference is not centered within the dimensions of objective and subjective guidelines of the religious, political, historical, cultural and economic interactions of Africa with the outside world. So, the searching question becomes: Why is the African's perception of reality not centered within the web of thought that grew out of the African people's existential universe? Or to put it another way, why are things the way they are?

The paradox of the concept race, its effect on the cultural outlook of the African people, and its subsequent interplay on the mental universe of the average African's conceptualization of the modern world is thus the focal point. This book is further intended to emphasize the undeniable unity of the African experience and the similarities of historical forces which have affected the nature of the dilemma under which the African people were born. We arrive at the point of departure when the forces that influence social conditions are analyzed and explained for the average individual. Until this is done, there is no meaningful corrective measure, in terms of improvement, that can be taken to alleviate such social problems. Consequently, the intent is to stimulate thought and provide meanings to the emerging corpus of theoretical reference structures necessary in understanding the mental and cultural conditions of the African people.

In this book, the terms "Black" people and African people are used interchangeably because they represent or have represented the overall historical pattern by which Africans at one time or the other have been known. The use of the term African people is based on the premise that all black people are Africans; and also, that all African people were one people in their general worldview, religion, culture, social law, legal system, and kinship. I have thereby approached the themes in the book from the standpoint that all African people are one people, and that whatever differences that may seem to exist between Africans—in terms of language, geographical distance, religious belief, philosophical outlook, etc.—are more or less products of the historical panorama of Africa and Africans.

This thesis is the germinated seed of my intellectual reaction to the precarious and traumatic nature of the mental and cultural socialization with which Africans have been encumbered. It is my revulsion to this state of existence of the African people that has given me no peace. In other words, it is the introspective and mundane encounters of incongruous forces by an African who has found the modern world in a bubbling cauldron of stupendous monomania. I have pondered some of the issues, raised in this book, ever since I was a youngster growing up in the midst of forces I could not understand. My parents and teachers alike could not provide my youthful, but inquisitive, mind with coherent or at least justifiable explanations for an understanding of this neurotic condition. I was forced to accept a philosophical ideology of life that negated my natural aspirations for a fulfilled and dignified life, and equally made me more or less an unrealistic dreamer in a distorted make-believe world.

I remember quite clearly the attitudes of many Africans in Nigeria with regards to those traditional religious custodians who stuck to their guns and continued to practice the traditional African Religion. These Euro-Christianized and Arabized Islamic Africans attempted to make me believe that the Africans who practiced the traditional forms of the African God-concept of spiritually were "pagans" who worshipped the "devil", and that they must repent and be converted to the so-called "true" religions.[1] As youngsters, we were indoctrinated to despise and see these proud Africans as agents of the devil. In accordance with such debasement, the indigenous African culture to which they conformed was made taboo, something that must be scorned and despised.

Instead of accepting the alien cultural debasement of my African heritage, I questioned the validity of such disparagement and degradation of the African culture. It was hard for me to understand why Africans had to be enslaved because they were neither practicing the Christian nor the Muslim religions. Why, in fact, Africans have to wait for the Eurasians to show them the way to the "true" religions. In primary and secondary school, whenever, reference was made of the Supreme Being in the African Religion, he (she) was always written in small letters. But when the textbooks discussed the Christian and Muslim supreme deities, capital letters were the rule. This made me more puzzled and confused.

As the ever-present graphic descriptions of "heaven" and "hell" became the bases upon which alien religions of Europe and the Arabian Peninsula were compared to the African Spirituality by the zealot alien cultural agents, I began to question them about my ancestors who were neither Christian nor Muslim. I would always ask: Given that my ancestors were neither Christian nor Muslim, have their souls rested in peace in heaven or hell? Tactful ones would find a way to answer my questions without implicating their religious beliefs. Some of them would say, since my ancestors were not leveraged to practice the "true" religion before their death, that their God would give them another chance to eternal life by reincarnating them again to the world. Whilst some others would tell me that each and every one of my ancestors had been in hell suffering for their unbelief. Now it seems to me, that the zealot cultural agents wanted to indoctrinate me into the ever growing blind crowds of Africans who worship the popular alien created images of the human mind. Conversely, I have never quite believed wholeheartedly the psycho-cultural religious beliefs that have the concept of "God", "angels", and all the good guys as white, whilst the concept of the "devil" and all the bad guys were portrayed as black. But these religions' degradation and debasement of the African Spirituality did make definite impressions on my mental and cultural universe.

Based on my growing understanding of the antagonistic nature of this ideological disparagement of Africa and other aspect of the African conditions, it became very cogent to me that there is an inter-connection of various features precipitating the African people's understanding of the modern world. Consequently, over the years, spurred by tireless intellectual pursuits, I have strived to discern many of the recurrent patterns of behaviors and prevalent conditions that have evoked my intellectual curiosity and puzzlement as suggestive of a larger force.

Therefore, the Theory of White Magic evolved out of my understanding that the European and Arabian ideologies, attitudes, and political, cultural, economic, and religious developments were based on the success of a spell of doom—White Magic---cast on Africans to alter their thought pattern. Wherefore, the Theory of White Magic should not be misconstrued in the same vein Europeans have used the term "Black Magic" and as they had applied historically their own theory of black magic. This is because White Magic is not only an abstract concept but also a concrete phenomenon that focuses on the African world experience; and how it has affected and influenced the extreme materialistic tendencies of the European development as a dominant force in the contemporary world.

In other words, White Magic is not humane. It is not the "miraculous force of the imagination through faith" and love, as some European writers have needlessly strived to assert.[2] Instead, White Magic is characterized by the materialistic extremities of greed, hate, jealousy, deceit, etc., that function as a brute force; and it has been used to subjugate and subordinate the Original People to an inferior status within the human family.

No doubt, the European's attitude and their understanding of the African world is eloquently engrossed in their definition of "Black Magic". It is the oft-repeated cliché that represents the adulteration of everything African. So that black magic was degraded and defined as "magic in league with the devil", precisely as anything that connotes evil, agony and backwardness.[3] It is the maddening fantasy of black negativity, such as the stereotypical notions of African's witchcraftism, fetishism, cultural childishness, and occultism. Whereupon, the depictions of the African character as trivial, devilish, and useless were imposed as "universal" truths. Blackness was indeed made to represent the embodiment of nothingness. These are, in fact, the over two thousand years old ubiquitous legacy of black degradation, devaluation and defamation.

Nevertheless, the effects of these assumptions on the African have been unbelievably profound. He has unquestionably accepted and adopted the European debasing nuances toward his heritage, and thus began his degeneration. As he began to despise his heritage, he developed a bitter hatred towards the virtues of his nature and lived a life bent on blind and disgusting imitation of his supposed mentors. Therefore, he became an object of caricature, an empty vessel, a buffoon, a sycophant, and a joke on humanity. On the contrary, however, we must not overlook the fact that if a lie is told often enough people would begin to believe it.

White Magic therefore is the mental and cultural state of most African people. It is the anti-African hysteria which has created and nurtured the patterns of black mental and cultural colonialism. This has been the effect of the Eurasian cultural bigotry and white supremacy on the African people.

Undauntedly, the panacea to this state of existence (violence, poor health, self-destructive behavior, intellectual and material dependence) amongst African people is sought upon the understanding that this is the congruent symptom of a deeper malady—a malady of the soul. For, it is the by-product of the ferocious human degradation, isolation, and the economic, religious and political chicanery upon which Africa and Africans have been subjected. Thereupon, the basic theoretical assumption of White Magic is grounded upon the idea that the European's imposition of the supremacy of whiteness has created a psychological negation towards blackness, especially by the African people.

One such assumption is that the principle of self-preservation as the supreme law of nature does not apply to most Africans. For one can only be capable of preserving self, if one knows one's self. The point of this argument is that White Magic is a malady or mental poison that inculcates a sense of self-disdain and self-alienation to its African victims.

Thus, the perceived antidote is that the process of self-preservation can only be accomplished by those who know themselves. Given that the prerequisite for self-preservation is the knowledge of self, White Magic becomes a fundamental root of the malady because it is predicated on depriving Africans the knowledge of self. Consequently, the end result has been the prevalence of self-destructive behavior amongst Africans over behavior that enhances self-preservation.

A second assumption is that since the mechanics of Eurasian racism is based on such superficial as the skin color, all African people are presumed victims of racism, directly or indirectly. Thus far, given this view point, it is upon this parameter that all African people generally are considered to be under the yoke of imperialism. (This also includes those Africans who have collaborated or are currently in partnership with the European power elites in the exploitation of Africa and Africa people around the world.) This approach is accentuated by the ethics of imperialism which are governed by the cultural, social, educational, economic, religious and political trappings of the imperialists. For, in order to rationalize not only the enslavement of Africans but also their dehumanization, fantastic theories of race were developed. For example, it was espoused that humanity are of two kinds, the superior and the inferior. The inferiors were supposedly divined by God to work for the superiors, for the enhancement of "the great and impassable gulf fixed by the Creator at the foundation of the world".[4] In other words, the superiors were allegedly the God's children created in the image of God and empowered by God to govern all of his creations. This pseudo-intellectual assumption of the African inferiority gained an incredible acceptance in the nineteenth century of the Christian era and has ever since been the ethical backbone of Eurasian imperialism. The sum total of my argument is based on the premise that White Magic has been racist in thinking and imperialistic in practical terms.

In writing this book, I have recognized that the overriding factor underlying the African people's state of existence is a myriad of forces, impregnated by the interplay of incongruent historical marginality and impacted by the African's overall contemporary economic, social and political conditions. Beyond all that, however, the book becomes a debunking motif, committed to reveal the bases of the deceptions and manipulations constantly at loggerheads with the mental liberation of the African people.

I do not, by any means, profess to have all the answers. Neither have I yet encountered a human personality who claimed to have an absolute monopoly to the knowledge of the universe. However, I believe that the Truth shall speak for itself. For, I am essentially doing what the circumstances of my birth as an African have impelled me to do. In sum, it is to say that this book is intended to expose within the limits of my intellectual capability the patterns of distortion, suppression, and debasement of the African character in the development of the world.

Blessings of Hotep (Peace)!
Chukwudi Okeke Maduno

NOTES FROM THE PREFACE

1. The term African God-concept of spirituality is introduced here as the most appropriate name for the African Spirituality and metaphysics as opposed to the term religion. In most African languages, there is no word for "religion" as we know it. This term embraces not only the unity and diversity found in the African cultural experience, but also demands the attention it deserves as the prototype of all human metaphysics.
2. Joseph Ennemoser, "White Magic and Truth", *The History of Magic,* Volume II(translated from the German by William Howitt), New Hyde Park, New York: University Books Inc., 1970, pp. 219-220; see also, Alice A. Bailey, *A Treatise On White Magic,* New York: Lucis Publishing Company, sixth edition 1956.
3. *The American Heritage Dictionary,* New York, N.Y.: Dell Publishing Co. Inc., second edition, p.73
4. *Quoted in James Weldon Johnson,* "The Autobiography of an Ex-Coloured man", *Three Negro Classics,* New York; Avon books, 1965 (C: Alfred A. Knopf, Inc. 1972), p. 498.

CHAPTER ONE
THE FORCES OF THE MODERN WORLD

"Rationalizing the slave trade eventually required Europeans to turn a self-blinded eye toward African life itself. If Africans were accursed and inferior, so the implicit argument ran, then they could not have produced anything that was not inherently inferior and accursed. Europeans in general held the view that slavery in the New World was better than "savage barbarism" in Africa." [1a]

----John Henrik Clarke

"The battle was first waged over the right of the Negro to be classed as a human being with a soul; later, as to whether he had sufficient intellect to master even the rudiments of learning; and today it is being fought out over his social recognition". [1b]

----James Weldon Johnson.

O Mother **Kemet**!
Whence did the centuries gone by?
The good ol' days that are no more
Your children thine cried
But alas!
They had been taken away from you
In your presence,
They were called half-devil and half-monkey.

The mistakes of their fathers
They paid with their blood, labor, and sweat.
Enslaved and colonized,
They were treated as wild animals
Wild beasts that were-
Incapable of being tamed and domesticated
Lo! They cried out to their mother
Why have they forsaken us?

Brutalized and dehumanized,-

They rejected thee.
And sought comfort in the God of their oppressor.
Behold, they lifted their face in sorrow.
And they prayed to their oppressor's God for protection.
Nay…
The oppressor's God said to them
Thou shall first lose thy Kemetic identity.
Reject thy originality:
Bleach thy skin, conk thy wooly hair
Lest thou become the servants of my children.
In serving my children,-
Thou shall be honored
Honorary white I shall make thee.
Second class white in your deeds and thoughts
Thou shall become the African that never was
The ego-trip and effigy of my children

Mother **Kemet** is weeping
She is crying
And wailing
For her children
Beckoning unto them to come back to her
In the spirit of MAAT for the sake of Truth.

----Chukwudi Okeke Maduno

I. INTRODUCTION

If one takes into consideration the overall image of Africa over the past five centuries, it will seem that the continent has a monopoly on negative controversies. But when one probes more deeply, it becomes apparent that the penchant for self-fulfilling prophecies has been the motivating force behind the controversial negative image of our beloved continent. The result has been the perennial one sided-view on the entire spectrum of the African life. Such has been the classic legacy of historical dynamics in Africa. Some of the manifestations of these misleading controversies range from the European fables of Africa as a "Dark Continent" (superimposed as Nothingness), and the concomitant or normative idea of Africans as a "Lost Race", to the question of whether Africans have the intellectual capacity for governing themselves.

In the ideological sphere, many of these self-fulfilling prophecies or controversies have since become entangled in the vibrant mechanisms of oppression, exploitation and domination. Thus, these misleading controversies have conditioned, constrained and predisposed certain understanding of most African phenomena.

The understanding of these one-sided controversies is exceedingly important today because the various impacts they had on Africa and Africans have continued to validate and demean the contemporary image of the African world. In short, the African image and integrity have been tremendously distorted and deformed by these premeditated wild speculations that the African is yet to fully recover from their compounding effects. Yet this fact is rarely taken into account by those who deemed themselves competent to study the contemporary African world experience. Indeed, except on few instances, the misleading European stereotypes of Africa have remained the bases for the conceptualization of Africa's image.

The main features of the foregoing discussion will constitute the point of departure in this text. In view of the causative implications of the controversies about Africa, the entire African's modus of existence have been constructed to suit the conceptions and self-interests of certain groups within and outside of Africa to become one of the most discussed continental regions in the modern world. Nevertheless, one is bound to ask: Have the subject matters of most of the controversial issues that relate to Africa clouded and muddled the image of Africa? Or, have these issues been detrimental to the survival ability of Africans, as one people. Also, can one say that some of these controversial issues have given better understanding to the conditions of the Africans? Given the tremendous perplexity of these controversies, it is not at all surprising that there is a multiplicity of views concerning the interpretations of these controversies. But what had been striking about these divergent views are the representations of three particularistic pre-eminent belief-systems that are diametrically opposed to each other in their construction and propagation of the African image.

These three different belief-systems are not only deep-seated in their different visions of the world, but can be categorized into three distinct images, i.e., Euro-centric, Arab-centric and African-centric. As the Euro-centric and Arab-centric images seem to have been dominant in Africa during the modern era, they have also contributed immensely to the development of the one-sided image of Africa that makes negative controversy a desired African way of life. Not only have these opposing images helped to shape the way Africans view world, they have also molded the underlying psychology of non-Africans in their interactions with Africans, whether in the Continent or in the Diaspora. Hence, the relative factors that have induced this imposed African reality go well beyond the realms of history, religion, economics, and politics. Rather, these factors constitute an amalgamation of various imbalanced forces that have encompassed all spheres of the entire African people's modus of existence.

In sum, these controversies have aptly dominated discussions of Africa and on Africans over the past five centuries. Therefore, they have influenced, to a large extent, the emergence of the contemporary image of Africa. This image of Africa arguably leads one to ask certain types of questions, seek certain types of answers and apply certain types of methodology when studying the phenomenology of the African's past and present. Consequently, the resultant conclusions drawn have inevitably encouraged and enhanced the perpetuation of this image of Africa and Africans. The outcome has been a gross misrepresentation and misinterpretation of the different roles our beloved continent had played in both the ancient and the modern world. The intellectual precursors of this image, misperception and misrepresentation, have therefore helped to shape this painstaking reality of our continent and its people. Similarly, through the labyrinth of time, this pervasive African bastardization has undercut, impeded and muddled the idea of a balanced interpretation of the historical authenticity of Africa and Africans. Thus, the overall outcome has encapsulated both literally and figuratively the persistent depiction of blacks as unfit and inferior human stock.

II. THE AFTERMATH OF GRAECO-ROMAN'S SOJOURN TO AFRICA

Historically, the derogatory depiction of blacks as unfit and inferior human stock had begun before the birth of Christendom. When the relatively backward and materialistic Greeks conquered ancient Kemet, they did not in any form feel superior to our ancient Kemetic ancestors; rather, they were overwhelmed by their own inadequacies. But the sophistication and spiritual nature of the ancient Kemetic civilization must have kindled a pathological hatred and inferiority complex amongst the ancient Greeks and Romans, that some of them found it necessary to counteract its effect on them after they conquered ancient Kemet by depicting blackness as an abnormality. This was the inordinate psychological and cultural inadequacies felt by the ancient Greeks, who were consistently referred to as 'children in spirituality' by the ancient Kemites, and later also by the Romans on their encounters with the cultural and physical ancestors of the present–day African people. This seething and deep reaction was bottled up by the mere fact that they lacked the natural ability to reasonably produce melanin, a serious factor for skin pigmentation, and compounded by the Kemetic ingenious development of a superior civilization that was grounded and organized on an in-depth understanding of the universe.

Heretofore, the influence of the ancient Greeks and Romans in the war against black imagery has immensely been underestimated. We have been indoctrinated to believe that this war was influenced by the political and economic prerogatives of the Europeans at the turn of the seventeenth century C.E. (Common Era or Christian Era). Nevertheless, now it has been increasingly clear, that the core of the problem between the Kemites (blacks) and non-Kemites (mostly the so-called whites) has been nothing but a concerted and deliberate effort to distort the origins of the legacy built by the ancient Kemites upon which the entire humanity have gained their salvation and knowledge of the universe. Thus, the Kemetic cultural universe as exemplified in ancient Kemet or what the Europeans call ancient "Egypt was the center of the body of ancient wisdom and knowledge, religious, philosophical and scientific spread to other lands through student initiates".[I] So, it was in the continent of Kemet that the fundamental precepts of the world civilization were invented: writing, medicine, philosophy, religion, astronomy, astrology, agriculture, mathematics, law, engineering, etc. There is no doubt that these significant inventions were not only the unequaled achievements of our ancient Kemetic ancestors; but, also that the evident impact of these discoveries had single-handedly helped to move humanity further away from prehistoric and uncultivated cultural existence.

For more than five thousand years, before the Christian Era, the ancient Kemites of the Nile Valley (ancient Kemet proper, Nubia, Kush, etc.) presided over the most complex philosophical system yet founded by the human spirit—MAAT or the supreme value of life—and made it a secret order. This Maatic system of supreme righteousness was based on a spiritual goal as opposed to a materialistic goal: The transformation of the human spirit to the broadest and highest possibilities of what it means to be a human being par excellence by striving to gain the knowledge of the highest Truth in the universe. Conversely, in order to be enrolled in the quest for self-knowledge—Know Thy Self—one must first be initiated, and this initiation had been based upon a ritual and an oath for secrecy. Thus, it was only the initiates who had sworn the oath of allegiance and had undergone all the necessary rituals that participated in the intellectual and spiritual exercises of mastering the governing laws of the universe.

This concept, "Man, Know Thy Self", was later attributed to Socrates (470-399 B.C.E.); but this concept which Socrates translated into Greek as "Gnothi Seuaton" is at least four thousand years older than Socrates. Not surprisingly, the now revered Socrates was "persecuted" by his people for teaching a version of the ancient Kemetic Philosophy. Hence, this philosophy has been part and parcel of the Kemetic socio-cultural complex before there was Greece. As a result the inscriptions, "Man, Know Thy Self" were inscribed in all entrances of the Holy Temples in the Nile Valley culture areas, many have survived to this day.[2]

In addition, it was based on the oath for secrecy and the practice of esoteric sciences that the ancient Kemet was known to the ancient world as the "Land of Mysteries" and the "Land of Gods". However, after many thousands of years the "House of Life" or "Mystery System" in ancient Kemet began to admit non-Africans (Eurasians) for the first time. The clamor by non-Kemites to study in ancient Kemet during the ancient time corresponded with many of the accounts of the ancient writers who documented the idea 'that ancient Kemet was not only the Holy Land but the Holiest of Lands or countries and that indeed the Gods dwelt there.'[3]

In the fourth century, 332 B.C.E., Alexander II, son of Philip of Macedonia, waged a successful military campaign against the Royal Kingdom of ancient Kemet and having defeated the two contending powers from imperial Assyria and Persia, he had limited obstacles taking over the kingdom of ancient Kemet. It must be noted that the Assyrians invaded ancient Kemet in about 661 B.C.E.; successively, after more than one century, the Persians equally invaded the Nile Valley in 525 B.C.E. However, the actual turning point in the history of the continent of Kemet began to crystallize when Alexander the Greek of Macedonia inflicted the devastating blow on the continent of Kemet despite all the previous foreign invasions from Asia. In retrospect, the defeat suffered by the Nile Valley civilization on the hands of Alexander was the defeat of the continental Kemites as a whole. This was because the Nile Valley not only occupied the seat of the most advanced civilization then known to humanity; but also because it occupied within that time frame the delicate and strategic geographical landmass of the Kemetic cultural universe in its interaction with the outside world. This contention is quite valid when one takes into consideration the demography of the continent of Kemet today, especially around the northern perimeter. The Arab hordes' military and Islamic incursions into the continent of Kemet, beginning from the Seventh century of the Christian era, was in fact a profound outcome of this European defeat of ancient Kemet. Moreover, the strategic importance of the Nile Valley civilization and its spiritual and material wealth evidently explained why ancient Kemet was continually invaded by different foreign groups. Thus, the stake and prize for a military defeat of ancient Kemet seemed to be the dream and ambition of those foreign cultures, which could not resist the temptation of sharing in the splendor and glory of the continent of Kemet's accumulated wisdom.

Although the invasion of ancient Kemet by the Greeks under the leadership of Alexander was the first recorded "European" military encounter with ancient Kemet, it was also the most devastating of all the foreign invasions that took place in the continent of Kemet, with the exception of the Arab invasion that began later in the seventh century C.E. Actually, the Greek's conquest of ancient Kemet began a new Era, an age of the African debacle with its later Roman introduction of the name Africa as a pejorative description of our beloved continent as a conquered territory. Consequently, the continent of Kemet was renamed Africa and 'ancient Kemet was then stolen and annexed as a portion of Alexander's empire; but the invasion plan included far more than mere territorial expansion; for it prepared the way and made it possible for the capture of the continental space of Kemet'.[4]

In 323 B.C.E., after the death of Alexander, one of his military commanders, General Ptolemy I, was crowned the Pharoah of Egypt. The Ptolemaic era (dynasty) thence began. The era that marked the decline of the continent of Kemet as the center of the world's wisdom began with a systemized plunder of the Kemetic creative legacy that had evolved over thousands of years of experimentations and careful observations of nature. This was not simply because ancient Kemet lost a war; rather, this was because Alexander saw an ample opportunity to use ancient Kemet's civilization as a means of creating a Greek civilization. In this sense, ancient Kemet which was the exemplar and glory of the continental Kemetic cultural universe was renamed Aeguptos (Hwt Ka Pth) or Egypt; and its cultural city Waset was renamed Thebai or Thebes. The royal libraries in this city's splendid temples were looted and plundered for most of all the accumulated intellectual books. This was the turning point for Alexander because the war booties led to the building of a new city and a new library which were called Alexandria, in the delta of the Nile River. Subsequently, with the help of Aristotle and other celebrated Greeks, the Royal Libraries of ancient Kemet were transformed into Greek schools or research centers and the new library built in Alexandria helped to further the goal of translation and transliterations of ancient Kemet's intellectual records into the Greek Language. It is in this particular sense that George G.M. James noted as follows:

"It is therefore an erroneous belief that the Greeks, on Egyptian soil, and through their own native ability, set up a great university at Alexandria and turned out great scholars. On the other hand, since it is a well known fact that Egypt was the land of Temples and Libraries, we can see how comparatively easy it was for the Greeks to strip other Egyptian libraries of their books in order to maintain the new library at Alexandria...."[5]

Thereupon, the authorships of Aristotle, Euclid, Callimachus, Erasistratus, Herophilus, Erastothenes, Archimedes, Appollonius, Hipparchus, Pythagoras, etc., were actually the plagiarized versions of the ancient Kemet's intellectual achievements. Essentially, the self-acclaimed Greek Philosophies' were therefore the Greek's interpretations of the several volumes of many centuries of the recorded accounts of ancient Kemetic scholarship found in the Kemetic House of Life. Indeed, most of the major Greek Philosophers were the interpreters and transmitters of ideas rather than being their discoverers. Current research has shown that many of these ideas that are attributed to Greek philosophy such as the Pythagoras theorem and the 3,4,5 triangle had been known in the ancient Kemet for centuries.

There are certain basic facts that one must remember: That this negation of Kemetic life expanded from the era of Alexander of Macedonia to the Roman Era, from the Arab Islamic conquests and penetrations to the ravages of the slave trade, and back again to the Napoleonic Era of formal colonization of Africa. But the ardent vengeance of Alexander on the Kemetic culture and spiritual life force had had an impetuous diatribe on the modern world. His enraged effort to obliterate and erase the outstanding achievements of our Kemetic ancestors in all spheres of life set the tone of the White Magic spell on Africans. The Ptolemaic era was actually the period when the relatively backward Europeans gained access to the sacred books of the Kemetic antiquity from the Royal Libraries in ancient Kemet and all the surrounding environs. Therefore, the plunder of the Kemetic classical works led to the emergence of an epoch, which can be correctly dubbed: THE ERA OF GRAECO-ROMAN'S INTERPRETATIONS OF THE KEMETIC CULTURAL, PHILOSOPHICAL, AND SCIENTIFIC ACHIEVEMENTS.[6]

III. THE AFRICAN ORIGINS OF WESTERN RELIGIONS

The Hebrew religion came into being because of its primary borrowings from the spiritual foundations in the cultures of ancient Kemet, Canaan and Mesopotamia.[7] But Hebrewism is yet to acknowledge that Moses borrowed the "Ten Commandments" from the already existing "Admonitions of MAAT".[8] It has been proven, beyond the shadow of doubt, that the indiscriminate use of the ancient Kemetic sacred books had salvaged humanity from barbarism, bestowing upon humanity the virtues of the human being. Given that no religion can develop in a vacuum, the legacy of White Magic began from the "chosen people" myth which was built upon the patriarchies of Abraham, Isaac, and Jacob. Insofar as the foundation of Hebrewism was supposedly laid by the mythical character named Moses (or Moshe) with his "Ten Commandments" from Mount Sinai and not from the ancient Kemet's "Admonitions of MAAT", the drama for the ideological invention and negation of Africa began with the origin of Hebrewism.

As a matter of fact, the origin of Hebrewism was based on the "oldest known" doctrines of eternal life found in the Kemetic teleologic system as recorded in *The Book of Coming Forth by Day (*or Papyrus Of Ani) and the *Men-noferite [Memphite] Theology System (*or "The creation of Ra as Ptah").[9] As the transcendental value of life and the belief in one Supreme Being were the threshold upon which Hebrewism, Christianity and later Islam were founded, we the Kemites have been noted to be the original cultivators of the true God-concept of spirituality throughout antiquity. And this was amplified by Chukwunyere Kamalu when he pointed out, that it is from the ancient Kemetic Holy Scriptures (above) "one will find the early sources of inspiration for the Holy Bible and the Torah".[10]

Contextually, again, the spread of Christianity was the result of the philosophy of life allegedly preached by the mythical character represented as the Christian Christ, who was the moving force behind the religious fervent, which engrossed the minds of his believers. However, the doctrines of life and the Ausarian-Heru archetype called Jesus the Christ, as euhemerized in the biblical scriptures, are later versions or outgrowths of the original Kemetic Ausarian-Heru (Osiris-Horus) mythical story. Indeed, there is a conclusive evidence to substantiate the argument that the historic Christianity has been a canonization of the mythos of the ancient Kemetic God-concept of spirituality. In other words, the religion of Christianity is a parody that is based on the historicization of the mythos of the ancient Kemet through which a man called Jesus the Christ is represented to take the place of the sun.

In the Kemetic mythical drama, Auset (Isis) became pregnant by Immaculate Conception. As a result, she gave birth to Heru (Horus) in about 4100 B.C.E. The date of this story demonstrates how it predates the biblical drama of the Immaculate Conception of Mary by more than Four Thousand years of history. Hence, the mythical Christ is none other than a later-day version of the Ausarian-Heru mystical prototype. Whereas the man named Yahshua, notably later canonized as Jesus Christ, is associated with the name "Karast" and may have been an historic figure who was educated by the Essenes in ancient Kemet.[11] By any rate, if indeed this man had ever existed, he may have been a figure that was reportedly tried and hanged in Palestine by the Jews when he was about 50 years old, and by juxtaposition would have been the basis of the deification that would later be associated with Jesus Christ, and through consubstantiation became identified as the mythical Ausarian–Heru archetype, i.e., Ausar the Karast. The word "Christ" is derived from the ancient Kemetic word, "Karast" and was rendered in Greek language as "Christos". Similarly, this word Christos is a Greek rendering for the ancient Kemet's Ausar the "Karast" which means the "anointed" or the "messiah". In addition, the name "Jesus" is a later invention that was derived from the Greek translation of Yahshua as "Joshua".[12] It is therefore categorical in stating that the celestial allegory or abstract personification of Ausar or "Christ" is a level of consciousness all human beings may aspire to attain, and not the name of an historical man *per se*.[13] But whether or not this noted historical Yahshua attained within himself the degree of spiritual consciousness necessary in order to be personalized as an Ausar is not within the scope of this text.

Upon the foundation laid by the ancient Kemetic God-concept of spirituality, ergo, came Hebrewism and Christianity from where the Muslim fathers borrowed extensively in the development of the Islamic religion. Thus, with the development of Islam came the crescent flag of Islamic Jihadist* marching amidst the continent of Kemet (Africa), conquering, pillaging and subduing many African communities to the Faith of Islam. (*The fertile Crescent of Allah found on every Islamic flag is an imitation of the Kemetic Star of Amenta.)

Consequently, in my opinion, the history of Hebrewism, Christianity, and Islam have not yet unfolded, if these religions do not acknowledge their Kemetic origins. What we know about these religions are actually the impact they have had on humanity. But the Kemetic origins of these religions hold a very significant key needed to unlock the many doors to the mysteries that have enveloped the African existence. As these religions were not equipped to understand and interpret the ancient Kemet's mystical sciences of the universe, they took them literally and "historicized" them. Similarly, I also think that these religions' failure to understand and interpret the ancient Kemet's astronomical allegory was based on the fear that such undertaking would expose the Kemetic origins of the world's most organized religions of Faith.

Due to many juxtaposing questions, there is the need when discussing the origins of the *Torah, Bible* and *Qur'an* to isolate the tremendous role ancient Kemet had played in their construction and composition. Not only in the abundant borrowing of her intellectual achievements but also by her provision of the authors with various uncredited documents of religion, morality, philosophy, social justice, astronomy, cosmology, mystical symbols, etc. One of the reasons why these mysteries existed in the first place was the direct result of the secrecy ancient Kemites had bestowed on spiritual knowledge: The ancient Kemetic Mystery System. Ironically, because of the plunder of Kemet by foreigners and the enemies of Kemet alike, these versed knowledge are now credited to the Judaeo-Christians and the Muslims who had raped and stolen the legacy of the ancient Kemetic civilization. No doubt, the ancient Kemetic God-concept of spirituality clearly laid the foundation upon which the world's self-proclaimed religions of Faith based their mythological and philosophical roots.

Nevertheless, the spell of White Magic has relegated the ancient Kemetic God-concept of spirituality to an obscure and insignificant constitution. But it was this God-concept of spirituality that has changed the world. It was the ancient Kemetic God-concept of spirituality originated by the ancient Kemites that inspired them to develop the most remarkable civilization that has transformed all humanity. According to Chancellor Williams, "The ancient [Kemetic] religion—gave birth to science and learning art, engineering, architecture, the resources for a national economy and political control—that same religion was the mother of history, of writing, of music, the healing art, the song and the dance".[14] The purpose of the ancient Kemetic God-concept of spirituality was centered towards man's understanding of the inner workings of the universe, for the salvation of the individual Chi.

IV. THE PROGNOSIS

Although we have recognized the destructive role of Arabism in the continent of Kemet and in the battle for our authentic Kemetic identity and heritage, this book will concentrate on the European's expansion of the anti-African jealousies and hatreds felt by the Greeks and the Romans in their encounters with the ancient Kemites. These jealousies and hatreds have been the invisible force upon which the myth of race was born, and now have been transformed to become the anti-African hysteria. The currency of their manifestations not only has been the basis of the African-European interactions, but also can be found in the gusto for terror and its inflictions by Napoleon and his contemporaries on Africans; and his command to his soldiers to blow off the nose on the Great Her-Em-Akhet at Gizeh (so-called Great Sphinx) and other Kemetic self-imposing monuments and to the transfer of Kemetic artifacts, tekhenw (obelisks), colossi, papyri, amongst others, to Europe and the Americas.[15]

Upon these backdrops of fundamental and philosophical truths we would proceed to state categorically: That the origin of the aforementioned controversies is primarily rooted in the European contrived creation of an African image that was from its inception anti-African, and the consequent African-European intercourse that took a dimensional shift in the middle of the fifteenth century of the Christian Era. The most explicit of these controversies or assumptions, however, were popularized and paraded as universal truths, at various historical periods within the time frame (and until the present generation), first through their dissertations as theories, concepts or social ideas. And the underlying motivation for this corpus of assumption is the total sum of conscious and unconscious distortions and misinterpretations of the seminal historical role the continent of Kemet has played and would continue to play in world history. Accordingly, this invariable schematization of Africa and the subsequent dehumanization of Africans were later legitimized through the vicissitudes of the print media, motion picture and every other conceivable propaganda device.

Furthermore, as indicated, these theories have been propagated and perpetuated, very often by non-Kemites, mostly by the Europeans. However, in the most provocative sense many fundamental elements of the

Kemetic world historical existence have been overlooked through this invented false African image. In other words, the calamities suffered by the African people, ever since the fifteenth century, have been made to become the logical manifestations of an alleged inherent inferiority, rather than the abominable negations to natural law. Indeed, over the past five centuries the name Africa has been reduced to a mere melodramatic giant with a toddler's limp. The continent of Kemet itself has been the scene of political, economic, and religious chicanery—a congruous upheaval of irresponsible interpretations of, and the mis-understanding of the continent's true historical personality and culture. It is no doubt that the continent of Kemet has been the sole recipient of the yoke of pernicious stigma of a supposed innate inferiority. Whilst on the other hand, the so-called Africans have been brutalized, dehumanized, and culturally humiliated (undervalued) for many centuries because of the perennial assumptions of race.

Therefore, the continuous debasement of the Kemetic continental world culture under the false and imposed African image and the subsequent dehumanization of its people are the central problems confronting all humanity. The abrupt defamation of the African's humanity and the consequent negation of all the things that are African constitute the catastrophic nature of the contemporary African world existence. Clearly, this anti-African hysteria or the hierarchical subordination and perversion of everything misconstrued to fit into the invented African image that never was is deeply embedded in the racial philosophies that have permeated all fabrics of the modern world. However, whether it is borne out of complete cultural negligence by the perpetrators or their naïve belief that their "culture" and its bigotry should be the accepted norm for humanity ultimately becomes the fundamental issues.

The false African image and the problems of the African people cannot be isolated to a particular geographical area in the world; hence, the problems of the African people constitute a global phenomenon. Their global nature stems from the forced dispersion, and the fact that every drop of "blackness" can be traced back to our beloved continent. In the following statement, for example, Chinua Achebe, one of Africa's renowned novelists, evokes this idea of Africans as a global people. As he puts it:

"Africa is more than a geographical reality; it is a spiritual phenomenon, born, truly enough, of a painful history—the history of slavery—but it is a history which, however uneasy we may feel about it, binds every Black person to Africa".[16]

Thus, the forced dispersion of Africans to the Western hemisphere for involuntary servitude created the African Diaspora—the African overseas community. The European human trade on Africans and the subsequent brutal enslavement of the African people legitimized the monomaniac era of white ideological schism of race over blacks. Conversely, the need to rationalize the institution of slavery heightened the desire to stamp the black image as an inferior character in relation to whites, and from this evolved the perversions of black negativity.

Consequently, the avid war on the black imagery is not superficial; instead, it is a deeply rooted warfare that has been permeated by the spiritual and material conditions of one against the other and could not have been possible without the imposed false African image. On the biological plane, one of the significant differences between black and white people is that there is a palpable distinction between their skin melanin pigmentations. Hence, the term black refers to those people who are the descendants of the ancient Kemites to whom the false African identity was imposed upon. These are the so-called Africans who are noted to predominate the entire humanity in the possession of melanin pigment on their skin. Plainly, melanin imbues varied skin pigmentation on humans. At the same time, the term white depicts a group of humans that exhibit a relative deficiency of melanin on their skin. Ultimately, white is a lack of melanin, an albinism. On the other hand, black is a profound presence of melanin. This attribute manifests in varied skin pigmentation based on the level of melanin content on the individual's skin. The struggle between the deficiency or lack of melanin as the norm for humanity against the possession of melanin, the imposition of imagery and the debasement of one for another, is buttressed in this invidious image warfare.

In other words, the blackness of the skin is the highest level of skin melanin content on the human body. At the same time, it must be understood that the pinkness or paleness of skin is the lowest level or the lack of reasonable melanin pigment on the human body. Therefore, the debasement of the black imagery by whites is a perpetrated effort to counteract and distort the natural reality of the human being. In the *Cress Theory of Color Confrontation and Racism,* Frances Cress Welsing forcefully lifts up the motif on the origins of the perennial degradation of blackness by whites when she writes:

"The white race historically has sought to hide its genetic origins in Africa amongst Blacks, just as it has sought to deny the origins of the white civilization from the culture of Blacks in Africa, seeking instead to proclaim an origin amongst the Greeks. Historically, whites also have sought to degrade Africa and everything Black. By doing so, Whites can avoid confronting the true meaning of skin whiteness as a mutation and genetic deficiency state from the Black norm—the 'hue-man' norm".[17]

VI. THE INVENTION OF THE SAMBO MYTH

Most certainly, from the outset of the enslavement of the African captives, the Europeans and their descendants in the Americas did set out to show the world that the institution of slavery was good for the black man. Consistent with this notion, they became determined to prove it, by creating many kinds of outrageous pseudo-intellectual theories, using the Bible and the media as objects of propaganda to prove their point. Its elaboration began with the contrived creation of the myth that the enslaved Africans were docile and as a result loved their condition and their masters. The initial standardization of the enslaved African's image was therefore vulgarized and made popular through literature and theater. This was the Sambo character which first appeared in a play called *The Divorce* in 1781, and subsequently in *The Triumphs of Love* in 1795. Sambo, a clown and a happy-go-lucky character in a black mask, was unable to talk intelligently, seemingly was a sing-song shiftless individual who was portrayed as the caricature of black males. The effect of the invented Sambo character on the image of blacks was sensational; and as a consequence, it inflamed the endless battle of persistent caricature of the African people as not only a subservient genetic stock but also as an inferior phenotypical group, in relation to the European.[18]

The Sambo or minstrel character thus became the archetypal image of the African people. Not only had the 'blacked-faced' white actors, who played the Sambo character, been able to fix a grotesque caricature of the African people, but their anti-African imaginations have also been the bases for the justification of the alleged docility of the enslaved Africans.

But, contrary to the Sambo tradition, the African enslavement was marked with continuous mutiny and rebellion on the part of the enslaved Africans to free themselves from the bondage imposed on them by their European masters. As William L. Katz puts it, "Of the myths that surround the institution of slavery, none has been as lasting as the claim that Africans wore their chains quietly". William Katz emphasized that "the owners' views of the happy, docile slave were refuted by a stubborn and sometimes daring resistance by families and group of men, women and children".[19] His explanation of these revolts went further to prove that the invention of the Sambo image of the enslaved Africans was an explicit contradiction to the historical reality of the European enslavement of Africans. But looking at the childlike and fun-loving Sambo-minstrel from the European or American viewpoint, it becomes clear that the Sambo character laid the groundwork for an organized racism and served as the justification on the alleged inferiority of the African people.

It is clear that this Sambo creation provided the pseudo-intellectual basis for many European writers of the nineteenth century of the Christian Era who seized the initiative to propagate and create needed literature for the myths of white supremacy and black inferiority. It was based on this type of premise that the myth of white superiority became intertwined with the ideology that a group of humanity were supposedly born to rule due to their skin color. In accordance with this ideology, all Eurocentric theories regarding Africa henceforth were meant to degrade the African and to perpetuate his material and mental conditions through lies and fraudulent means. Apart from that, the Machiavellian doctrine of the end justifying the means was popularized and made relevant to the struggle of the white supremacists. As they employed any means necessary to keep Africans in physical and psychological bondage, many Africans were violently murdered or brutalized in the process. This was amplified by William L. Katz when he observed that "to justify enslavement, masters bent history, truth and the Bible to their purposes. They also created their own "scientific evidence".[20]

Was the European enslavement and colonization of the African a blessing in disguise to the African people? The quest to answer this question stemmed from the knowledge that the institution of slavery had helped to enhance the development of the European economic hegemony. So, if chattel slavery was economically an enormous blessing to the Europeans, why not the Africans? On the one hand, did chattel slavery help in the entrenchment of an African economic, social, psychological, or political order? On the other hand, what are the consequences and repercussions of the massive enslavement of Africans? Beginning from their arbitrary dispersal as price tagged chattels to the Americas, 'the suppression of their language, religion, culture and kinship patterns and their victimization under the inhuman conditions of plantation slavery, and the pernicious stigma of "racial" inferiority on the mentality of the African people should serve as the basis of rationalization of the theory of White Magic.[21]

The complexities of these questions notwithstanding, this book will attempt to trace the historical pattern from the fifteenth century of the Christian Era to the contemporary present to ascertain if there is a correlation between the European and the African slavery experience. This issue is not only vital to black people but also to white people. It will help us to re-evaluate our beliefs and will foster a thorough understanding of the historical context upon which "race" was used to determine one's social and economic involvement in the society, with the consonance of the modern world. Moreover, it is my belief that until we begin to present accurate information on historical, sociological, anthropological, and cultural facts that are devoid of racist and stereotypical tendencies shall it be possible for the correction of conditioned and environmental false images of an invented Africa that never was can be erased and transcended.

Thus, the seed for the understanding of the historical reality of the African people must be planted to usher in the truth. Consequently, the knowledge of the truth will ultimately unshackle the mental and cultural colonialism in order to foster a sense of dignity and to set the path for the freedom of the African people from the spell of White Magic. The freedom of the African people from the spell of White Magic would transform the continent from the image of an Africa that never was to the image of the people of Kemet from the continent of Kemet that has always been a major factor in world history.

I am convinced that a new kind of awakening is needed, if Africans living in the continent and in the Diaspora are to be redeemed from the malaise comprising their existence. The euphoric existence of the African people all over the world, with its implications, and the constant struggle by the Western Establishment to suppress and exacerbate the African conditions constitute the underlying motive for this theoretical framework and analysis. The corrosion of the imposed African image and the falsification of the Kemetic origins to the scientific and philosophical legacies, handed down to them by their ancestors have become a mental-agony-debacle for Africa and Africans. The isolation, the psychological and the economic manipulations ring like a conspiracy impregnated by over two thousand years of history of an invented Africa that never was.

VII. THE PLAN OF THE BOOK

When one thinks or tries to understand the core of things, one must become humble. This humility makes it possible for one to understand the dynamics of the human existence. It is important to understand this concept called the "Establishment" within the context of this book. The embodiment of the Establishment consists of all people who have strived to keep the African people inferior—in economic, social, cultural, political and psychological terms. The Ekwensu people who want to maintain and preserve the present global status quo. I refrain to prejudge anybody because of skin color, national origin, religion, or any other beliefs or backgrounds. Thus, the Establishment is the Ekwensu people or entities who have contributed in any capacity in the depiction and dehumanization of the African people as chattel, savage, inferior, primitive, backward, uncivilized and uncultured. In other words, the Establishment constitutes the structure of the present global status quo. It is the dynamics upon which the modern world was defined and is being operated by those who have a false claim of being in control of the forces of human development or by their stooges.

Nevertheless, we have to recognize also the role of the Europeans in the structure of the contemporary world of color prejudice and black degradation. As Joseph E. Harris stated, "It must be emphasized, therefore, that one of the greatest contributions Europeans made to the new world was the expansion and entrenchment of the concept of black inferiority".[22] Thereupon, throughout the pages of this book, the terms Establishment, European*, and the white man are used interchangeably. (*The term European denotes all people of European descent.)

On the other hand, the use of this concept—the Establishment—is to reinforce the ideas articulated in this book: That the present order of things or the status quo does not represent the African world's interests. Hence, it does not favor the greater majority of the African people and does not represent the accurate historical contributions of Africa to the world. So the negation of the tremendous contributions of the African heritage to humanity has been enthroned as the character of the modern world.

The modern world is organized and regulated by particular sets of ideas which when indoctrinated on individuals become the guiding principles of their behavior and knowledge of the universe. The African has no special interest to protect in the existing global order of things. He can only free himself by attacking the ideas that govern the modern world, by overcoming all the kernels of the anti-African hysteria which have been entrenched to negate his human potential, and by imposing the Kemetic worldview as the precondition for a new world order.

Insofar, as the dilemma of several centuries of historical debauchery and political chicanery on Africa have left her and her people naked and exploited, African people must yield their mind and body to the resurgence of the Kemetic cultural re-birth. Similarly, historical change constitutes the established order of the universe. In fact, the organic nature of the universe is governed by dynamic forces that make change inevitable. The role of man and woman in manifesting these forces in the world is the underlying precursor of change. The African people must understand that historical change is an integral part of the nature of the universe; and since the present state of affairs has defined Africans as inferior, we must work towards changing our general status by yielding our mind, body and spirit to the Truth. For the truth shall set us free, and thereby will glorify the yet unequaled achievements of our ancestors. Inasmuch as no historical condition can transform itself, it is our duty as Africans to rise above our present marginalized condition by transforming the world beginning with the name of our beloved continent.

The components of data contained in this essay are divided up into seven basic segments of concise information dealing with the origins and ideas of **WHITE MAGIC.**

Chapter One dealt with the forces of the modern world and how the interactions of these forces have affected the African people's contemporary image of the world and themselves. It is a general overview grounded in the ongoing development of the Kemetic World Identity and induced by the trends of the revolutionary impact of the philosophical origins of the world mission of Nzoputa Uwa.

Chapter Two treated the different aspects of historical relationships and how they have affected the African's reality and worldview.

Chapter Three discussed the paradox of the concept of race, and the dynamics of this phenomenon on the definition of the African condition.

Chapter Four is an overview of the European Slave Trade imposed on Africans, which is erroneously called the Atlantic slave trade. It is an analytical vis-a-vis synthesized understanding of events and factors that not only precipitated the imposition of the slave trade but also made it inevitable from the European standpoint.

Chapter Five dealt with the issue of language in relation to the enslavement of Africans. The historical impact of politics in the European language praxis and its understanding within the reality of blackness is fundamental.

Chapter Six discussed why colonialism and neo-colonialism are integral to the European's practice of White Magic. This chapter treats the African colonial experience, with emphasis on the Africa's colonial Agents, based on their understanding of reality.

Chapter Seven is the conclusion. This is the European legacy as it has affected most African people's understanding of the modern world. The issue of inter-connectedness should come to the mind of the readers at this point of the book, in order to understand the relationship between the African past, present and future. The brief exposition on religion is an acknowledgement of the role of religion and how religiosity has affected the understanding of the African experience. Its evident impact has very much relegated the African cosmography itself as an irrelevant structure of the African's perceptions of reality.

VIII. WHO INVENTED CIVILIZATION?

The word, *civilization*, is contemporaneously a misnomer, a self-protecting euphemism. This word, *civilization*, has been misused and abused with obsession by the world of Ekwensu to the detriment of the African people. The mechanics of this word have permeated every facet of the ideologies of the modern world. But contemporary Europeans are hypocrites whenever they talk of civilization. It is the Indo-European civilization that they mostly talk of. The contemporary Europeans, who by their self-proclaimed heritage of the Graeco-Roman's civilization hope to keep millions of Africans in the periphery of human existence with their invention and propagation of an Africa that never was. By denying the heritage of the ancient Kemetic civilization to its African descendants and at the same time claiming the heritage of the Graeco-Roman civilization, the contemporary Europeans have made a mockery of the true meaning of the word *civilization* and consequently have made it to become a self-protecting euphemism .[23]

Without due regards to the authentic historical and archaeological facts, Europeans have consistently dramatized the idea that it was Greece that introduced civilization into Europe. But how did Greece herself become gifted with the knowledge of a civilized life? They have invariably failed to answer this crucial question.

Despite this European's attitude, ancient records have proven that without the ancient Kemetic world civilization there could not have been anything called European civilization—there is no Western civilization. The Europeans, no doubt, have understood this historical fact for centuries, and had gone out of their way to obliterate and wipe out all the conceivable traces of the link between the ancient Kemetic civilization and the contemporary European civilization with their invention of an Africa that never was. Thus, the dramatizations of the glory of the Greek and Roman civilizations were necessary in their premeditated effort to distort and confuse the historical facts of the human development. The "glory that was Greece" and the "grandeur that was Rome" became an important part of the European's propaganda machine. These civilizations very well could have evolved in a vacuum. As they put it, they were the "master race"—the master builders of great civilizations. But the endless distortions notwithstanding, the visible impact of the ancient Kemetic civilization in Europe is still quite impressive.

Therefore, the residual ramification of this European's false notion of Europe as the originator or standard of civilization is exemplified in its impact on their perception of who is an African. As a result, they used the false African image to remove our people from a dignified commentary of history. But the so-called Africans were wrong to accept the false image and its interpretation of their humanity which had made them victims of malicious propaganda. Thus, the idea conveys the attitude that the African through Western indoctrination was supposed to become honorarily "civilized", when he acquires the Western status symbol: Western Education. He was supposed to wear the so-called "civilized" outfit, suit and tie, and also to speak in the language of his masters, coupled with professing or adhering to the pseudo-Christian tenets of Western lifestyle. At the same time, his European counterparts were supposed to be innately civilized from birth—that they are congenitally civilized. Hence, the idiosyncrasies of a civilized life, attitudes and notions, are natural and part of their existence for they inherited genetically the "glory" of Greece and the "grandeur" of Rome. However, the obvious is that Europeans seem to exhibit ambiguity between individual mastership and the underpinnings of civilization—between a broader understanding of the world and apathy regarding the wider scope of cultures constituting humanity. Nor is Eurocentrism the only index of a civilized state.

In other words, by exploiting the differences in culture, the European debases the culture of the African, degrading those attributes peculiar to and/or antithetical to his own by assigning false and inferior traits to the African image. The implication of this imposed false African image is that it has become a major challenge imposed artificially by history for the people of the continent to redefine and/or define themselves and to be engaged in this self-definition is fundamental in the ultimate aim of the people asserting their humanity. Therefore, the redefinition of the name of our beloved continent and by identifying with the new name, Kemet, constitute the beginning of a fundamental process that would ultimately destroy the false notion of separating ancient Kemet and North Africa from the rest of the continent and would henceforth make such malicious notion fallacious and untenable. It would then become apparent that our mission to link and integrate ancient Kemet as the classical civilization of the continent of Kemet would now become a matter of serious scholarly concern.

Unambiguously, there are historical, anthropological and archeological evidence that civilization and humanity began in the continent of Kemet. It is without any doubt that the continent of Kemet is the cradle of human civilization and the original home of humanity. The various kinds of stone tools uncovered from the land of Kemet, the cave paintings, the temple and pyramid paintings, the shattered pottery, the records in the rocks, the records in the tekhenwy (obelisks), the self imposing monuments, the various learned papyri, the survived ancient Kemet's artifacts, the bone and fossil remains in Kemet are all parts of the scientific and archeological evidence that Kemet is the mother of human civilization. We the Kemites were the creators of agriculture, the use of tools and the early culture which we later spread to Asia and Europe. In this respect, the Hapy (Nile) River was one of the first highways for the transmission of the early culture to other parts of the world. And so, the myth depicting Africa as a 'Dark Continent' and Africans as 'savages' who contributed nothing to human civilization is a grand premeditated fable and a gross misrepresentation to the scientific and factual evidence that is found in the science of archeology, anthropology and history. According to the world renowned anthropologist, L.S.B. Leakey, "... men of science today are with few exceptions satisfied that Africa was the birthplace of man himself...

Africa's first contribution to human progress, then, was the evolution of man himself".[24]

The invention of an Africa that never was became necessary as it was used to distort the historical role played by the continent of Kemet in the evolution of human civilization and the invention of an Africa that never was also had helped in the creation of anti-Africanism. The emergence of anti-African hatred and jealousy had created a world in which everything that is black is supposed to be negative, morally inferior, and a depiction of darkness. Thenceforth, this darkness (i.e., the Dark Continent euphemism) has been superimposed to become an unmistakable emptiness—which has been translated to imply that blacks lived in a perpetual intellectual vacuum. As W.E.B. Du Bois described it, 'the African has long been the clown of history; the football of anthropology; and the slave of industry'.[25]

The late Arnold Toynbee was supposed to be an historian of his own right. Yet when you begin to read his works, it would dawn on you that he was a product of his environment—an environment contaminated with anti-African hatred and white supremacy. He was blinded with prejudice having been caught up between the bigotry of Eurocentrism and the resultant conditioned environmental euphemism of anti-Africanism. In this context, it was therefore unwarranted for him to separate himself from the environment that nurtured and educated him about the facts of life. Toynbee's most popular and equally controversial historical work was his conclusion that 'the black race alone have not contributed positively to any civilization'.[26] Indeed, his fallacious conclusion was not an isolated case, because he derived his analogy from the five century-old tradition of excluding Africa from serious anthropological, historical and archeological study. The persistently held view of the Europeans that Africans had no history before their contact with Europeans and the false belief that Africa is a 'Dark Continent' inhabited by biologically inferior people formed the bedrock of the Eurocentric ideology towards the African people and their history.

Whilst contemporary Europeans seemingly appeared indifferent to the role of Africa in human development, almost all the major celebrated astute European observers: from Socrates to Plato, from Pythagoras to Aristotle, from Nicolaus Copernicus to Galileo, from Francis Bacon to Isaac Newton, from Friedrich Hegel to Karl Max, and from Benjamin Franklin to Sigmund Freud, have been those who had devoted most of their life studying the classical accomplishments of ancient Kemites in the Nile Valley culture complex. This ambivalent attitude partly explained why Europeans went out of their way to steal ancient Kemet from our beloved continent having integrated most of the precepts of that high civilization into the fabric of their culture without giving credit to our Kemetic ancestral originators.

In order to separate the Nile Valley classical civilization from the African cultural universe, European racial anthropologists divided the African people into different racial categories. It was based on this scheme of separating the Nile Valley high civilization from the invented Africa that never was could ancient Kemet be classified as an integral part of the "Caucasian" cultural achievements. First to be mentioned is the use of the terms "Mediterranean", "Near Eastern", "Hamitic", "Semitic" or "Caucasoid" to describe the biological grouping and geographical location of ancient Kemet. Plainly, this framework exemplifies the European's arrogance, and racist disregard to geography and culture of the African people. But the intentions are quite clear. Thus, the imperatives of historical falsification and obliteration are high on the agenda of domination and oppression. This aspect of the language politics has in the main been to the advantage of the Europeans whose languages have become part of the media for intellectual pursuits amongst most African people due to their slave and colonial experiences.[27]

Secondly, when the evidence of the African pioneering role became overwhelmingly clear, the question arose "how could Africans have achieved all these?" Of course, the records were there to show that much of what we know as the components of Western civilization were built upon the ancient Kemetic cultural achievements. It is to say that the continent of Kemet is not only the birthplace of humanity but also the original source of human civilization.

Thirdly, when the Great Wall of Zimbabwe (the Acropolis or Great Enclosure as called by the explorer who confirmed it) was made known to the world, in the nineteenth century C.E., fantastic explanations were used to obscure the validity of the African's place in the history of the world. This nauseating fact was grounded upon the belief that "all signs of civilization in Africa were to be attributed to outside influence"; that Africans had no intellectual capability needed for the development of a high civilization.[28] Yet the modern world owes its origin and foundation to the ancient world; whilst the ancient world owed its existence to the ancient autochthonous (African) Kemetic ancestors of the Nile Valley classical civilization. In the *Ruins of Empires* (1793), the eighteenth century(C.E.) French scholar, C.F.C. Volney reminded the world as follows:

"There are a people, now forgotten, discovered, while others were yet barbarians, the elements of the arts and sciences. A race of men rejected from society for their sable skin and frizzled hair, founded on the study of the laws of nature, those civil and religious systems which still govern the universe".[29]

There is nothing new with the preceding observation by C.F.C. Volney even at the time it was noted. It has been a well documented fact.[30] What is important is the fact that the Western historical tradition invented an Africa that never was and had continued to use it as its platform to deny the precise nature of the continent's relationship to the evolution and development of human civilization despite all evidence to the contrary. The image of Africa created and projected to the world by non-African outsiders has reflected a standardized response of mainly Eurasians in their economic, intellectual, political, religious and social interests. The basis of the distorted history of Africa is not hard to find. Thus, the European cultural hegemony has been ill-equipped to deal with the idea that Africa's contribution to the development of humanity has not so far been equaled in recorded history. The European premeditated fables about the role of Africa in human development depict the Eurocentric mental phantasm of the human historiography. This European state of mind has been exposed by G.K. Osei, when he stated that:

"Whatever the European man has today he borrowed or stole it from Africans. There are no monuments in any part of the world that are older than those built by the wise, intelligent and proud ancient Africans. Show me any monument that is older than the Great Pyramid of Giza. As a true born African I don't have and will never acknowledge the superiority of the white man in anything, above the African. After all, we are the originators. The European man is an imitator".[31]

In addition, to these, the civilization of Mesopotamia, which was by all evidence influenced by the Kemetic world cultural complex, was alluded to have given the world writing, the sixty minute hour, the 360-degree circle, and the codes of law, so long as the continent of Africa is not within the picture. This tacit Eurocentric "race" baiting is, nevertheless, uncouth and definitely will not stand the test of time. On the contrary, the more objective account has unequivocally revealed that the world owes the Nile Valley civilization for its current civilization, and not Mesopotamia or even Sumeria. As Margaret A. Murray puts it:

"It is to Egypt that we owe our divisions of time; the twelve months and the three hundred and sixty-five days of the year; the twelve hours of the night are due to the work of the Egyptian astronomers. The earliest clocks the clepsydrae were the invention of Egyptian physicists. The earliest known intelligible writing is the Egyptian, so also are the earliest recorded historical events".[32]

Inasmuch as most historical indicators have proven that the classical African civilization was the beginning of world civilization, its unfolding impact weighs like a curse on the infamous European's notion of a "master race". The fact that it was our ancient Kemetic ancestors who framed and designed the future development of the world was something the Eurocentric scholarship does not yet want to confront due to their continued belief in an invented Africa that never was. This is so because the knowledge that the Nile Valley classical civilization almost pioneered single-handedly the foundation that made possible the development of the world contradicts the erroneous theories of white supremacy. For this reason, this world's oldest civilization was then stripped of its significance when it became clear that it was founded and maintained for several millennia by the autochthonous Africans, who now must be called the ancient Kemites. Hence, the fact that the ancient Kemites were the originators of human civilization and the architects of the most remarkable and the oldest human-made institutions in the universe negate this very existence of white ideology of Europe as the origin of the contemporary Western civilization. Therefore, the ancient Greek civilization was given all the credit as the beginning of what is now considered as Western civilization. "It is impossible", commented Cheikh Anta Diop, 'to stress all that the world, particularly the Hellenistic world, owed to the ancient Kemites. The Greeks merely continued and developed, sometimes partially, what the ancient Kemites had invented. By virtue of their materialistic tendencies, the Greeks stripped those inventions of the religious, idealistic shell in which the ancient Kemites had enveloped them'.[33]

It is without a shadow of doubt that the enslaved and colonized African people were the target of the Eurocentric ideology. For as long as they believed that they have not contributed anything to human civilization, then they would accept their inferior mundane status with gratitude. Denying the Africans their contributions to humanity and civilization was channeled to inflict the ever-present psychological trauma of self-hate, to alter their thought pattern and to make them think and believe that they were worthless. However, by misrepresenting and distorting the Kemetic world history, Europeans may have benefitted temporary. But the repercussions have begun to indicate that they had very little foresight in their judgments and expectations regarding Africans. This is, ironically, because the destiny of a people can be delayed but cannot be denied. Evidently, they were equating political and economic power with the nature of man. Thus, this European framework conveys an acute disregard to human nature and an incredible narrow-mindedness. In fact, their attitude indicated that they failed to understand that political and economic power positions are constantly changing phenomena; whereas human nature is the natural state of the human being. Notwithstanding, the actualization of the European economic and political power would not have been possible without the role Africans played in the European development.

It should be remembered that the fundamental basis of all European predatory designs against Africans are buried or buttressed on the static view of the worldly conditions of man. Therefore this lack of foresight within the European thinking in terms of other groups is indeed deeply rooted. It was inherited from the European's traditional Judeao-Christian dogma of an Africa that never was and sanctified by the ever present false assumptions of their alleged innate superiority. So, whenever Europeans talk about "progress", they usually mean "progress" in terms of strengthening their power positions in the world, to suit their goals and ambitions. Within the European belief system, there is this sense of insecurity and a deepening desire for absolute control of the forces of human development and survival. This type of thinking has no room for a conceptualization of an eventual re-emergence of the continent of Kemet and its people as a dominant group in the world affairs; because this mode of thinking resists change as a natural process. It is then no surprise that the Europeans equated political and economic conditions of the African people with the state of nature of man. Given the inherent subtleties that characterized this ideological aloofness and prejudice, David G. Du Bois has this to say:

"To justify the extremely profitable trade in Africans during the 17th, 18th and 19th centuries slave trade, the evidence that Africa was the site of man's beginning and progenitor of European civilization was ignored, suppressed and denied in Europe, and the myth of white or European supremacy was born and widely propagated".[34]

The impact of this goal, that is, the mental and cultural subordination of the Africans has been the most atrocious, barbarous, and the most stupendous the human world has ever witnessed in its entire history. The skin color of the Africans, consequently, became the rallying ground for this outrageous European folly. Henceforth, the skin color, history and humanity of Africans were debased and bastardized as the root of the supposedly African inferiority.

In other words, the historical antecedents of the African condition can be stretched to the time period when the European Slave Trade and the enslavement of the Africans interchangeably led to the triumphant development of the European material and spiritual conditions. The successful adjustment of the social and economic conditions of the Africans to suit the European interests and needs of a given time period had developed an egomania syndrome amongst the Europeans that they began to parade themselves as the "gods" of the universe with their invention of an Africa that never was. The modification of actions, within the same frame of things, became not only vital to the European interests of survival, but the seemingly modified actions also suited their holier-than-thou moral gimmick.

The resultant effect of this hideous drama on the Africans is the beginning of a new page in human history. Beginning from the time of the European Slave Trade to the era of the political colonization of Africa, many enslaved and colonized Africans demonstrated their repudiation of these European designs. However, the vast majority of the African world masses more often than not, found themselves believing this Eurocentric negation of their humanity. Whichever way one looks at it, one can equally empathize with them. Because the concrete material accomplishments of the Europeans at the expense of the African's humanity and labor have not only changed the world order but also have impaired the definite understanding of certain phenomena.

Therefore, it became a fact of history that most Africans in the Diaspora and in the continent of Kemet were deceived to accept the contrived European disparaging and ahistorical negative image of Africa. The result has been a rejection of the continent of Kemet, which is the mental and cultural rejection of themselves—a rejection of their historical authenticity. This rejection has obviously manifested itself, in both the

African people's social and psychological expectations, and has subsequently affected the characters and images of the African world's mundane interests. In any case, this has been the manifestation of the brutal nature as found in the systems of slavery and colonialism, interlocked by the subsequent effect of racism upon the psychology and culture of the African world experience.

Unquestionably, this has been the inescapable attitude of many Africans albeit unwittingly, and had made their mental and cultural colonization inextricable. Clearly, this pathology is indeed inherent in the African people's ambivalent view of the modern world. Nevertheless, if Africans accept the Eurocentric ideology towards the continent of Kemet, then they are acquiescing to the notion that their ancestors were not only ignorant, but also that their ancestors were actually "savages" as had been entrenched in their indoctrination.[35]

IX. RECONSTRUCTION AND RECOVERY

The application of modern science is wading humanity towards a renewed understanding of itself. Over the past twelve decades intellectual arguments and anthropological researches have been waged by prominent scholars in various spectrums—in order to trace not only the geographical location but also to determine the phenotype of the original human stock. The true historical currents of this important intellectual investigation have ranged from the scholarly expositions of Gerald Massey's works on *A Book of the Beginnings*(1881) and *Natural Genesis*(1883) to Albert Churchward on *The Origin and Evolution of Primitive Man*(1912), etc., and to the more substantive archeological and anthropological discoveries of Zinjanthropus Boisie in Olduvai Gorge in northern Tanzania, and the discovery of "Lucy" in 1974 in northern Ethiopia by Donald C. Johanson, to the present invariable scientific acclamation of Africa as the mother of humanity.[36]

The validations of this significant scientific milestone have been nothing but consistent. This has thus far rejuvenated and reinvigorated the ancient Kemet's understanding that somewhere in the continent of Kemet is located the abode of the original Great Mother, which they called allegorically Het-Heru: The principle of surrogate motherhood. Given the current body of research, the plausibility of this contention is quite impressive. Indeed, when all is said and done, when all modern techniques are applied, it is hoped that this corpus of scientific evidence on the continent of Kemet as the cradle of humanity will lead to the development of a new theory for the modern world. Certainly, the modern world will only be reinventing what the ancient Kemet priest-scientists had known and documented since the time of Ausar and Auset. Thus, the contemporary affirmations of the old notion of the ancient Kemites that they originated from the P*apyrus of Hunefer's* "Mountain of the Moon" (Mt. Kilimanjaro) have renewed the idea that the continent of Kemet was the home of the original Great Mother of Humanity. And that black people are the cultural and physical descendants of Het-Heru in her true allegorical context and meaning.

However, the importance of this modern "African Origin" theory to the modern world and especially to the modern Africans is that it will finally dispel and disprove the myth of race and the inhibitions of the superiority of low melanin pigmentation over high melanin pigmentation which was devised and propagated by the Europeans. In fact to be precise, the African origin theories have re-affirmed the well known fact around many circles that black people are the only biological group with the genetic properties necessary to produce other human stocks. This is to say that at one point in human history, that all human beings were black, Suffice it here to mean that human blackness is the natural phenotype of humanity. This fact of life not only stands as a testament to the authenticity of the continent of Kemet as the original home of humanity and civilization, but it also re-validates the pioneering spirit of many thinkers of modern African thought—such thinkers like Africanus Horton, Edward W. Blyden, Martin Delany, Marcus Garvey, Carter G. Wooden, W.E.B. Dubois, Leo Hansberry, J.A. Rogers, Nnamdi Azikiwe, George Padmore, Cheikh Anta Diop, Chancellor Williams, George G.M. James, John H. Clarke, Y. Ben Jochannan, John G. Jackson, Aime Cesaire, Leopold Senghor, Kwame Nkrumah, Adu Boahen, Theophile Obenga, Frantz Fanon, Joseph E. Harris, Walter Rodney, Amilcar Cabral, Chinua Achebe,

Wole Soyinka, Ivan Van Sertima, Jacob Carruthers, Chinweizu, Maulana Karenga, Ayi Kwei Armah, Molefi K. Asante, Na'im Akbar, Asa G. Hillard III, Wade Nobles, Frances C. Welsing, Charles S. Finch III, and many others.

So far, the most recent re-validation of this historical truth has come from prominent Western scholars who also may have been driven by the desire to find accurate and more objective origin of humanity. In 1987, a group of U.S. Anthropologists grounded the "African Origin" theory when they put forth an authoritative data and findings in support of this argument. In retrospect, when a team of U.S. researchers converged in Washington D.C., on September 27, 1991, many people speculated that this day may be very significant for the 1987 U.S. theory. On that day, the researchers comprised of Anthropologists and Bio-chemists from Pennsylvania State University and the University of California in Berkeley, unequivocally re-validated the theory that all human beings originated from one Great Mother around 200,000 years ago. This "strongest confirmation yet" given was based on the scientific use of an analysis of the genetic material mitochondrial DNA.

This important scientific research was made possible by the profound use of a "tree of evolution" combined with an ingenious application of the mitochondrial DNA material. Randomly, 189 people from all parts of the world were tested with the comparing sample of mitochondrial DNA material, the result was traced back to a common ancestor, a woman that was predicted to have lived between 166,000 and 249,000 years ago. In fact, the outcome of this experimental study would lend further credence to the original U.S. theory in 1987, that all humanity originated from one African Great Mother: The surrogate motherhood of Het-Heru. The researchers noted that she probably lived in southern Africa, Southern Kemet. However, Mark Stoneking the co-author of the 1987 study emphasized that she and her people were "dark skinned, shorter, and stocker than modern humans."[37] According to the ancient Kemetic classical thought, there is a direct correlation between the Twa people (incorrectly called the Pygmies) and the original humans. The Twa people also were recognized as the people who laid the foundation of the ancient Nile Valley classical civilization of Kemet.

A whole wide range of new areas of scholarship and research is now open for scholars. A new understanding of the world is imminent, and the threshold of these intellectual pursuits will be focused in re-shaping and re-molding the basic understanding of the world and the forces of human development: the re-structuring of the already accepted ideas and the undeniable emergence of a new outlook towards the continent of Kemet. Accordingly modern Africans must now endeavor to lead the way in not just rejecting the false imposed African image. Not only in the spear-heading of this emerging intellectual pursuit, but also they must be equipped to use these developments to confront and totally dispel the persistently held view that the continent of Kemet is inhabited by "childish" and "paganistic" people. Another aspect of this development constitutes the debunking of the myth of the European superiority and the purging and regeneration of many mentally and culturally colonized modern Africans who ought to embrace the new name of our beloved continent. The dynamics will first evolve within the confines of academic scholarships, which will later be permeated by the trends of theoretical developments. Indeed, this academic scramble on Kemet as the milieu of the world has already begun to inflame the minds of many scholars.

There is no doubt that this theory, when proven beyond the shadow of doubt, will have a tremendous impact on the modern world. In my view, it will rank as the third outstanding intellectual development that will infuse and engender dramatic changes in the modern world, the third intellectual revolution that would shatter the preconceived notions of "race" and humanity. The first and second revolutions were of course the Nicolaus Copernicus' theory of the "Heliocentric Solar System" of 1543 C.E., and the Charles Darwin's theory on *The Origins of Species by Means of Natural Selection,* published in 1859 C.E., respectively. Both theories comprised the two major intellectual revolutions that have had dramatic effects in the modern world. They are the two theories that Europeans used to conquer the world and to justify their alleged superiority. Copernicus' theory of Heliocentricity underscored the massive rape and plunder of

Africa; whilst the Darwin's theory of Natural Selection later helped to justify the European crime against the humanity of Africans

X. THE TWO THEORIES THAT CHANGED THE MODERN WORLD

The theory of "Heliocentric Solar System" constitutes what many have called one of the most dramatic changes in human intellectual existence. It is regarded in many circles as the catalyst that spurred the European scientific revolution. Nicholaus Copernicus used his theory to prove that it is the sun that is the center of the universe, and not the earth. He concluded his theory by emphasizing that the universe is Heliocentric and not Geocentric. It should be remarked, however, that Copernicus used the ancient Africa's (Kemetic) Civil Calendar as the basis for the Lunar and Planetary Tables of his theory, thus indicating that the ancient Kemites had understood the position of the sun in the divine order of things from antiquity. This understanding may help to explain why they called themselves the "Children of the Sun". Because they not only knew that the sun is the key to life on the planet, but that their blackness (high melanism) of the skin was the testament of the divinity of the sun.

Also, Charles Darwin established through his theory that human beings are an integral part of nature. Thus, this idea of being an integral part of nature has been able to diffuse the European preconception of the human race as being separate from nature, and equally contradicting the Biblical notions of creation and nature. He used the theory of the "Natural Law of Selection" to trace the intricate nature of the evolutionary trends of man and other species. These principles of evolution have since begun to influence every aspect of the modern world. In fact, the principles of evolution have become the foundation of all modern science disciplines, and these principles are based on the premise that man is a product of a purely natural process.[38]

This doctrine of the Natural Law of Selection with its ramifications as exemplified in the concept "Survival of the Fittest" found fertile ground in the minds of those who wanted to justify the brutality and dehumanization of the African people.[39] Not only was this theory a handmaiden for imperialist pursuits, it also became the harbinger upon which the concept of Social Darwinism was developed, with Hebert Spencer as its Chief proponent. Thus, it is hard not to acknowledge the fact that Charles Darwin himself was indeed a product of his environment. It is an environment that professes physical and material aggression of man on the planet for the expansion of self. This contention is further illuminated by Bernard Makhosezwe Magubane as he writes: "It is quite obvious that the rise of Social Darwinism, with its doctrine of evolution, offered the best rationale for the status quo in 19th century Europe and the white dominated dependencies".[40]

However, it is important to mentally note the date the first theory (Heliocentric Solar System) was published, in order to understand the historical pattern that led to the evolution of the European economic, political, cultural and intellectual hegemony. The first theory developed in 1543 C.E. was after about one century of interaction between the Africans and Europeans had already begun. This date is very significant because it will help us to understand how the development of Europe underdeveloped Africa. How Europe was developed at the expense of Africa. What made it possible for Europe to develop at that pace and the debilitating effect this development had on Africa. Why in fact Africans had to pay the gruesome price. Hence by 1543 C.E., the fruits of the European Slave Trade have begun to change and revalidate every sector of the European life. What was later termed the European Renaissance was actually the beginning effect of the incredible wealth garnered from the European rape of Africa. This resulted in a dawn of a new era, an era Europe and the entire humanity had never witnessed before. It resulted in a tremendous overhaul of the social, economic, intellectual, religious, political and traditional values of the European people. Therefore, the institutions created after 1441 C.E. in Europe, have a direct or an indirect correlation with the overall impact of the European rape and plunder of Africa. This is very important because many scholars have failed to recognize the revolutionary impact the European Slave Trade and the enslavement of Africans have had on the contemporary world. Thereby they have deviated from the facts, which on the whole have become detrimental to the understanding of the very important role Africans have played in the evolution of the modern world.

Furthermore, it is important to pay close attention to these dates, because from them we can get a better picture of even how the prevailing attitude of European superiority influenced and affected the Darwin's theory on the "Natural Law of Selection", in the nineteenth century. So that we can begin to understand how the modern world evolved, and what roles Africa and Africans have played in the manifestation of this "manifest destiny". For, as W.E.B. Du Bois has argued, 'it was not a mere case of parallelism but of cause and effect: The European Slave Trade of the sixteenth and seventeenth centuries gave birth to the Industrial Revolution of the eighteenth and nineteenth centuries'.[41] Then the benefits of the European Industrial Revolution affected the minds of many Europeans and this accomplishment equally began to shape the European culture and attitudes. Thus, the Europeans did not resist the concomitant temptation, their attitude invariably mandated them to become the devil's advocate: to see themselves as a more superior being by choosing to forget what in fact made the European development possible. They deliberately ignored or consciously mis-interpreted the fact that Europe was developed at the expense of Africa. Subsequently, they tried to alter the history of the human world, to isolate the African people from the human family and to perpetuate their conditions. From this standpoint the African's "labor was degraded, [his] humanity was despised, the theory of "race" arose. There came a new doctrine of universal labor: Mankind were of two sorts—the superior and the inferior; the inferior toiled for the superior, and the superior were the real men, the inferior were half men or less".[42]

Walter Rodney in his book, *How Europe Underdeveloped Africa,* contended that the gruesome price Africa has paid for the development of Europe is what has kept Africa "stagnated" and "underdeveloped". He based his premise on what he called the "multiplier effects" of the European asymmetrical relationship with Africa. These multiplier effects represent the dynamic attribute of capitalism where growth creates more opportunities for further growth. The author used concrete historical data to substantiate his analogy, and explicated his premise based on the conclusive evidence of many cause and effect variables. To illustrate, he stated that the massive European Slave Trade on the African human was not only initiated by Europeans, but was also defined and controlled by them. As a result, the African labor and human power were hijacked from the continent in order to render involuntary labor services needed for capital accumulation. In the process, the under population and social dislocation that resulted from the forced dispersion of Africans to the European controlled landscapes made Africa to wane whilst Europe waxed stronger.

Thus, the rapid growth of the capitalist system was because of the massive influx of captive African labor which in itself intensified the need for stable sources of raw materials for the capitalist industries. Africa so far has been the carcass upon which the greedy vultures have fed their insatiable needs. The economic partition of Africa around the conference table in Berlin, Germany, in 1884-85, demonstrated the propensity of the European's acquisition mentality. The end results were the dismemberment, deinstitutionalization and colonization of Africa, which heightened the expropriation of Africa's factors of production to Europe.

So long as capitalism is the monopoly of mineral and natural resources for the production of capital, with the sole preoccupation of furthering the creation of more wealth for the world's minority, so long will exploitation and discrimination be the names of the game. The historical fact of the European and Arab plunder and rape of Africa not only has implanted the idea that Africans are exploitable, its repercussions will continue to define the basis upon which the world interacts with Africa. The role Africa played in the development of capitalism is diabolical; because whilst Africa aided in the development and enhancement of European capitalism, European capitalism has been the most profound phenomenon in the underdevelopment of Africa.

If human life is only defined in economic terms, then one can draw the conclusion that the African life is indeed underdeveloped. Not only have the social formations in Africa been deformed and distorted, some of the vibrant components of Africa's survival ability have been destroyed and replaced by foreign forces that have rendered the continued exploitation of Africa inescapable.

Using the neo-Marxist theoretical framework, Walter Rodney had attempted to show the futility of the African people's capitalist association with the metropolitan centers. His basic argument is that Africa is not only hampered by the unequal economic strength and bargaining positions between the periphery and the capitalist centers, but that Africa can remain weak and underdeveloped because of Africa's lopsided structural pattern which has tended to favor the metropolitan centers in their one dimensional economic and trade relations with Africa.

XI. CONCLUSION

In the first place, we seem to live in a make-believe world that is defined by interest. Therefore, the configuration of two extreme opposite forces necessitated the cultural distillation, vacillation and genocide on Africans which have been buttressed by the spell of White Magic. However, we must say that the Leakey's anthropological discoveries and other related scientific findings have already qualified the argument that Africa gave birth to humanity. These discoveries which have been accepted most favorably within the scientific community proved that the issue of race is unintelligible. It also proved, as Cheikh Anta Diop pointed out, that the 'African has been here from the beginning, for several millennia he was the only one in existence. Nevertheless, on the threshold of the historical epoch, the Eurocentric scholar turns his back on him, raises questions about his genesis, and even speculates "objectively" about his genetic inheritance'.[43] The so-called "great and impassible gulf fixed by the Creator at the foundation of the world", is nothing but a desperate attempt to manipulate and perpetuate the almost expired era of the European's epoch of mindless euphemism.[44] In short, the creation and conditioning of phenotypical hierarchy by the European can be qualified as amoral and pseudo-intellectual. It will thence be looked upon not as a biological phenomenon but as an extreme materialistic impasse where a particular group has created and stigmatized certain attributes in people to suit some imbecilic system. Race, in other words, not only becomes a European device for power monopoly and social control, but also an ideological system that uses European standards and phenotype as the bases for measuring social and human worthiness.

In the second place, the adaptation of the Kemetic religious, economic, political, scientific, philosophical and cultural achievements by the Greeks and the Romans led to the short spanned Greaco-Roman's era (Hellenistic and Roman civilizations). But since the Europeans lacked the spiritual essence of the ancient Kemetic civilization, these adopted ideas could not flourish for a long time. This lack of comprehension of the African philosophical complex necessitated the Theodosius' Edict of the Fourth century C.E. and the Justinian Edict of the Sixth century C.E. In these decrees, Europeans were forbidden from practicing many of the Kemetic religious and intellectual doctrines. On the other hand, the Europeans lacked the spiritual life force upon which the order of the Kemetic life was organized. On the other hand, because of the political Edicts, the Europeans relapsed back into their historic Middle Ages. It took more than one thousand years of bitter evolution for the Europeans to become able to adapt these ideas and make them effective to their materialistic tendencies.

In fact, this is the irony of the African White Age. It took Europeans almost one thousand years to create a workable and responsive system within the same framework of the ideas found in the original civilization of humanity: The ancient Kemetic civilization. It is therefore very indicative of how long it will take Africans to evolve a responsive system, if they will choose to continue imitating and aping the second hand doctrines the ancient Greeks garnered from the ancient Kemetic civilization, certainly not less than two thousand years. Hence, many of the efforts to suffocate the African re-awakening have been conjugated with the ideologies of the modern world: for example, the emasculating psychology of the African Third Worldism. Thus another contradiction of the European global ideology becomes manifest: the philosophy behind the categorization of sovereign countries into first, second, and third worlds. The contradiction inherent in such categorization has been the topic of many heated debates. Subsequently, some Europeans have rationalized these categories on the basis of the attainment of higher technological advancement. This assumption of "underdevelopment" of the so-called "Third World" nations based on the European model, presupposes that whatever may be the characteristics of Western development is not only the standard, but also the ultimate progression of human development.

However, one is bound to ask the inevitable questions: To what extent does technology improve the lives of the lot of humanity? Is technology an integral part of the cultural and natural advancement of man to higher spiritual consciousness? What happened to the eternal ideals of sustainable development and environmental responsibility through spiritual consciousness? Or, is the spiritual and material balance of the human spirit irrelevant? Clearly, these nagging questions must be integrated into the framework of the ongoing discourse concerning the need for humanity's interrelationship with the universe of life. Michael Bradley was emphatic when he noted "that progress doesn't really have much to do with technology. Technology is only the means of progress. The motivation is something else".[45] It is the idea that technology is only a means and not an end in itself. That it is one of the means through which human beings can realize their human potentials.

Moreover, the discordant is what is wrong with the modern world. It is obvious that technology will not save the human family; but it can destroy the entire inhabitants of this planet. Eurocentrism has distorted the governing laws of the universe, and has abused the order of creation. We have as a result misplaced our priority. This wishful thinking is indeed palpable in the attitude of those who consider the modern time to be superior to the ancient time in all aspect. It is the idea that through the use of modern technology that man has or is capable of conquering nature—that man through his transcendence over nature has created a world according to his needs and desires. But, far from this euphoria, man's aggression on the planet is on the verge of creating an environment that will not be conducive for most of the inhabitants of this planet to survive. Consequently, the world of the Kemites would have only one choice, if they are to be redeemed from the spell of White Magic. This is the idea that, at collective and individual level, we must begin the rehabilitation, reconstruction, rediscovery and re-authentication of the dynamic ethos of the Kemetic worldview. Hopefully, this could be the only panacea for humanity as a whole.

Finally, the inexplicable desire to dominate, manipulate and control the intellectual resurrection of the African people has led to the mosaic stampede to discredit many African-centered scholars. The fact that the African-centered scholars are determined to reconstruct the history of the African past, which many European scholars have sadistically distorted, has created an intellectual pandemonium. It has become a common argument for those who oppose the idea of the African people taking control of their history to condemn and denounce the intrinsic value of the African struggle to overcome evil by doing good. Certainly, their intention is not only to discredit African scholars but also to implicitly battle for the preservation of the status quo, which has doggedly ideologized the belief that Africans are neither capable of taking their destiny into their own hands nor able of contributing to the human civilization in the contemporary world.

But we do not necessarily have to rebut such illogical and irrelevant argument from the descendants and colleagues of those who had attempted to obliterate and confuse the history of ancient Kemet, to the detriment of Africans.[46] In fact, it will constitute a vain reaction. That is to say that the arguments are not germane. Thus, it is my contention that such irrelevant argument is unfounded and as such does not even deserve a serious attention in this book. Indeed, most Eurocentric scholars have failed to offer scholarly critiques to the arguments on the primacy of ancient Kemet in human development. But have resorted to popular culture propaganda in their reactions to the idea that there was essentially nothing like Greek philosophy, but the Greek's interpretations or transmissions of ancient Kemetic philosophy.

Moreover, some of the Eurocentric scholars seem to pretend that there has been no such scientific argument confronting the intellectual realm of the Establishment. Conversely, the current contention by adamant Eurocentrists on the need for the application of the principles of "universalism" and "multiculturalism" in intellectual and academic scholarships is a cynical but a desperate attempt to hold on to the fundamental vestiges of what Martin Bernal and others have called the white supremacists "Aryan Model".[47]

To sum it up, I will reiterate the following conclusion from George G.M. James: 'The ancient Greeks were not the authors of what has been called "Greek Philosophy", but the Black People of the Nile Valley, The ancient Kemites'.[48]

CHAPTER ONE
NOTES

1A. John Henrik Clarke, "Time of Troubles—C.1492-1828", *The Horizon History of Africa,* II (eds.) Alvin Josephy, Jr.et al., New York: American Heritage Publishing Co., Inc., a subsidiary of McGraw-Hill Inc.,1971, p. 393.

1B. James Weldon Johnson, "The Autobiography of an Ex-Coloured Man", *Three Negro Classics,* New York: Avon Books, 1965. C. Alfred A. Knopf, Inc., 1927, p. 434.

1. George G.M. James, *Stolen Legacy,* Newport News, Virginia: United Brothers Communications Systems, 1989. p. 12
2. Yosef A.A. Ben-Jochannan, *Africa: Mother of Western Civilization,* Baltimore, Maryland: Black Classics Press, 1988, pp. 381-382.
3. Goerge G.M James, *Stolen Legacy,* Newport News, Virginia: United Brothers Communications Systems, 1989, p. 36.
4. Ibid, pp.153-154.
5. Ibid, p. 46
6. Ibid, pp.1-173; see also Yosef A.A. Ben-Jochannan, *Africa: Mother of Western Civilization,* Baltimore, Maryland: Black Classic Press, 1988, pp. 375-452.
7. Modupe Oduyoye, "The Spirits that Rule The World: African Religion & Judaism", in *African Origins of the Major World Religions,* (ed) Amon Saba Saakana, London: Karmak House, 1991, pp. 65-79.
8. Yosef Ben Jochannan, "Moses: African Influence on Judaism", *African Origins of the Major "Western Religions",* Baltimore Maryland: Black Classics Press, 1991, pp. 138-195; "Moses: African on Judaism", in *Africa Origin of the Major World Religions,* (ed.) Amon Saba Saakana, London: Karnak House, 1991, pp. 1-32.
9. Gerald Massey, *Ancient Egypt the Light Of The World,* Baltimore: Black Classics Press, 1992, p. 186.
10. Chukwunyere Kamalu, *Foundations of African Thought*, London, Great Britain: Karnak House, 1990, p. 4.
11. According to Gerald Massey, the Essenes or Nazarites belonged to a religious sect which practiced spirituality as a way of life as opposed to preaching refurbished doctrines of life.

12. Charles S. Finch III, "Osiris, the Egyptian Funerary Ritual and Birth of Christianity", Echoes of the Old Darkland, Decator, Georgia: Khenti, Inc., 1991, pp.179-210.
13. Gerald Massey, *The Historical Jesus and the Mythical Christ, Edmonds,* W.A: Sure Fire Press, 1990, pp. 4-27*;* for a more detailed analysis see Gerald Massey (1907) *Ancient Egypt The Light of the World*: A Work of Reclamation and Restitution in Twelve Books, Vols. I and II, Baltimore: Black Classic Press (reprint 1992). It is unfortunate that many people take the stories in the Bible literally as historical facts. Nevertheless, the continent of Africa has produced many Ausaru or Sages; that is people who had studied and mastered the inner workings of the universe and have become the embodiment of Divine Intelligence, for example, Ani, Imhotep, Pepi I, Kagemni, Ptahhotep, Neferti, Ogotomeli, etc.
14. Chancellor Williams, *The Destruction of Black Civilization,* Chicago, Illinois: Third World Press, 1976, p. 97.
15. From 1798 to 1801, a French expeditionary force commanded by Napoleon Bonaparte occupied and looted Egypt.
16. Chinua Achebe, "Our Mission", *African Commentary*. Vol. I, Issue I. (Amherst, Massachusetts: October 1989), p. 4.
17. Frances Cress Welsing, The Isis *papers: The Keys To The Colors,* Chicago: Third World Press, 1991, p. 128.
18. Jannette L. Dates & William Barlow, "A War Of Images*", Split Image: African Americans In The Mass Media*, Washington, DC.: Howard University Press,1990, pp. 1-8.
19. William L. Katz, *Breaking The Chains*, New York: Atheneum 1990.
20. Ibid, p. X.
21. Rupert Lewis *Marcus Garvey: Anti-Colonial Champion,* Trenton, New Jersey: Africa World Press, Inc., 1998, p. 125.
22. Joseph E. Harris, *Africans and their History*, New York: Penguin Books USA Inc. (Mentor), 1987, p. 21.
23. Quoted in Wulf Sachs, *Black Anger,* Westport, Connecticut: Greenwood Press, Publishers, 1968, p. 161
24. Quoted in Dorothy Blake Farden, *Message To The White Man & Woman In America,* Hampton, Virginia: United Brothers & United Communication Systems, May 1991, p. 17; see also Charles Silberman Crisis in Black and White, New York: Vintage Books, 1964, p. 170.

25. W.E.B. Du Bois, *Black Folk: Then and Now*, New York: H. Holt, 1939, Kraus-Thomson Organization Limited, Millwood, New York, 1975, p. IX.
26. Quoted in Charles Silberman, *Crisis in Black and White*, New York: Vintage Books, 1964, p. 170; see, Arnold Toynbee *A Study Of History*.
27. It is a fact that Europeans have used linguistics reconstruction to link Graeco-Roman antiquity with the rest of Europe as a demonstration of their supposedly predialectical common ancestry. Whereas in Africa, on the other hand, European Linguistics and the likes have strived to use the same linguistic tool to segment and divide Africa into different linguistic "racial" families. Thus linguistic tool was used to validate the false assumptions of "race". Similarly, biblical myths have been used by Europeans insofar as they can facilitate their domination of Africans. For instance, the enslaved Africans were called "Hamites" when it was necessary to justify their enslavement. But the same term was used as "Hamitic Hypothesis" to deny Africans their contribution in human development. The "Hamites" of slavery were black because they were allegedly cursed by the God of the Hebrew; whilst the "Hamites" of Egyptology were "white" who built the Nile Valley Civilization. It is in the nature of oppression to continuously create contradictions through lies!!!
28. Basil Davidson, *The African Slave Trade,* Boston Atlantic-Little, Brown Co., 1961, p. 101. Most eighteenth and nineteenth centuries' works of European anthropologists, explorers, missionaries, etc, typify this view of "outside influence" and later have been standardized by such known works as C.G. Seligman's *Races of Africa* (London: T. Butterworth, Ltd 1930), and D.H. Westermann's *The Africa Today and Tomorrow* (London: Oxford University Press,1949). Thus the "Hamitic" or "Semitic" invaders
29. C.F. Volney, *The Ruins or, Meditation on the Revolutions of Empires:* and *the Law of Nature*, reprint Baltimore, M.D: Black Classic Press, 1991, pp. 16-17; see also George Wells Parker *The Children of the Sun,* Baltimore, Maryland: Black Classic Press, 1981, p. 3.
30. The Greek and Roman writers, for instance, had testified to the phenotype or ethnicity of the Kemites: from Homer to Herodotus, from Aristotle to Lucian, from Apolodorus to Aeschylus, from

Achilles Tatius of Alexandria to Strabo, and from Diodorus of Sicily to Ammianus Marcellinus. The ancient Kemites themselves through their abundant literature described themselves to the world as autochthonous and black in comparison to non-blacks. In addition the Hebrew Torah and its derivative, the Bible, affirmed that Mizraim (i.e. ancient Kemet), Canaan, Cush and Put were the sons of Ham, the black one. For a detailed account, see Cheikh Anta Diop, "Origin of the Ancient Egyptians" in UNESCO *General History of Africa Vol.2,* (ed) G. Mokhtar Berkley: University of California, 1981.

31. R.W. Haskins, *The Arts, Science and Civilization*, Buffalo, New York: A.W Wilgus, 1844, "Introduction" by G.K Osei, 1983.
32. Margeret A. Murray, *The Splendor That Was EGYPT* New York: Frederick A. Praeger Publishers, 1964, p. XVII.
33. Cheikh Anta Diop, *the African Origin of Civilization:* Myth or Reality? (Edited and translated by Mercer Cook), Chicago, Illinois: Lawrence Hill & Co.1974, p.230.
34. David G. Du Bois, "Racism, U.S. Foreign policy and the Rising Tide Of Color", *African Commentary,* Vol II, Issues 4 & 5. Amherst, MA: African Commentary Corporation, (May 1990) pp. 23-24.
35. If Africans reject their cultural heritage, and adopt alien cultures, ideas, and conventions, it could be argued that such is an aberration of human behavior. Frantz Fanon notably made the argument that mentally colonized persons cannot become truly liberated until they stop using their colonizer as the model of development.
36. Charles S. Finch III has done an important analysis of this scholarly development in his book, *Echoes of the Old Darkland.* This is particularly emphasized in his "Race and Human Origins" in pp. 7-34.
37. Quoted in Arab News, Vol. XVI NO.305.Riyadh, Saudi Arabia: Saudi Research & Publishing Co., (Saturday, September 28,1991) p. 16; see also, Lorenzo Forbes, "Mitochondrial Eve: Critical Reflections on an African Basis to Science and Religion", *Journal of Black Studies,*22, 4, (June 1992) pp.593-616; U.S. *News & World Report*, (September 16,1991) pp. 53-60.
38. See John G. Jackson, *Man, God and civilization,* Secaucus, New Jersey: Citadel Press, 1972, pp. 28-29.

39. Herbert Spencer coined the expression "Survival of the Fittest" in his article, "A Theory of Population, Deduced from the General Law of Animal Fertility", *Westminster Review,* LVII (1852), PP. 499-500. This was later elaborated by Charles Darwin's theory of Evolution.
40. Benard Nakhosezwe Magubane, *The Ties That Bind,* Trenton, New Jersey: Africa World Press Inc., 1989, p. 53.
41. W.E.B. DU Bois, *Black Folk: Then and Now*, New York: H. Holt, 1939, p. 127.
42. W.E.B. DU Bois, *The World and Africa,* New York: International Publishers Co. Inc., 1965, p. 19.
43. Cheikh Anta Diop, *The African Origin of Civilization: Myth or Reality?* Illinois: Lawrence Hill & Co., 1974. P. 274. See also L.S.B Leakey, *The Stone Age Race of Kenya*, Oxford: Oxford University Press, 1935.
44. James Weldon Johnson, "The Autobiography of an Ex-colored Man", *Three Negro Classics,* New York: Avon books, 1965. (C: Alfred A. Knopf, Inc.1927) p. 498.
45. Micheal Bradley, *Ice Iceman Inheritance,* New York: Kayode Publications Ltd, 1991.
46. It is repugnant that some Eurocentric scholars are accusing the African-centered scholars with the invention of an African past that never was. Indeed, there is abundant evidence that can testify to the fact that it was the Europeans who created the "Africa that never was". It will be a disservice to humanity, if genuine African scholars will allow the Eurocentric propaganda machine to distract them in their morally bound project of restoring the humanity of Africans.
47. See Arthur Schlessinger, Jr., "When Ethnic Studies Are Un-American", *Social Studies Review* 5(Summer 1990), pp.11-13; *The Disuniting of American,* New York: W.W. Norton & Co., 1992. Arthur Sclessinger's argument is for a dubious reason equating Afrocentrism with Eurocentrism. Instead of acknowledging that Eurocentrism is not only "narrow", but also has been an ideology of domination and a 'phychotherapy' for people of European extraction, the author seems to be equating 400 years old Eurocentic chauvinism with the not more than two decades of humane Afrocentric history in the above listed essays. It is therefore my honorable opinion that genuine multi-culturalism is

incapable of being applied in the curricula of institutions of learning until the fundamental history of humanity has been rewritten and corrected.

48. George G.M. James, *Stolen Legacy,* Newport News, Virginia United Brothers Communications System, 1989, p. 158

CHAPTER TWO
AFRICA IN THE TWILIGHT ZONE

"I have to disabuse the mind of some of you who came here as black-white and brown-white men, who are everything else except what they are." [1a]

---Marcus Garvey

The expansion of Western Europe has been the basis upon which human development is contemporarily being interpreted and misunderstood. They are calling it either the product of class struggle or the natural dialectical process. But the history of European colonialism and imperialism reveals that it is mostly the issue of culture, as embedded in the color line, which has been their focus of consciousness rather than class in the real sense of the word.

The European historical expeditions into Africa, Asia, and the Americas have been implicitly used as the standard for the Hegelian theory of dialectical natural process. As a result, the European feudal economic organization was made to become the exemplar for justifying the atrocities committed by Europeans as they emerged from their many centuries of internal struggle for self-definition and stagnation in what was then a severe and hostile environment. From the viewpoint of a Kemite, there are serious flaws with the Marxist's theory of an evolutionary unlinear process with its inherent notion of "progress". Its inability to account for the processes that led to the ancient high civilization of the Nile Valley gave Marx and other Marxist theoreticians no alternative but to categorize the ancient time as inferior to the modern time—which is purely Eurocentric. The Marxist five evolutionary types of production relationships—communalism, slavery, feudalism, capitalism and socialism—do not have any universal value. [1] For Europe in particular cannot in any form be considered an appropriate model in human development. How can Marx explain the long historical standing of many civilizations in the ancient time, especially the Nile Valley high civilization? Or, if economics is the basis of human development, why is it that European cultural bigotry takes precedence over economic development? The case in point is that the Marxist's typology like most other European notions of "universalism" distorts and strangulates African realities as we will find out soon in this chapter.

I. THE CRYSTALIZATION OF EUROCENTRISM

The year was 1441 C.E. (Christian Era) when it all started. This year marked the beginning of the Africa's most traumatic metamorphic debacle. The plunder and the intensive exploitation of Africa heralded the iniquitous interaction between Africans and Europeans, which began in this year 1441 C.E. Europe was emerging at this time from the last Christian Crusade. The first Christian Crusade began in 1095 C.E. The end of the crusade brought about the decline of Muslim Moorish control and power on the Mediterranean ocean. In addition, the social conditions emanating from European feudalism triggered a new economic upheaval. This resulted in a new social organization which radicalized Europeans and created the desire for a new life. The first impact of this phenomenon could be described as the emergence of urban life in Western Europe.

Thus, many European nations began their numerous explorations in their quest for trade and commerce. These expeditions no doubt would begin an era the entire humanity had never witnessed before. For, these unprecedented developments would change the world forever. It was an era of hope, challenges, new ideas, and economic manipulations in the European continent. The need to expand coupled with the desire for commercial ventures may have been the motivating factors, which led to the European explorations of Africa and Asia. The great demand for silk, spices and gold made these expeditions inevitable. Thereupon, when the North African city of Ceuta was captured from the Moors in 1415 C.E., Europeans began to control not only the Mediterranean but also the Atlantic oceans. Because of this development, the Portuguese began to explore the Africa's west coast.

Prince Henry, a son of the Portuguese King, became the governor of Ceuta, the town that was captured from the Moors in 1415. As the governor of Ceuta, Prince Henry came in contact with seamen and traders who told him stories about the gold trade with Guinea. When Prince Henry returned to Portugal, he became determined to find the sea route to Guinea so that the Portuguese merchants can be a part of the gold trade in Guinea. As a result, Prince Henry the Navigator of Portugal was supposedly commissioned to find the sea route to Guinea. However, it is important to remember that during the fifteenth century in Europe, the accepted belief was that the earth was the center of the universe, which was a wrong cosmological perspective. This perception and its underpinning equally was a reflection of the overwhelming impact of isolation on the European people's mentality. These problems were even compounded by the European's belief that the origin of many European realities is "universal". This is a one dimensional view of the world. Invariably, this Eurocentric approach assumes universalism of almost all European phenomena, rooting the origins of certain kinds of European realities as universal. Plainly, they believed that their worldview had been universal; that is why, anything beyond their comprehension and understanding has been qualified as barbaric and uncivilized. This understanding of life and the cosmos had manifested in their relations or interactions with all non-Europeans. To them, Europe represented the center of the universe and the model of human development. But the European worldview lacks an apprehension of the universal spiritual principle of the cosmos, and even though inflated with the notion of "universalism" is narrow and extremely materialistic.

Therefore, the evident European's dogmatic beliefs that there are particular phenomena which have withstood the tide of time and this in Europe are, for example, the historic time and the European "classical" music. The music of Beethoven is a European phenomenon; it is a European classical music experience and not a universal classical music experience. Hence Beethoven music phenomenon is inspired to revere Europeans, cases in mind are the "Eroica symphony in honour of Napoleon, or Sergei Prokoview composing an oratorio based on the deeds of Alexander Nevsky".[2] Thus, these emphases lend credence to my repudiation of the vociferous use of the European traditional and cultural experiences as the accepted standard for Africans. The Beethoven phenomenon for many centuries has been dangled at Africans as the epitome of "civilized" music; and consequently it has become the standard flag bearer for the justification of the cultural superiority of Europeans.

In fact, most ethnic groups or nations of Africa have their own classical music experiences that have withstood the tide of time. The difference between the African classical music experience and the European Beethoven experience is that most African ethnic groups or nations have unique experiences; whilst the European Beethoven experience often transcended many European ethnic or national boundaries. That, in a sense, qualifies it as a collective European experience shared by many European nationalities. The same reasoning is applicable to the European historical periods and records. Historical records have been kept throughout antiquity in ancient Kemet; accordingly, the ancient "Egyptian temples were the first observatories of history".[3] The Europeans asserted that Herodotus was the 'father of history'. But Herodotus could be the father of European history, and not the father of African or universal history. From the same standpoint, the European Middle Ages (Dark Ages) was also interpreted to be a global Age of intellectual emptiness. They sufficed it here to mean that the universe went through the "Dark Age" period at the same time with Europeans. But correctly interpreted, the European "Dark Age" meant the period when Africans dominated the intellectual life of Europe whilst Europeans struggled to survive their stagnated state. On the other hand, the African's White Age began during the historical epoch that witnessed the European Slave Trade, slavery and colonial exploitation of Africans.

Nevertheless, the African existence must be interpreted from the view point upon which the ancient and traditional Africans had defined their world. It must be accorded its due recognition to enable the integration of the African's historical perspective. Unlike Europeans, however, history is the embodiment of the African culture and traditions; as a result, the Africa's historical periods are African; and they do not bear any qualitative or quantitative resemblance in meaning to the many European historical concepts. This is because history like the African God-concept of spirituality is the authentication of man's existence through intellectual and cultural celebrations of life. In other words, the ancient and traditional African life had been a continuum of the past, the role history played in this existence is of utmost importance.

Furthermore, the imposition of the European frame of reference as the standard for the African intellectual universe has impaired and obscured the idea of an authentic inquiry on African life. No doubt, the essence of creation is reflected on all corners of the globe; it is not segregated to a particular area in the world as many Europeans have needlessly strived to assert.

The above discussion is a set of ideas that is meant to serve as the background to the following essay. The Europeans did not have a pre-knowledge of the geographical composition of Africa and Asia before they set out on the expedition that brought them to the West African coast in 1441. So the arrival of the Portuguese in 1441 on the West African coast was not in isolation but was connected with their past. Because almost all the major changes in Europe since the time of the ancient Greeks and Romans have had direct connections with Africa, we can understand why Africa was the key to the European quest for trade and expansion.

Nonetheless, since 1441 C.E., when Prince Henry the Navigator and his gang began their exploration of the West African coast, there has been an impetuous transfer of power and a universal dimensional shift in the world order. That journey signaled the beginning of an era of competitiveness, where the African and other peoples of the world have been subjected to an inferior status within the human family. It created a considerable psychological impotence on them and their relation to what is considered real. The constitution of the interaction that emerged immediately relegated the African to the subservient role of which a simple interpretation can only mean the distinction between the master and the servant.

The economic, political, social, historical, and religious roles of the African have become insignificant ever since the fifteenth century. This inferior status and its justification again made the African the laughing stock of the world. The parallel then becomes clear: that if the European has to consider himself superior somebody must have to be inferior. The African was made to be inferior to provide the polar contrast for their assertions of superiority. Na'im Akbar remarks that "it is necessary for them to somehow define themselves as superior on the basis of somebody else's inferiority. In order to do it, they had to distort history, they had to distort records, they had to go out and wipe out the signs of the greatness of our history".[4] Thus, it has been proven that one of the most important factor in the psychology of oppression is the "complete control" of the oppressed mind by the oppressor. This complete control of a collective group's mind can only suffice if the history and the culture (collective memory) of the oppressed were disfigured, distorted and destroyed. It is "only when a man has no knowledge of the past can he become fully an instrument with all resistant extinguished" for the manipulations of the oppressor.[5]

This dialectical tension between the oppressed and the oppressor was the frame of mind or dynamics upon which the modern European civilization came to evolve. This pattern of thinking became the pinnacle and the springboard from where the contemporary Western civilization was built. For this process of development involved the aggressive and imperialistic encroachment of Europeans into the landmass of Africans and Native Americans; the destruction and decimation of Native Americans; the enslavement and cultural dislocation of Africans; the construction of "civilize" and "primitive" paradigms as contrasting pair for "progress" and "nothingness"; the development of white supremacy system and the expansion of anti-Africanism to exemplify black inferiority; the elevation of Europe (originally a peninsula of Asia) as a continent; the hierarchization of all peoples based on their level of melanin skin pigmentation (using Europeans as the model); the economic division of the inhabited lands into first, second and third worlds; and finally, the creation of a dichotomy between themselves the "haves" and those they consider the "have nots": the North and South dichotomy. Of course, they imposed the "standard" and expect the world to follow, believing that their superiority is demonstrative on their ability to put all people where they should or actually belong.

II. WHITE MAGIC IS WHITE POWER

The problem of Africa and African people today is rooted in the historical past of an Africa that never was. Its current transformations created a chain reaction that has overtaken events as evidenced in the patterns of the European Slave Trade, Slavery, Colonialism, Imperialism and the contemporary misrepresentation and isolation of our beloved continent in the global affairs. The stereotypical tendencies, the patronizing overtures and the paternalistic inclinations thus have become the dominant principles imposed by the Establishment for the nurturing and conditioning of the minds, attitudes, and development of the African people.

What is the contemporary relationship between power and skin color? What is the reality of the association of wealth with whiteness and poverty with blackness? As Marion D. de B. Kilson puts it, "The tradition of dependence enforced by slavery and perpetuated by the persistence of plantation agriculture within the rural South has contributed in the contemporary impoverished urban context to the development of a culture of dependence upon public institutions" amongst blacks in the United States.[6] In Africa and the Caribbean, colonialism and involuntary servitude created a socio-economic culture that depended on their European conquerors for survival. Through formal colonization, the remaining elements of the declining African power were destroyed and wiped out into the oblivion of history. The importance of power in human existence does not need to be overstressed. Thus, it is the stimulant of historical change. Not only is power the basic utility that galvanizes societies to control their vested interests, it is also paramount in the regulation and definition of the cultural and historical process. Whenever a people's culture is violently and persistently disrupted, it is safe to say that the people have figuratively ceased to exist. For, they essentially would have ceased to make worthwhile history. Walter Rodney was correct when he stated that, "Colonized Africans, like pre-colonial African chattel slaves, were pushed around into positions which suited European interests and which were damaging to the African continent and its peoples".[7]

The continent of Africa since it lost power to White Magic had lost the center–piece of its existence to the outside influence of the capitalist centers. That is why, despite the revolution in the technological discoveries, many African countries have not yet felt the impact of this global dimensional shift in the production of goods and services. On a contemporary context, the same principle of subordination or dependence is behind the concept of "Tied Aid" and other so-called foreign-aid programs, which characterize the development of many African countries—"Third World Aid". These Aids usually are used to promote and entrench economic dependence. They are also imposed in order to finesse political problems. Thus, these countries' dependence on these exploitative Aids overrules their sovereign rights and authority. Obviously, the resultant brainwashing has culminated with the total degradation of the entire people of African descent. This has resulted in confusion, crisis in identity, warped sense of destiny, hatred of self, and lack of cultural cohesion, reducing the individuals to an aberration of behavior contradicting norms of self-growth and human fulfillment.

Moreover, there is the mistaken belief that black people in Africa had achieved power and sovereignty through political independence. Nevertheless, the black man ruling a dependent country within the white imperialist system has no real power. He is simply a lackey, stooge, or pawn of the white metropolitan power structure, with an army and police force that were designed to maintain the imperialist way of things in that particular country. Besides the enormous control exercised by the metropolitan power elites in perpetuating the colonial apparatus, the role of the United Nation's agencies, World Bank, International Monetary Fund, and European Economic Community in enforcing direct and indirect controls through their aggravating conditionality cannot be overemphasized in this process of maintaining absolute control of power and wealth by the whites against the black masses. In addition, many of the contemporary African leaders are also the puppets of the Arabian power structure. Some of these leaders have indeed become the instruments for the Arab Islamic domination of Africa.

Considering the inherent duplicity in the system of oppression, one of the major designs of European domination is embedded in the nature of their ***lies***. And these lies are the one particular aspect that I am yet to reconcile with. ***This is because when it comes to Africa, the gulf between what Europeans preach and what they practice widens***. Not only are these differences between what is preached and what is practiced, diametrically opposed to each other, they are in all purposes mutually exclusive. Thus in their rhetoric, Europeans always profess to support African development; whilst at the same time they have consistently created and fostered ideas and policies that suppress possibilities of genuine African development. This hypocritical dichotomy between what is preached and what is practiced is not simply racism. It is rather a phenomenon called White Magic. Whereupon, W.E.B. Du Bois outlined this anti-African obscurantism of hate, greed, and deceit when he described the schema: "A system at first conscious and then unconscious of lying about history and distorting it to the disadvantage of the Negroids became so widespread that the history of Africa ceased to be taught, the color of Memnon was forgotten, and every effort was made in archeology, history, biography, in biology, psychology and sociology, to prove the…assumption that the color line had a scientific basis".[8]

Why is it necessary to fabricate and exacerbate the African people's existence? Could it be that the Establishment did not deem it necessary to tell the truth because the consequences might contradict many centuries of the anti-African propaganda? If not, maybe the Establishment has internalized these false images and theories, becoming itself imprisoned with these ideas. In either case, an acknowledgment of the authentic reality of the African people would seem capable of upsetting the status quo

The status quo is the belief that black is inferior, devilish, malignant, primitive, deadly, baneful, sinister, savage, etc. These anti-African beliefs were founded upon the false notion that black people are beggars, always looking for handouts and cannot create or manage modern technology. It is the understanding that blacks are anti-Establishment; and as a result, they must not be given a fair chance for self-determination because the Establishment derives its power from the continued illusion of the invented Africa that never was. Moreover, that if encouraged blacks would discover the truth about the invented Africa that never was, leading to an upset in the balance of power, ensuring a power struggle. This is the reason why anything that promotes and cherishes the black genius, positivism or resurrection is considered anti-Establishment. Therefore, it must be disorganized and discouraged.

How long will this **lie** last? This ***White Magic*** will prosper so long as the African people remain passive sleeping partners in their own development. And what precisely is this ***White Magic***? The motivating schemes behind ***White Magic*** are fear and jealousy. The Establishment is afraid of the African people, insecure about their development, afraid that it may lose the chance of exploiting them in the future. They are jealous of the African people because they knew that Africans are truly the Kemites who were the founders of human civilization; and also that Africans are the cultural and physical descendants of the ancient Kemites.

What is clear, now, is that the Eurasian's monopoly of ***White Magic*** against Africans insures their control of the political, economic, religious, intellectual and social functions of this agent in the world. Consequently, the guiding principle of ***White Magic*** is self-hatred; whilst the phenomenon of ***White Magic*** is an outgrowth of the resultant debilitating effect of the cultural and mental colonialism on all African people. It is an action-reaction syndrome, where the Eurocentric value system is constantly being reinforced by the slave and colonial experience and had become the dictum used for the emasculation and demoralization of the psychic of the African people. It had paralyzed the collective initiative and impoverished the energy needed in the fight for better conditions of life. Thus, it had hitherto made the victims dependent on the world of Ekwensu for survival—blind imitations and adoptions of all the disposed and anachronistic cultural attributes become evident. Such an attitude is disastrous, and makes development and self-improvement a theoretical phenomenon. Certainly, the emulation of other cultures within bounds is part of the historical realities of the human life. Despite this fact, like the old saying, charity should begin from home. The black culture not only needs to be flexible and creative, it must be seen from the standpoint where liberation and freedom are the cardinal virtues of the human life. For in spite of the strides made in many aspects of the African existence, especially during the 1960s, the struggle of the African world masses for human rights and self-determination has been hitherto limited to the design and interest of the Establishment.

III. THE MEDIA

The mass media is one of the most powerful vehicles of human communication. Its role is at once vast and it dominates, controls, conditions, shapes and molds the values of the defenseless masses. The masses who are constantly being bombarded by its contrived imagery become victims of its malicious propaganda. The advent of motion picture and television have aided in the enhancement of the false African image as an inferior antithesis of Europe. The Establishment has been very successful in using the audio-visual media to reinforce and recreate images detrimental to the African people. It is the ongoing process of the anti-African propaganda that diminishes the worth of all African people. The negative subliminal messages became the tool that is being used to enslave the minds of young blacks: The systematic imposition of the European materialistic doctrines and the contrived creation of anti-African imagery. Accordingly, the perpetrators of black negativity are the enemies of the African image. They use the media as a weapon to inculcate a sense of inadequacy, and thereby help to heighten the material aspect of the individual condition. This systematic conditioning breeds and perpetuates a morbid state of mind which characterizes the negativity that has enveloped blackness.

IV. THE CASTING OF TARZAN AS AN ANATHEMA TO AFRICA

As we have previously shown, before the debut of the Tarzan Movie Series, the Sambo image of the African people had gone through a profound legitimization in the Western hemisphere. However, it was lacking a dependent origination—which is the African terrain. The gap created by this factor intensified the desire to connect Africa, and to condemn Africa that never was as the root cause of the alleged black inferiority. This symptomatic alienation from the truth led to the conception of the first Tarzan Movie, which was an instant success. The clear message in the movie was that Africans were savages, evil beasts and unclean brutes. This infused and generated the need to make the Tarzan Movie a major Movie/TV Series. Hence, the Tarzan Series were the contrived creations of Hollywood based on the popular American folklore of black condemnation and later blessed by the need to justify racism by whites.

The author of the Tarzan Book Series, Edgar Rice Burroughs, published in 1914 (copyrighted in 1912) the first of the Tarzan's book series called *Tarzan of the Apes*, which became an instant literary success, (Interestingly, Edgar R. Burroughs did never travel to the continent of Kemet before his death but obviously "invented" his own Africa that never was.) Subsequently, the fantastic need for a visual justification of racism coupled with the book's overwhelming success made it an inevitable choice for the Hollywood's desire to cash in on the increasing need for a truncated view of Africa and Africans. Understandably, this anti-African yearning of the Establishment created an impressive economic crucible not only for Edgar R. Burroughs who captured the imagination and fantastic racial dreams of his brethren and therefore published twenty-six Tarzan books before his death in 1950; but equally Hollywood, which used the Tarzan Movie Series as the foundation upon which a strong American Movie base was built around the world.

The Tarzan Book Series, therefore, were like one stone used to kill two birds. Firstly, the book was first designed to be used as an intellectual paroxysm for the sole purpose of fulfilling the white supremacist wishes and desires–fantastic dreams—of the Eurocentric imaginations of the African as an unusually depraved and backward character. Secondly, the ability demonstrated by Hollywood in the transformation of the Edgar R. Burroughs' books (written words) into sublime negative imagery resulted in the subsequent use of highly contrived motion pictures to pacify and immutably settle the African's agitations for equality in the United States (which the most prominent of black leaders that were accepted by whites, Booker T. Washington, supposedly had blessed many years earlier in his famous "Atlanta Expositions" speech or the so-called "Atlanta Compromise" of September 18, 1895)*.[9]

Thereupon, to a large degree, propaganda of this nature were used to strengthen the willing ego of the white collective and to weaken, at least, psychologically the African people's understanding of themselves.

A critical retrospective look at the Tarzan Movie Series confirmed this idea of the Establishment's effort to use the Movie Series to settle the race question, especially in the United States where they were used amongst other things to mold public opinion. Firstly, the Tarzan Movies' black characters resembled more or less the century-old ignoble Sambo characters of eighteenth and nineteenth centuries. This resemblance is much eloquent in the unintelligible speech as perpetrated by the servile Sambo. Secondly, the overall appearance and gesticulation of the slow-witted Sambo was equally in-line with the Tarzan characters (although the Sambo characters were white actors in black masks, whilst the Tarzan characters were black actors.). However, the common denominator was that both the Sambo characters and Tarzan Black characters were paraded as blamelessly fornicating black males. Perhaps these black caricatures were made to act within the fantasy and imagination of what the perpetrators would want the African people to be like. This is because prejudice only produces stereotype and not the actual historical personality or character. That is why, in both characters (Sambo and Tarzan), Africans were depicted as unfit, shiftless, indolent, dirty, unclean, stupid, weak, barbaric, and savage. Thirdly, although quite subtle, both Sambo and Tarzan black caricatures were portrayed in such a way as to reinforce the racist myth that Africans did not fully evolve as full human beings. This is the belief that Africans were generally "part-human and part-monkey". This was very apparent in the way these black caricatures were made to walk, not upright but rather their walks were seemingly like that of either an anthropoid chimpanzee or gorilla. They used these negative and false images in a sublime manner, thus depicting Africans as hedonistic wild brutes of partly or in the resemblance of human beings. Therefore, the Tarzan Movie's success and its impact on the mental universe of black people is within bounds with the European ideology towards the Africans and their belief that their notion of a superior race cannot manifest into an eternal domination if Africans were not reduced to white sycophancy and economic subservience.

The power of the Western media: The systematic conditioning enhanced through television and motion pictures have become the tools that are being used to perpetuate African demoralization and isolation. The Western Eurocentric media is the African people's image maker outside Africa. Hollywood movies like the "Tarzan", "Out of Africa", and "Gorillas in the Midst" have created a disparaging image of Africa. It took a concerted and determined effort between Hollywood and the racist intellectuals to embark on African mythmaking. The Tarzan Movie Series and other Hollywood-made movies about Africa, supported by Television became the organs used in the creation and reinforcement of African stereotypes. In addition, the Tarzan movies have played a significant role in impacting the negative images of Africa by setting an unprecedented record in depicting Africa as a jungle terrain, inhabited by animals and half-naked cannibals. Thus, the Tarzan movies were bestsellers and to a degree have established the yard-stick for the future African image making. Obviously, the fact that Africa is a continent made up of different nations and ethnic groups is overlooked. Equally, neglected is a common factor in human nature: the fact that all African people are not monolithic in character. Of course, that would have made their objective of creating an African stereotype more or less impossible. Hence, the movie producers branded the African people as either good or bad "natives"—gook natives. The intent was to distort, misinform, degenerate, confuse, and paint African people as primitive, backward, uncivilized, and as savages. Thus, the extensive use of Walter Lippmann's brainchild, the media centered concept of the stereotype, has helped to advance the already created Sambo image of the African people.

The cards were stacked against the African, and there was nobody to defend or seriously challenge the stupid distortions of Africa's image. Although there are few Africans in the Diaspora who challenged these distortions of African image, the overwhelming majority believed and internalized the false images as authentic depictions of Africans in the continent. Typically, the effect was devastating to many African Americans, who then would rather be called "colored". The African American's petty-bourgeois class (black middle class) had been then emphasizing the idea of getting away from being black.

The authors of this concept of "colored" were partly on the one hand influenced by the Brazilian, South African and the overall Eurocentric understanding of the term "coloured" or "colored". Whilst on the other hand, the societal pressures imposed on the term Black as seen in the demeaning connotation that has encompassed the totality of blackness became the motivating factor. Perhaps, they must have thought that a change of name and a total surrender to Eurocentrism might lead to the assimilation of Africans into European-centered America. But as the late Carter G. Woodson stated, "they hope[d] to make the Negro conform quickly to the standard of the whites and thus remove the pretext for the barriers between the races. They do not realize, however that even if the Negroes do successfully imitate whites, nothing new has thereby been accomplished".[10]

No doubt, the motion pictures invented an Africa that never was and used such a false image to consistently cast aspersions that confirmed what had been the accepted African image in the curricula of most American public schools. Thus, the motion pictures from Hollywood enhanced and perpetuated the age old liberal belief that the salvation of Africans must come from playing subservient roles for whites. So most African Americans, having been incessantly exposed to the Eurocentric cultural prism of race, accepted what they like the continental Africans, since the formal colonization of Africa by Europeans, had been taught: 'That the continent of Africa was a cultural vacuum, a jungle from which they should consider themselves lucky to have escaped'.[11]

The false image of the African in the American public school textbooks and in the Hemingway short stories depicted the African as more of an Ape than a human being. The authors sufficed it here to mean that "the…African had somehow managed to survive in primitive squalor and simplicity, a little better than animals but not much—and not enough, in any case, to justify regarding him as a man who deserved the same respects as other men".[12] Contrasting the African image to the other "races", it becomes clear that there is a pattern; and in this pattern the African would always be the "scapegoat" or the outsider in the human family, as long as the Europeans dominate the forces of human development. Part of the reasons for this premeditated European idiosyncrasy towards the African had been explained by the German scholar, the late Janheinz Jahn. He noted as follows:

"But prejudice has created types in the mind of the public. Only the most highly cultivated person, humane, cosmopolitan, enlightened, progressive, counts as 'real' European'. A 'real African', on the other hand, lives in the bush, carves 'primitive' sculptures. Can neither read nor write, goes naked, lives carefree and happy from day to day and tells fairy stories about crocodile and the elephant. The more 'primitive', the more 'really African' ".[13]

The same principle of the European imposition of an Africa that never was as their twisted vision of the "real" African is applicable in African history. Many Europeans who by their epistemological presuppositions seemingly lack genuine understanding of Africa have imposed themselves as academic authorities in the study of the African life, both past and present. They have taken it upon themselves to decide what is, and who gave the "real" account of any aspect of the African experience. Also, these Eurocentric scholars have managed to continue this deception by indoctrinating fellow Africans as their buffer system.

But to understand how deeply ingrained this ideology has become, a popular Textbook that was once used most commonly in the United States summarized what it called the "five races of man" with perceptible images. The five races of man as shown in this Textbook are as follows: "The Emersonian white man, the Japanese aristocrat, the Malay nobleman, and the Indian Chief, who were all obviously selected to depict the highest social rank in each case".[14] However, according to Professor Isaacs, the "African image was chosen to represent "a prehistoric figure, naked, stepping out of primeval ooze, carrying an ante-deluvian club and shield".[15] This demonstrates what has become a tradition to the European's self-serving African imagery. Thus, when it comes to the African the rule changes and the reverse or opposite becomes the case. This imposed false "African" image was definitely from an imagined figure from "prehistoric" time as the good Professor noted. Evidently, there is no doubt that even the lowest socially ranked African does not qualify as a "real" African to the European cultural bigots who had invented their own African.

The Professor (Isaacs) analyzed the compartmentalization of the images that were associated with the pictures of "the five races of man". His explanation of the categories was that the states of man as "savage" belonged to "all black or red" peoples, "barbarous" were "chiefly brown" peoples, "half civilized" were "wholly yellow" peoples, whilst the "civilized" state exclusively belonged to the "white" peoples. As we can see from these illustrations, the projected "savage" image of the African is depicted to serve as the inferior or deficient antithesis of the exclusively "civilized" European image. Both of the images have been allegorically orchestrated to complement the two extreme opposites of good and bad: The "civilized" European and the "savage" African.

In consonance, with the European ideology of the "real" African or of an invented Africa that never was, the Tarzan Movies were produced for the purpose of complementing the already established false image of the "real" African: the "uncivilized" or "depraved" figure. So the movies provided the "real " life visual picture, the last straw that broke the camel's back, with regards to the image of the Africans in the Motherland in particular and Africans in the Diaspora in general. It helped to establish the image of black people as "a shiftless and of indolent character, living either in a primitive mud hut or in the more deplorable shanty town, and meeting all life's problems with a flashing smile, a sinuous dance, and drum-assisted song".[16] A simple summation of the African people's established false image by the European racists implied one thing that black people "were physically, mentally, socially, and culturally inferior".[17]

This contrived false image of the African people has had devastating effects on the continent of Kemet to the extent that many of Africa's own people felt ashamed of their African ancestral heritage. In the United States of America, where this image warfare has been very intense, Africans suffered tremendously as a result. In this sense, we can only generalize on the untold repercussions this false image of Africa have had on individual African's integrity and pride. But one thing can be observed, the image's impact on the African American was natural. Hence, he has been conditioned over the centuries of mental and physical abuse to believe that the white man may be "progressive" and "superior". (This same notion also is evident amongst continental Africans who often looked down on things African as "backward" and "inferior".) For, it is one thing to uproot individuals from their ancestral roots for the purpose of using them as economic tools, but it is another thing to perpetuate their exploitation and isolation because of their genetic ancestry to the same cultural roots they were uprooted in the first place.

Not only was the system of chattel slavery dependent on the control of the enslaved minds by means of dehumanization, the imperatives of segregation and discrimination, after the demise of chattel slavery, also were based on the isolation, degradation, and exploitation of the descendants of the Africans. Africans were not only degraded, exploited and isolated from the respectable world community, the resultant inferior condition had been overstressed as a testimony to support the propaganda of their alleged inherent inferiority. In other words, the African American was not in a situation where he could know any better, at that time. Similarly, it was a natural reaction; because for "so long had Africa been described as something shameful, barbaric, a land in which one went about naked, a land in which his ancestors had sold their kith and kin as slaves—so long had he heard all this that he wanted to dis-associate himself in his mind from all such realities…."[18] In view of that, he considered himself a different "breed" from the continental African.

Nonetheless, he had enough of his own problem trying to survive by 'staying in his place'. This was imposed either by the de jure segregation in the old Southern States of America, or by the de facto segregation in Northern United States. More so, he was very much aware of the terrorist regime of the infamous Ku Klux Klanners, who executed lynch murder and other violent acts on persons and properties of many African Americans without being held accountable by the legal system. The Ku Klux Klanners were understandably very unpopular amongst most African Americans because they were noted for committing these atrocities that went unpunished. There were unjust trials; sometimes, there were no trial at all. The organization of Ku Klux Klan was founded as a secret society in 1866 in Pulaski, Tennessee, by its first leader Nathan Bedford Forrest. Henceforth, it began its terrorist operations against blacks and was notorious in the old Southern states of America

In short, the negative depictions of Africa in every facet of the Eurocentric American culture were bound to have a psychological impact on the African Americans. In addition to that, also, the "Tarzan and Jane" stories of the Tarzan Movie Series therefore constituted a trumpet volley of the African bastardization which had invariably created a persistent negative image of Africa amongst blacks in America. This process of psychological annihilation warranted that a greater proportion of the African American's population believed, without any doubt, that their ancestral homeland was inhabited by primitive cave-like people who lived on trees, swinging alongside the animals. Malcolm X went on to explain this idea during his speech at the Harvard Law School Forum of December 19, 1964. He stated that most African Americans saw:

"Africa as a jungle, a wild place where people were cannibals, naked and savage in a countryside overrun with dangerous animals. Such an image of the Africans was so hateful to Afro-Americans that they refused to identify with Africa".[19]

The message was loud and clear! It had delivered the expected results which the traducers had envisioned. Definitely, the message carried the hand writing on the colored wall, which declared that Africans in the Americas should be happy to have been enslaved; that their condition was much better than the Africans in the continent; and that slavery was a necessary process of bringing them into civilization. This rationale supported by the Hamitic myth was encouraged even in the universities, to the extent that a considerable proportion of white Americans believed that blacks would always be subservient to whites.

As a white college president puts it, "The Negro is a child race… The Negro here is bound to be under the tutelage and control of the whites. It would be a cruelty greater than slavery to leave this helpless race, this child race, to work out its own salvation… the Negro… must aim at white civilization, and must reach it through the support, guidance, and control of the white people among whom he lives".[20] In fact this point of view was one of the primary rationale used by whites during slavery to keep blacks in institutionalized bondage. Thus, Graham Knox contended that during slavery "many whites believed that the plantation was a vital agency for civilizing the black masses and ought to be kept alive irrespective of economic considerations".[21] The expectations were for the enslaved Africans to be grateful, patient, and complacent until the completion of their evolutionary phases—becoming a "civilized" man. That is to say, a Europeanized African who is mentally and culturally dislocated. Accordingly, William L. Katz noted that, the slave "masters liked to think of themselves as kindly ladies and gentlemen converting childlike, ignorant heathens into civilized, Christian workers".[22] Therefore, it could be deduced that the Eurocentric point of view is that the enslavement of Africans, ironically, was a blessing in disguise to the descendants of the enslaved Africans. That they should be content with their life in the European West; after all, if there was no enslavement of Africans, they would have been running around naked, poor, and with bare feet swinging on trees in the alleged African jungle terrain.

In this argument, a very important point is usually overlooked; and this point is that without the European Slave Trade and the institution of chattel slavery Europe would, like China and other cultures, be developing at an approximate parallel, with most cultures of the world. Not even like China, because most argument on development by Europeans had been based on the idea of the attainment of a feudal stage. But China and many African national groups definitely had longer years of feudalism than Europe. In any case, by mis-interpreting the interplay of forces evident in human development the Eurocentrists conveniently side-tracked what in fact made Western hemisphere to dominate the forces of human development since the dawn of the sixteenth century. As a result, they suppressed the fact that it was the European rape and plunder of Africa that created the wealth necessary for their global expansion; in addition, that it was the African involuntary labor that made the system of mercantilism triumphant as it became the mother of capitalism, which led to the European settlement in the Americas. As one observer noted, it is true that "interest in national and sectional history has often obscured the significance of Negro slavery in the overall development of the Americas… Given the lack of an alternative labor supply, it is difficult to see how European nations could have settled [in] America and exploited its resources without the aid of African Slaves."[23]

The fact that the development of what we now know as the Americas has been, and would always be, the consequences of the brutal enslavement of Africans has not escaped the attention of the most informed observers. For instance, Harold Cruse noted that "the American civilization, as we know it, could not have been built without African slavery".[24] It is without any doubt that the settlements of Europeans in the Americas had made it to become the satellite of Europe. On the contrary, during the initial encroachment of Europeans to the Americas, most of the European settlers had no plans of settling in it on a permanent basis. Their main objective initially was to exploit and extract all the mineral and natural resources as much as possible for the benefit of their home country.

Moreover, the tradition of comparing and contrasting the lives of Africans living in countries like the United States and South Africa with other black-controlled African countries is a painful tragedy. These Eurocentric intellectuals are carrying on the enslavement of the African minds in a contemporary context. They are imploring and employing all the tools used by their ancestors to divide and rule. Whenever they deem it necessary, they use their bias comparisons to send messages to a specific black community, electing them to be happy that their condition is better than other Africans. When will somebody tell these pseudo-intellectuals that Africans are human beings and not species of experimentation or degradation. I am yet to see any of those people comparing English people and French, or German and Italian, justifying the obvious differences because of inferiority of some kind; rather their comparisons always stressed diversity, common culture, and respect amongst these nations. The argument raised by David Lamb is not new, "that the south African Black is, on the whole, the best educated, best dressed, most prosperous, most literate black on the African Continent."[25]

Evidently, Lamb made these judgments in terms of the European culture and also in keeping with the Eurocentric values which are fundamentally intrinsic in his view of the world. This understanding must be viewed essentially as cultural which, for example, exemplified in large measure the Westerner's interpretation of the African cultural values. On the other hand, it is clear that such supposition of "progress" for continental Africans then living under the white supremacy system of Apartheid misses the point. In my opinion, this aspect of the Eurocentric subterfuge has been going on for centuries. Because all those issues are relative, and are dependent upon what angle of human existence one looks at them, it must be dismissed as baseless. It is a baseless assumption that many people would very much find repugnant. Nonetheless, his value judgment is not a surprise, because as usual he was looking at issues from his Eurocentric chauvinism and arrogance. This type of hype is what Frantz Fanon would have called 'narcissism' At any rate, the tradition of implying that the salvation of Africans must come from playing subservient roles for Europeans has become an unconscious attitude for many people. However, I am sure that many indigenous South Africans knew better than to believe such innuendo. The same argument has been used persistently ever since the beginning of the African enslavement to foster a complacent attitude within the African community in the United States. "Your counterparts in Africa are much worse off than you in America", they would say. All things being equal, I will infer categorically that the argument lacked foundation; and secondly, that those who put forward such argument are only basing it on the framework of preserving the status quo.

V. TO BE OR NOT TO BE: AFRICANISM OR EUROPEANISM

Most Africans in the Americas are products of the historical conditioning effects of a dualistic culture that came into existence because of the European and African experience. Indeed, it is a culture that grew out of the psychological dehumanization of the millions of captured Africans who were brought into the Americas as 'hewers of wood and drawers of water'. It is a culture that grew out of resistance and survival. Historically, this in time has gradually been elaborated and transmitted into the general ideology of life, giving way to new ideas of survival. Thus, these conditional ideas and projects of survival have been perpetuated from one generation to another. Consequently, this African's ability in adjusting to severe conditions of survival in servitude also left him no choice but to become partly internalized in the oppressor's values.

Eurocentric values were not only adopted by many of the enslaved Africans, they were gradually echoed in many facets of their life. In the United States, the late Franklin Frazier had argued that the enslaved African was almost stripped of his ancestral heritage. The following is the basic reflection of his argument: "The character which the Negro family acquired under the system of slavery was due to the exigencies of servitude rather than surviving African patterns of behavior".[26] Even if this view is accepted, the issue still remains whether or not the transplanted African family accepted the false European theory of the African inferiority? Despite considerable individual variation, it is safe to state that many enslaved Africans, consciously or unconsciously, accepted the false theory of the African inferiority and simultaneously as a result accepted their own inferiority in the process.[27] It may be said, however, that this acceptance and its underpinning could in fact be the turning-point in the continuing physical and cultural suicide of Africans in the Americas.

Because implicit in this acceptance of the false theory of the African inferiority lies the penchant drama of anti-Africanism—the snowballing effect. Its impact thus began to affect the cultural and psychological stimulations of most Africans in the Americas. Hence, this manifested first in the relationship between the "mixed" and the "unmixed" blacks, thereby aiding in the development of the so-called "mulatto hypothesis". Similarly, this acceptance of the false theory of the African inferiority partly resulted in the elevation of the lower melanin pigmented individuals (least--African–looking) as the logical leaders in many sectors of the socio-economic endeavors of Black America, reinforced also by the Eurocentric white supremacist ideological complex.

There seems to be enough evidence to support the argument that a considerable proportion of the African population believed and accepted their inferior status because their Europeanization had left its "foot prints" on their cultural instincts. Conceptually the name Africa became poison on their throat. The use of the name "Africa" to refer to a black person became the curse of the highest order, as a result. Subsequently, many black families began to arrange family trees that included an individual from the European biological group, or somebody from the Native American group. A deep-seated and complex psychological makeup was nurtured and was often dominated by a systematic alienation from the truth. This probably later affected or influenced the use of the concept "integration" as a civil rights Ideology in the North American continent. The definition of the word civilization was the narrow and parochial Eurocentric understanding of the term "good life", i.e., individualism and materialism. The prevailing attitude suggested that in order to be civilized one must be Europeanized: one must look like the European, dress like the European, talk like the European, and conceive life from the European's perspective. The most affluent vacationed most frequently in Europe. The continental Europe, where they were treated as temporary "honorary whites", became their second home. Accordingly, their understanding of the real world revolved around the Americas and Europe. This attitude obviously justified the notion that enslavement was a necessary process of bringing Africans into "civilization". Thus, many have unconsciously succumbed to the suggestion that their historical existence had been wholly the result of their African ancestor's contact with the Europeans. That is to say that their African ancestors had no history before their contact with the Europeans. Consider what Lerone Benneth, Jr., correctly stated many years ago, "Our thinking—and the scholarship which undergirds that thinking—is Europe-centered, white-centered, property and place-centered. We can now see through a glass whitely, and there can be no more desperate and dangerous task than the task which faces us now of trying to see with our own eyes".[28]

However, the main thrust of my argument is not isolated to any geographical area; for White Magic is rather an affliction that has affected every community in the African world. In fact, we all are the products of the engulfing White Magic, engulfing the whole suffering black world, there may be an overlap and a considerable individual variation. Typically, it is a cankerworm that is sucking the life blood of the African cultural existence. The disaster caused by this parasite has dominated, with varying degrees, the minds of all African people, whether in the Motherland or in the Diaspora. It must be seen as a global problem confronting all African people in the entire universe. This mental and cultural colonialism is the by-product of the disdainful reality of the effects of racism and white supremacy on the mental and cultural universe of all African people. Equally, it is the vehicle which has created and nurtured patterns of black inferiority complex and derision. The scope of the social implications is high; for as long as there are dysfunctional cultural perspectives and lack of cultural identity amongst African people, there can be no positive identification of this malady. But cultural identity is not a given, it must be created, nurtured and sustained through the use of knowledge and ideas in their fundamental exegeses of human experience.

VI. THE SOCIOLOGY OF WHITE MAGIC

The sociology of White Magic nurtures the lack of knowledge of self. It then breeds the lack of appreciation to the virtues of cultural authenticity, and equally inculcates black disdain on its victims. This imperialistic "venom" when discharged concentrates on the mental and cultural universe of black people, just like the biblical devil, encouraging black folks to imitate and worship anything that is either white or a product of the European "lily-whiteness". This attraction to most things that are European-centered affects the perception of self and has shaped the attitudes of many Africans towards the modern world. Perhaps, it can be summed up as partly a collective unconscious neurotic behavior engendered by the incessant global white supremacists negative attacks on the images of blackness. It is this creation and maintenance of anti-African ideas that has clearly distorted the African people's relationships with reality. For instance, many young blacks today think that to seek knowledge, to be a scholar, is to be less black. Far from the truth, Africans have been historically the founders and leaders of major academic disciplines in the world. They invented writing, philosophy, art, science, astronomy, medicine, and mathematics amongst others. Therefore, to search for truth and knowledge has always been the backbone upon which the classical civilization of Africa was built. The black youths, despite the efforts of the traducers, must be taught that to seek knowledge is a genuine African tradition.

Human civilization began in Africa. It is then an historical fact that all the major precepts of the contemporary educational system originated in Africa—such as writing, arts, science, philosophy, astronomy, medicine, engineering, mathematics, architecture, etc. So, if there is one center of the universe, as far as contemporary education is concerned, surely it will be in Africa. For, it is ancient Kemet that gave the world the knowledge that have civilized all humanity. The continent of Kemet is indeed the cradle and the home of the original human civilization—and not Europe. Secondly, it is the ancient Kemetic God-concept of spirituality that laid the foundation of the first human civilization. In fact, it is correct to say that it was the ancient Kemet's cosmology and cosmogony that changed the world. Thus, it was the ancient Kemetic God-concept of spirituality that inspired the development of the original civilization of humanity. The dynamics of this spiritual consciousness not only presented the proper conditions for the development of all the precepts of a high civilization, but also became the prototype of all God-concept of spirituality.

Abdju (Abydos) is the Holy Land where the first recorded doctrines of eternal life, the Immaculate Conception, Virgin Birth, and the Resurrection of Ausar, were symbolically dramatized. Thus, the first creation story was ancient Kemetic in originality. It was recorded in the Temple of Seti I in Abdju (Abydos), Kemet, so also was the first Immaculate Conception story of Auset (Isis) and the Resurrection story of Ausar (Osiris). At the Kemetic temples in Dendera and Philae, the principle of surrogate motherhood, Het-Heru, was also celebrated as the original symbol of Virgin Birth and Immaculate Conception. The moral principle of MAAT stood as the foundation of the divine order of things. Therefore, if there is one holy land in the universe, it definitely must be in the continent of Kemet—and not in the Southwest Asia. Above all, the so-called major religions of Faith seem to lack scientific origins, since they have failed to recognize the scientific bases of their origins. Also, it is often suggested that the so-called major religions of Faith misunderstood the astronomical mythology of the ancient Kemetic God-concept of spirituality. And so they took the ancient Kemetic mythos literally and historicized them. It is important that these points are clearly understood. For any well meaning African must not only be awakened to the Truth of the divine birth of EKUMEKU, he/she must also realize that Kemet is our cultural window to the wider universe. That is why, I am in total agreement with the late Cheikh Anta Diop's basic thesis: That the ancient civilization of the Nile Valley (especially ancient Kemet) should serve as the foundation of philosophy and epistemology of African history.[29]

The epistemological and methodological premises of the African world scholarship have begun to capture the imaginations of young scholars, who are inspired not only by the pioneers of modern African thought but are equally moved by the juxtaposition of instilling ethical and moral postulations within the academic world.

Yet in Africa, contrary to reason, most Western educated continental Africans, who also constitute the majority of the petty-bourgeois class, are the agents of White Magic. To these ultra elitist Africans, Western education somewhat inculcated a sense of disdain to the umpteen African traditions and customs, which had invariably sustained their ancestors for generations. Their mis-education creates in them a sense of inadequacy and ambivalence in relation to their understanding of human reality and their Africanness. Psychologically, most of these continental Africans gave up the African mirror or criterion of beauty and moral standards, frequently emphasizing the European model. Thus, these so-called educated Africans live in a dilemma of two worlds without belonging to either one. They are cultural hybrids who are caught in the web of two opposing sets of worldviews, two sets of human conditions, characterized by the materialistic expansion of self on the one hand, and the spiritual basis of the African life in the other hand. And this ambivalence creates a void, psychological and spiritual emptiness of purpose, which has dislocated individuals from realizing their avowed knowledge for the benefit of the African masses. The degree of their Eurocentric indoctrination has tended to impose corresponding mental and cultural alienation between them and the productive agencies of the African spirit. Nevertheless, the existence of this condition can be attributed to the fact that most Western educated continental Africans, consciously or unconsciously, are still partly looking at themselves through the eyes of the Europeans. In short, the legacy of the European historical bastardization and degradation towards the African culture is still predominant.

Furthermore, the continental Africans with Islamic education, who conform to the Arabian cultural norms are also part and parcel of the agency of White Magic. Many at times, there is this attitude of overlooking the fact that although Islam may have been based on the principles of the ancient Kemetic God-concept of spirituality, the Arab Muslims just like the European Christians have used their religion as political machines for the singular objective of an Arab Islamic domination. They have frequently camouflaged their political, cultural and economic imperialism in Africa under the banner of the spiritual salvation of man. And whilst the objectives of subjugation, colonization and suppression of the African personality are high in the agenda of Islamic domination of Africa, the African religious experience and culture were debased as animalistic.

There is no major difference between Western education which is rooted in the idea of Europe as the center or standard of civilization and Islamic education which is grounded in the idea that Mecca is the number one Holy City and Arabic the only language of the angels and as such of God. Thus the dogma that the Qur'an and Islamic prayer, dress, divination, pilgrimage, baptismal and funeral rites must conform to the dictates of the Arabian culture has nothing to do with the spiritual salvation of the adherents, but rather had been meant to enhance the Arab's political, cultural, and economic imperatives in the African world.

It is indeed analogous to state that although the continent of Kemet provided the cosmological and mystical sciences for the so-called world major religions of Faith, these thematic and spiritual sciences were later embellished with patriarchal pantheons that stress the superiority of man over his fellow humankind (woman). These embroidered pantheons, such as Yahweh (Jehovah), Jesus Christ, and Allah, were then exported back to the African people as the only authentic media for the salvation of the soul. The outcome of this outrageous religious contempt invariably has contributed in no lesser degree to the bastardization of Africa and African people.[30]

As a consequence, the sociology of White Magic has not only contradicted the African thought pattern, but its evident impact within the African world has created and nurtured the alienating patterns of mental and cultural dislocations. The sociological pattern of White Magic, with regards to the Africans, is the total negation of all creative human potential. This mysterious force contributes in no lesser degree to the catastrophic nature of the African existence today. For it is a force that separates an African away from himself, and thereby dislocates him away from his mental and cultural universe.

But to live in a world with thought and actions that contradict one's basic human value is a dangerous negation of human potential. Similarly, to be African in the so-called modern world is to be born in a world that contradicts the essence of your being. It is a world that deprives you the right to be a productive human being. Indeed, it is a world that deprives you the human opportunity to live for something recognized by you to be significant. This is a fact that attests to the life of most Africans on a general level; a life characterized by a constant fight or struggle to survive on a daily basis within the threshold of human existence. Thereupon, the 'African has been assigned to the lowest drudgery as the sphere in which the majority must toil to make a living; and culturally, economically, and politically the African people had been generally proscribed'.[31] However, this is not to say that there are not a minority of Africans who have profoundly used their ingenuities on this planetry level. In fact, it will be a disaster to solely depend on the intellectual elitism of the so-called "talented tenth" amongst African people to liberate and regenerate the entire community of the marginalized and endangered African people.

VII. NEWS ABOUT AFRICA MUST BE NEGATIVE.

The contemporary pattern of global media information service is dominated by an interlocking network system which is controlled by the Western business interests. This exclusive control of mass communication by Europeans and their descendants has tremendously affected the popular image of Africa. An important television news commentator, Gil Noble, has observed that "The foundation of today's news information is the wire services. Associated Press, United Press International, and Reuters are the major ones. They are privately owned. They are not owned by journalists, but by business men… none of whom is Black. These wire services have news bureaus by the hundreds, all over the world".[32] His commentary about the monopolization of the contemporary media information reporting and its implications in the entrenchment and perpetuation of anti-African hysteria went further. He pointed out as follows: "Music, language, writing all had their beginnings in Africa. Hardly, a conduit of basic communication exists that doesn't have its origins in Africa. Yet when you examine today's mass communications and the people who control them, you'll find that the African is excluded".[33] Thus it is these wire services that decide what is deemed "newsworthy", but also of how the images of the news reports are presented to the public.

The effects of the Western media have totally devastated the African image. Headlines like "Famine in Africa", "Starvation in Africa", "African Green Monkey's Origins of AIDS", "AIDS: Africa's Number One Killer", "Corruption: The Embodiment of Governments in Africa", and "Black Gunman Shot a Pregnant White Woman", have become part and parcel of how Africa and Africans are perceived today. Questioning Journalists about their news framework of Africa or black people in general, the assertion was that the only news about Africa that can make sensational headline must be negative. Such an image must contain intrinsic contradictions to the norms of human aspirations and existence. Consequently, it has become an attestation of an inferior biological phenotype, which arguably necessitated dominance. In other words, the Western media have been projecting the false African image from the standpoint that the continent of Africa and her indigenous people are "abnormal" and "inferior" to Europe and her people. And this stimulant or the lubricating wheel common in the Western media is the conjecture of the Eurocentric imaginations of Africa as the inferior antithesis of Europe, and thereby in contradistinction to Europe's self-image.[34]

It is a seeming confrontational news framework that had been ingrained in the belief that balanced image news-making on Africa is not economically viable. Thus, the experiential basis for the "gloom and doom" framework on Africa has been explicitly justified by implication: That the conditioned expectations of people on the news regarding Africa and black people must be something that is related to failure, agony, or backwardness. These selective news reporting have remained largely the character of the Western media coverage in Africa. That this underlying mechanism is wrought in anti-African undertones is not contestable as it has helped to reinforce racial stereotypes about blackness.

It is understandable that the Eurocentric understanding of blackness goes back to the fifteenth century C.E. when most Europeans began to have close interaction with black people. Firstly, the reader must note that the almost ten centuries of the European Middle Ages had isolated them from the outside world. Secondly, that the European intellectual knowledge of the Greek's and Roman's encounters with the continent of Africa, then, were intentionally or consciously suppressed to lend validity to the controversial biological speculations about the African phenotype. Finally, that the domination of the Iberian Peninsula by African Muslims for several centuries seemed to have had considerable psychological impact on the European's perceptions of their pink skin pigmentation. So the root of the European fantasy of blackness may be embedded in the unconscious wishes of the European society to shake off the lethargy of their domination by the black Moors. Hence, when the biological speculation of skin blackness was becoming an issue in Europe, in the early part of the fifteenth century, many knowledgeable Europeans turned a blind eye to the growing fantasies of blackness because the fantasies suited their political and economic ambitions.

Meanwhile by debasing and degrading blackness, it seems, Europeans came to realize that they can counteract the obvious physical deficiencies of their skin pinkness. Therefore, it is no surprise that "the all-pervading desire to inculcate disdain for everything black" became a maddening fantasy as a result.[35] They tried to explain what they conceived as blackness within by referring to the apparent worldview and cultural differences between Africans and Europeans; and also, on what they understood as blackness without by alluding to the skin color of Africans. All the foregoing formed what they had projected as negative abnormalities. These supposedly negative abnormalities they speculated were caused by the blackness within and blackness without. Consequently, they imagined that the African God-concept of spirituality was defective; and envisioned the Africans to be sexually promiscuous, because they were not wearing lots of clothes (overlooking that the dressing mode of Africans in the continent was of course mutually mitigated by the African tropical weather—mostly hot and sunny).

Howbeit, the Europeans' initial justification of their maddening black fantasy was that women had sex with gorillas which resulted in the evolution of the African's blackness.[36] In the meantime, this "fantasy of blackness immediately became elaborated: These people were black; they were naked; they were unchristian: ergo, they were the damned".[37] This was summed up in a popular phrase: Blacks "in color so in condition are little other than Devil's incarnate"[38] But this negative African News making is not a new phenomenon. However it is like putting the new wine in the old wine bottle. For, white supremacy is wearing a different cover. It is more sophisticated, more subtle and insidious, more mind controlling and more demoralizing to the victim. Therefore, the use of imagery as a weapon is powerfully stimulated by the European desire to limit the human potentials of, and to reinforce anti-African stereotypes about, people of African ancestry. Explicit in this manipulation of images is the assumption that Europe is the standard of civilization and Africa the embodiment of nothingness. Thus, it is within this context that the role of the Western media in the enhancement and perpetuation of white supremacy system has been fundamental in nature.

Images are either symbols of strength or that of weakness. Whilst they are strictly the creation of the human mind, they are very effective in the creation and dramatization of what is, and how the social order should be preserved. To the extent that the image of Africa is subordinated and controlled by the Europeans, it is to that extent that the interest of Africans in the global affairs is subordinated or limited to the designs and needs of

Europe. The appreciation of this historical dynamic is in retrospect the primary reason why in March 1827 *Freedom's Journal,* the first African American press, was founded. In the premiere edition, its editorial responded to the exigency of that historical period by asserting the rights of Africans to speak for themselves.[39] Although the resistance to the European definition of African imagery has persisted ever since the inauguration and later demise of the *Freedom's Journal,* it has been limited in its scope and ability to stem the tide of the European battle against African imagery.[40] This failure to combat the European imposed anti-African imagery is critical and it underlies the basic premise of White Magic.

The world is a universe of ideas. It is like a market where ideas are the goods for sale and images the media used to sell the goods to buyers. As Africans, we must not settle for a secondary role in the marketplace of human ideas. The African image will not change until Africans begin to propagate their own vision to the world. The negative African imagery is the European vision.

It is the entrenchment of anti-Africanism amongst Africans that facilitates the European control of the African thoughts and global information necessary for the mental and cultural liberation of the African people. Therefore, the print, radio, television, motion picture, etc., are the dominant agents that have had an overwhelming impact in the shaping and molding of the African people's consciousness. These media and their operators dictate how we think and in that sense control our minds.

The world is the market place of ideas; and it is the moral obligation of the African people to articulate and propagate their own values of what it is to be human. The European propagation of a mono-cultural human world warrants us to ask: Where is the African's place in the marketplace of ideas? If the world is defined by ideas, then the African people must propagate the African vision in the marketplace of ideas.

The black print, radio, television, motion picture, etc., must reflect the African vision in the marketplace of ideas. They must be controlled by Africans and should be focused to represent the needs and aspirations of the people they are meant to serve. They must not be imitations of the Eurocentric media networks; rather, they should be capable of counteracting the invidious false images of Africa and Africans. This is the challenge that confronts us as we move toward the historical process of **Nzoputa Uwa**; and it is a challenge that needs creativity, cost effectiveness, organization, expertise and courage.

VIII. WHAT ARE WE DOING?

Africans have been called all kinds of names, of which the most common are Sambo, Nigger, Heathen, Kaffir, Pagan, Negro, etc., and unmistakably these names have stuck with Africans like a leech. In addition to that, the mass media have created an ever present African mythology that negates Africa and Africans. Raped, murdered, plundered, tortured, bartered, conquered, exploited, isolated and deprived, Africa must be ready to tell the traducers that the "party" is over. We ought to stop and ask ourselves: What are we doing? What is Africa and Africans doing about these enveloping catastrophes that are undermining the humanity of all Africans? Above all, many Eurocentric scholars have continued to perpetrate the black negativity, using Africans as anthropological specimen. Africans do not need their bias and highly opinionated racist views, because they can only do one thing: favor the conservation of the status quo. They spend volumes trying to prove the African's humaneness. It is ridiculous. Why is it necessary to prove that Africans belong to the human family? Who are they trying to prove this to? Who set the standard of what makes somebody human? And why do Europeans consistently disregard the humanity of the African people?

These concerns have led to my concomitant conclusions: that there are many reasons why the Establishment intends to keep Africa isolated with the spell of White Magic. First and foremost, is the impact the upsurge of the African diasporic experience will have on the world, if Africans in the Motherland and Africans in the Diaspora unite for the world mission of Nzoputa Uwa. Secondly, unlike the Jews the Diasporic Africans will never be assimilated into the Eurocentric culture totally. Their cultural and physical attributes make them distinct in every respect.

Thirdly, by the same token, Western civilization was built on racial superiority, racism underlay the social stratification in the society.

Fourthly, the inhuman aspects of the enslavement of Africans have made it hard for the Establishment to justify slavery and so have heightened the need to dehumanize and subordinate Africans. This lack of a convincing justification has created an intense power syndrome and a sense of insecurity on the Establishment.

The underlying factor used in the justification of the social and psychological de-culturalization of the African people has been Eurocentrism. It was developed and imposed on the African people during the European institutions of slavery and colonialism, as the case may be. Slave and colonial mentality evolved and became the *sine qua non* that nurtured the African people's cultural and mental inadequacy. At any rate, therefore, these slave and colonial experiences are the magic wands. For the cause of the behavioral virus found amongst African people is the impact coupled with the exigencies of the European's enslavement and colonization of the African. The effect is the potent force of White Magic: The adoption by definition of the European value system, consciously and subconsciously, by most African people. This adoption of the oppressor's logics (thought patterns), worldview, knowledgeview and valueview, has imposed on most Africans a different philosophical rationalization, concerning the pervading conflicts inherent in the dialectical tension between the oppressed and the oppressor. Understandably, this compulsive materialistic tendency warranted the cultural distillation of the African heritage to suit the paternalistic manipulations of the Establishment. Again, this void triggered by the cultural and mental colonization of most African people created an incredible opportunity for personal predilections of individual Africans to grab the fallen crumbs, from the European paternal overtures, for their selfish ends.

Therefore, the New generation African people have a great task ahead.[41] They must be the architects and advocates of African revisionism. The New generation Africans must learn how to deal with the world from a position of strength. They are the only people who can save Africa from this ever present conspiracy. They are the only hope for a New Africa. It is a New Africa that will purge out all the shackles of the contemporary image of a giant with a toddler's limp. It is a New Africa that is now called the continent of Kemet, where its borders will be opened for the rising sun; a New Africa where the sun will shine during the day and brighten its wilderness with an everlasting glow of life, happiness and progress during the night. The continent of Kemet is a unified Africa where people from all nooks and crannies of the world will come to learn the ways of life. It is our beloved continent of Kemet whom all her descendants will stand proud to proclaim our Kemetic heritage. Mother Kemet is bleeding; she is weeping, and crying for her children all over the world begging them to come back to her. Mother Kemet needs help from all her children, not because she is incapable of helping herself, but due to the obvious reason: she has been raped, oppressed, exploited, enslaved, and isolated from the world.

Consequently, it is the duty of the New Africans who are the Kemites to organize Africa's resources, natural and human, efficiently in order to interact with the world from a position of strength. They must neither bank on the goodwill of the exploiters of Africa, nor remain in a position of weakness. In other words, their objective must be strength through self-knowledge and self-improvement which also must be unbiased about acknowledging who we are as a people. That is the reason why this New African's role must be grounded upon the correct interpretation of the true nature of our oppression and how it had influenced the political, economic, and cultural realities of our lives. This undertaking should presuppose the continuous development of the world mission of ***Nzoputa Uwa*** as the ultimate mechanism for the total liberation of Africa and Africans, from all neo-colonial domination and corrupt leadership.[42] Furthermore, the indisputable role of the power of knowledge must be employed as a weapon in the education of individuals on the panoramic view of the past, present and future history of the African people. This form of thinking is envisioned capable of unleashing individual creative energies which on the whole will crystallize thought into action. Knowledge and ideas thus must be geared towards self-discovery and self-mastery. The discovery and mastery of the unlimited potentials endowed unto us by the One Creator of the universe would enable the recovery of all the ancient and traditional Africa's achievements and the creation of many new ideas of human existence.

At the same time, as freedom of the mind continues to elude most black people, there is an urgent need to salvage this problem. This is a necessary step in the journey for the recovery of our due respect from the rest of the entire human family. From the outset, the African people must first have respect and faith in themselves. They must become comfortable with their past and strive to seek a better future for themselves and their succeeding generations. The renowned black scholar Carter G. Woodson amplified this idea when he noted that, 'the lack of confidence of the African in himself and his possibilities is what has kept him down'.[43] In other words, the New African who also is the Kemite must not neglect our cultural ability to chart the course of our destiny. But it is the persistency of anti-African propaganda that has destroyed the African's confidence in our potential as African people.

In other words, when the African people rejected who they were, they rejected the virtues of their nature. Hence, when the white man told us Africans that our spirituality, political structure, health care system, counseling techniques, educational system and family structure were not good, many of us believed him, and immediately rejected our line of thinking and our understanding of life. Our degeneration thus began. Then he realized that we were insecure about ourselves and resorted to take advantage of those insecurities we had manifested in our actions.

It is a known fact that the economic control of a people is mostly predicated on their cultural and political subjugation. Thus the cultural conflict between the African and the Establishment, today, is enshrined mainly on the use of the mass media as a racial or politico-cultural machine. In order to liberate the African people from anti-Africanism, the influence of the mass media on the behavior and existence of black people has to exist within the control of black people.

We are an extension of the continent of Kemet; for whether we admit it or not, whenever there is an unnecessary assault on the image of our beloved continent, it is an assault on all African people. Thus, black people must understand that the common bond that holds them together is their cultural heritage, color, and ideal shared from the African ancestry. The dynamics must be to liberate the shackles of anti-Africanism permeated by centuries of slavery and colonialism. So the philosophical outlook towards the African existence is the New Africa, that is destined to create a redemptive value and a new spiritual base conducive for the African people's regeneration and that would foster an African cultural and intellectual dignity.[44] The rehabilitation of the African classical and traditional wisdom of our beloved continent, would thus forge a marriage between the African slavery and colonial experience. It would become the paradigm for the African people's redemptive spirituality and ideological assertiveness.

In other words, the debunking of the internalized Eurocentric values and the transformation of the African cultural and traditional ethos would become the iconoclasm for the African cultural rebirth and regeneration. "Consequently" as Cheikh Anta Diop has correctly argued, "the Black man must become able to restore the continuity of his national historic past, to draw from it the moral advantage needed to reconquer his place in the modern world".[45]

Unquestionable, the future is now, a time of rekindled optimism, a time for recapturing our suppressed humanity. Thus, the African image, the destiny of Africa, and the role of Africa must be what the African people make them to be. For, we must overcome the extreme materialistic force that seeks to suppress our humanity, turning us into cultural hybrids in order to destroy our culture, thus taking on the self-righteous posture of a "civilizer". This is the force of White Magic.

In summation, this is a crucial period in the history of the African people. This historical period calls for the African epistemological clarification, systematization, and specification. But it goes further. For it beckons the African to rise above his current predicament in order to recapture his rightful place in the world. It demands that we as African people are morally bound to rehabilitate the African worldview, and requires the relocation of the African people within the universe of the African heritage. However, this must not be a geographical initiative; it must be seen as a global re-awakening, to redeem and reclaim all the mentally and culturally colonized Africans at every nook and cranny of the world. It is this commitment for an African world cultural revolution that would create the basis of unity amongst people of African descent.[46] So the challenge of African unity is intertwined with the mission of an African epistemological, ontological, ideological, intellectual reconstruction and exposition of knowledge.

CHAPTER TWO
NOTES

1A. Rupert Lewis, *Marcus Garvey: Anti-Colonial Champion, Trenton, New Jersey:* African World Press, Inc., 1988, pp.79-80

1. See Karl Marx and Frederick Engels. *The German Ideology*, part one (edited by C.J. Arthur), New York: International Publishers, 1970, pp. 42-48. Karl Marx was wrong in his unlinear typology of the production relationship, even from a conceptual framework. The history of Europe is a typical example of this understanding. The institution of slavery, for instance, has played an important role in the establishment of the Greek, Roman and now Western civilization. In other words, slavery is not a stage in human development but may be termed a process; that is to say, a process that facilitates man's exploitation of his fellow man.

2. Ngugi wa Thiong'o, *Devil on the Cross,* London Heinemann Educational Books Ltd, 1982, p. 132.

3. George G.M James, *Stolen Legacy,* Newport News, Virginia United Brothers Communication Systems, 1989, p. 119.

4. Na'im Akbar, *Visions for Black Men,* Nashville, Tennessee: Winston-Derek Publishers Inc., 1991, p. 28.

5. Felix Gilbert, *The End of the European Era, 1890 To the Present,* New York: Norton & Co., 3rd edition, 1984, p. 515.

6. Marion D.de B. Kilson, "Afro-American Social Structure". *The African Diaspora.* Cambridge, Massachusetts: Harvard University Press, 1976, p. 447.

7. Walter Rodney, *How Europe Underdeveloped Africa,* Washington, District of Columbia: Howard University Press, 1982, p. 230

8. W.E.B. Du Bois, *The World and Africa,* New York: International Publisher Co. Inc., 1965, p. 20.

9. Booker T. Washington, "The Atlanta Exposition Address", *Up From Slavery: An Autobiography.* New York: Carol Publishing Group, 1989, pp. 218-225. *In the Atlanta Exposition of 1895, Booker T. Washington made a very compelling speech. In this speech Washington used the metaphor "cast down your bucket". This metaphoric phrase was directed to both his black and white audience. To the white group, he said, "in all things purely social we can be as separate as five fingers, yet as one in all things essential for mutual progress". In saying this Washington hoped to pacify the Southern whites into helping to regenerate black people

economically, rather than looking outside the country for the labor, human power, etc., needed for the industrial development of the South. On the other hand, when Washington used the same phrase for black people he was intoning his belief that blacks should give up at that time political agitation, civil rights, voting and participation as equals with the whites in the development of the South. His concerted effort was to stifle black political activism, to subsume them to a lower cadre in the mobilization of the South for Industrial Advancement. Again, this was because Mr. Washington believed that gradualism and the idea that beginning from the bottom is the essence of life and development.

Be that as it may, this address has been the topic of many controversies, debates, and conflicts. However, it is arguable as to what extent this one address may have affected the public opinion with regard to the conditions of blacks in the then South. The late Booker T. Washington, no doubt, loved his people and as a result was committed to the development of his people, as the address illustrated. Nevertheless, it is important to state that for a very obvious reason the effect this address had on the Southern whites was different from how the black community perceived of this speech. At least initially, to the Southern whites, their perception of the speech was that of an unequivocal support for their race fantasy of making the "Negro stay in his place". Thus, they proceeded to circumvent every policy action necessary to fulfill this goal. Indeed, there was over dramatization of this address to the effect that it shifted public opinion with regards to the African people's condition in the South. Many scholars equally, have argued that the political rancor of this speech affected the Supreme Court decision on *Plessy versus Ferguson* of 1896, which legalized segregation in the South. However, this speech was not an ideological speech but a tactical one. Although during the historical period, the white power structure chose to take the speech to represent the core of Booker T. Washington's ideology.

10. Carter G. Woodson, *The Mis-Education Of The Negro, Hampton,* Virginia: U.B. & U.S. Communications Systems, Inc., 1992,p.7.
11. Victor C. Ferkiss, *Africa's Search For Identity,* New York: George Braziller Inc., 1966, p.84.
12. Basil Davidson, *The African Slave Trade, Boston:* Atlantic-little, Brown Co.1961, p.120.

13. Janheinz Jahn, Muntu: African Culture and the Western World (translated by Majorie Grene), New York: (C.) Faber and Faber. Grove Weidenfeld Press, Inc., 1989, p. 20.
14. Quoted in Charles Silberman, *Crisis in Black and White*, New York: Vintage Books, 1964, p. 168; see Isaacs, The New *World of Negro Americans,* New York: John Day, 1963.
15. IBid, p. 168.
16. E.R. Braithwaite, *To Sir, With Love*, New Jersey: Prentice-Hall Inc., 1959, p. 111.
17. IBid, p. 111.
18. Richard Wright, *Black Power,* Wesport Connecticut: Greenwood Press Publishers, 1976, p. 66
19. Quoted in Archie Epps, *Malcolm X: Speeches at Harvard*, New York, N.Y.: Paragon House, 1991, pp. 167-168.
20. Quoted in Earl E. Thrope *The Central Theme of Black History,* Durham, North Carolina: Seeman Printery, 1969, p. 8; also, see "The Relation of the Whites to the Negroes",, *The Annals of the American Academy of Political and Social Science (July,1901).*
21. Graham Knox, "Political Change in Jamaica (1866-1906) and The Local Reaction to the Policies of the Crown Colony Government" in Caribbean in Transition, F.M. Andie & T.G. Mattews (eds.), Institute of Caribbean Studies, Puerto Rico, 1965, p. 149; see also Rupert Lewis, *Marcus Garvey,* Trenton, N.J: Africa World Press, Inc., 1988,p. 27.
22. William L. Katz, *Breaking The Chains,* New York: Atheneum, 1990, p. 26.
23. David Brion Davis, *The Problem Of Slavery in Western Culture,* Ithaca, New York: Cornell University Press, 1966 pp. 9-10.
24. Harold Cruse, *Plural But Equal: A Critical Study of Blacks and minorities and America's Plural Society*, New York: William Morrow and Company Inc., 1987, p. 33.
25. David Lamb, *The African,* New York: Vintage Books, 1987, p. 319.
26. E. Franklin Frazier, *Black Bourgeoisie,* New York: Collier Books-Macmillan Publishing Company, 1962, p. 101; see "In the House of the Master", *The Negro Family in the United States*, Chicago: University of Chicago Press, 1939. Although E. Franklin Frazer's perspective contradicts the case of African continuities, retentions, and syncretisms as advanced by Melville J. Herskovits, it may be

understood within the context of the sociology of scholarship. This sociology of scholarship is relevant in the comprehension of White Magic. This is because the epistemological basis of Frazer's perspective is still having pervasive influence in the thinking of the considerable proportions of the Africans in the Diaspora, amongst others.

27. Fortunately for us, the enslaved Africans left a body of literature that can attest for itself, amongst which are the testimonies of Ottobah Cugoano, Olaudah Equiano, Phillis Wheatley, Mary Prince, Frederick Douglass, etc. Christianity was the primary rationale used to condition Africans to accept the European theory on the alleged inferiority of Africans.

28. Lerone Benneth Jr., *The Challenge of Blackness*, Chicago: Johnson Publishing Company, inc., 1972, p. 36.

29. Cheikh Anta Diop, *The African Origin of Civilization,* New York: Lawrence Hill, 1971, p. 140.

30. Male and Female principles are equals that make one complete whole. As a result, their different roles in society must always stress this equality that is inherent in the duality of nature. The patriarchal Pantheons of God as masculine are inconsistent with the nature of the universe and are debasing to the humanity of all women. All human spirits are equal from the Truth of the One Creator of the universe, whether female or male.

31. Carter G. Woodson, *The Mis-Education of the Negro,* Hampton, Virginia: U.B & U.S Communications Systems, Inc.1992, p.133.

32. Gil Noble, "*Who Controls Media Information?", Freedomways* Vol.14, No.4, 1974 (Fourth Quarter), p. 317

33. IBid, p. 317.

34. Behind these headlines lay an overwhelming distortion of facts to the disadvantage of the descendants of Africa. Firstly, the "Black Gunman" that was sensationalized as the cannibal-like murderer was not only framed by Charles Stewart, the white man who killed his wife for insurance money. But when it became known that it was the white husband that killed his wife, most media houses refused to carry it as headline news. From their racist viewpoint, the reason is obvious. The mere fact that the culprit was white has made the whole story to lose its sensational attributes.

    Secondly, as the origin of AIDS looms in the mind of many observers, one thing is becoming very clear: the idea that this catastrophic disease may be a "man-made" biological weapon for mass destruction. It is very probable that AIDS may be the lethal weapon that is hoped to exterminate the "undesirables". There is strong indication that just like racism. AIDS was developed to be the new phenomenon that is capable of continuing the destruction of those the power-that-be (Establishment) deemed the undesirables in this universe. When the existence or the preservation of self is threatened by extinction, it shows to what extent the Establishment is determined in their desired goal to destroy Africa's children. But when this possibly human-made instrument for warfare was introduced, theories of its African origin flooded the Western news media. How long shall their LIES last?

Thirdly, in the case of famine and war related starvations in Africa, I am not putting down "humanitarian" gestures of the Network mass media but it is important for the mass media to be reminded that Africa is more than a continent engulfed with famine and starvation. We recognize that Africa has had its own fair share of natural and human-made disasters. Yet African people also have a strong tradition of survival and struggle against overwhelming odds. The mass media must always endeavor to balance the unfortunate or negative aspects of Africa's struggle to survive with the positive aspects of Africa's existence. This is because Africa is not just a continent where the indigenous people cannot feed themselves. The projection of a consistently negative image of Africa has a hidden agenda and it is morally wrong.

35. W.E.B Du Bois, "The Souls of Black Folks", *Three Negro Classics*, New York: Avon Books. 1965, p. 219.

36. Aristotle's pedagogy and the notion that Africa was a continent inhabited by monstrous beings who were products of the sexual union of humans and wild beasts were used as the pedigree to justify the schema of part-human and part-monkey stereotype of Africans. Indubitably, this myth of half-beast and half-human qualities of the African has been integrated into the overall projection of black image by the Establishment.

37. Joel Kovel, *White Racism: A psychohistory,* New York: Vintage Books, 1971, p. 63.

38. Quoted in Joel Kovel, *white Racism: A psychohistory,* New York: Vintage Books, 1971, p. 63. For the record, I do not hold any

grudge against the European fantasy towards the African, because I also do have my own perception of the pink European. However, what worries me is that this European fantasy of the African has been the primary basis upon which the Europeans have based their various historical interactions with the Africans.

39. The following is *Freedom's Journal* premiere editorial on March 16th 1827: "We wish to plead our own cause. Too long have others spoken for us. Too long has the public been deceived by misrepresentations in things which concern us dearly, though in the estimation of some mere trifles: for though there are many in society who exercise towards us benevolent feelings; still (with sorrow we confess it) there are others who make it their business to enlarge upon the least trifle, which tends to the discredit of any person of color; and pronounce anathemas and denounce our whole body for the misconduct of the guilty one". Quoted in Jannette L. Dates and William Barlow, *Split Image,* Washington, D.C.: Howard University Press, 1990, p. 346.

40. Janette L. Dates' "Print News" in *Split Image* is a fair summary of Black Print News media in the United States, from 1827 to the Late 1980s. Although her analysis is far from being critical, it has provided an important overview on the origins and purpose of the African American press.

41. The New Africans have now begun to emerge from the "Renascent Africans" or the so-called "New Negroes". Unlike the former, the New Africans understand their Kemetic heritage, both ancient and modern, and know that Africa's future must be defined within the self-interest, self-image, and worldview of Africa's cultural legacy. The "Renascent Africans" or "New Negroes" have been those who lacked a complete African vision; and therefore have continued to adjust and submit the African people to exploitation, degradation, stagnation, and impotence.

42. For an historical understanding of the concept of Pan-Africanism, please refer to P. Olisanwuche Esedebe, *Pan-Africanism: The Idea and Movement 1776-1963,* Washington D.C.: Howard University Press, 1982.

43. Carter G. Woodson, *The Mis-Education of the Negro,* Hampton, Virginia: U.B & U.S. Communications Systems, Inc., 1992,p.109.

44. Study, Chukwudi Okeke Maduno, *Nnamdi Azikiwe: The Vision of the New Africa,* Oba, Anambra: Ekumeku Communication

Systems, 2018. Also, read Molefi Kete Asante, *Afrocentricity*, Trenton, New Jersey: Africa World Press, Inc., 1989.

45. Cheikh Anta Diop, *The African Origin of Civilization: Myth or Reality?* Chicago, Illinois: Lawrence Hill & Co., 1974, p. 235.

46. We have to begin to work towards the unity of ideas through a commitment to the African-centered ideas. For, any unity that is not built on African-centered ideas and principles may not be able to survive the onslaught of our anti-African antagonists. The world mission of Nzoputa Uwa is our reason for existence.

CHAPTER THREE
THE PARADOX OF RACE

"The world was thinking wrong about race, because it did not know. The ultimate evil was stupidity. The cure for it was knowledge based on scientific investigation."[1a]

---*W.E.B. Du Bois*

It is my conviction that despite more than two millennia of interaction between Africa and rest of the world, the world of Ekwensu has continued to manifest an overwhelming ignorance as to Africa's true existence. I have therefore come to the conclusion as to why this ignorance still exists, basing my analysis on my personal experience, my intellectual endeavor, and my many years of careful observation and study. Thus, this book calls for a challenge against the racist elements of the Western tradition which have viewed and continued to view the African cultural experience as backward and inferior. It is a challenge to the status quo, for slaughter is better than oppression, and submission to oppression is a mental sickness. Whether the oppression itself is psychologically or physically inflicted does not make any difference. Therefore, it is urgent that the African people understand this reality and begin to adopt attitudinal, social, economic, intellectual and political changes from whence a new world order would emerge.

I am quite aware that this task would be difficult at the beginning for the modern world is organized on the assumptions of racial superiority (phenotypical hierarchy) and race sadism (cultural bigotry). In addition, it has been built on the labor, sweat, blood and the oppression of the African people. This status quo is at the bottom the celebration of not only the physical and psychological subjugation of Africans, but also the degradation, devaluation, and subordination of Blackness. However, it is a cultural dilemma because it takes two parties to have racism. In fact, Mahatma Gandhi developed his theory of non-violence based on the premise that oppression and injustice, "exist only insofar as we support them; they have no existence of their own without our cooperation, unintentional or intentional, injustice cannot continue".[1] This is based on the understanding that "as long as people accept exploitation, both exploiter and exploited will be entangled in injustice. But once the exploited refuse to accept the relationship, refuse to cooperate with it, they are already free".[2] On the other hand, I.K. Sundiata noted that "the problem of black-white relations lies not only in the field of economic exploitation and competition, but also in the tension engendered by the creation of Black men encapsulated in white minds".[3] Thus, these men with their self contempt for African people, not minding that they are members of the same aforementioned group, constitute a barrier to an equitable cultural intercourse.

"To whom does the world belong" is a philosophical question and a personal name in the Igbo Language.[4] The answer is simple but significant: The world belongs to those who claim it as their own. If the Africans have claims to make of the world, they must re-evaluate their interactions with the Establishment by becoming aware that the development and advancement of the African people would depend on their collective effort to work for the rehabilitation of the African culture and traditions. It is no gainsaying the fact that the African influence in Western civilization has always been downplayed. The obvious fact that the most progressive time in the West has been the period since Europe and Africa began their strange bedfellow-like interactions is most evident. This conclusion stems from the knowledge that the Slave Trade ushered in the modern world, and the subsequent role played by Africa and Europe interchangeably calls for closer examination and analysis.

I. UNVEILING THE CURTAIN OF RACE

The connection between the European economic development and the gradual growth of surplus capital value that was necessary for the triumph of mercantilism and the development of capitalism is causatively interweaved with the economic rewards of the Slave Trade and Slavery to the Europeans. Eric Williams, Walter Rodney, Karl Marx, Kwame Nkrumah, W.E.B. Du Bois, and many more others have shown through their numerous writings that the common denominator between the European economic hegemony and the Africa's economic underdevelopment had been the overwhelming effect of the Slave Trade on the people of both continents.[5]

The economic benefits derived from the "rape" of Africa had an incredible impact on the emergence of several seaport towns in Europe—for instance, Bristol, Liverpool, Nantes, Bordeaux, and Serville. The role of these towns in the development of capitalism can never be overemphasized. Take for an example, the seaport town of Liverpool was a major slave trading port within the English Lancashire County. The European Industrial Revolution known to have revolutionalized the world began in this county in England as a result of the economic stimulations engendered by the European Slave Trade on Africans. Since Great Britain was the indisputable leader of the Triangular Trade, it was not a coincidence that the European Industrial Revolution began in England, in the area that had benefitted immensely from the Slave Trade. The spread of the industrial machines not only added much impetus to the capitalist system of colonial economics, but also had gradually led to the demise of the slave labor as the backbone for the accumulation of capital.

Hitherto, the history of human existence can be qualified as the history of the continuous migration of people. There has always been migration throughout the history of humanity. Africans must start to explore the world. The impact global expansion has in the world today is the resultant effect of the Eurasian Slave Trade, Slavery, Colonialism, Imperialism, and Internationalism. The survival of Africa and Africans is dependent on their role in this world political economy. Therefore, Africans must be an integral part of this world economic and cultural competitiveness. Hence, Africans should not be doomed to confine themselves in their immediate environment alone. They have every right to move around in the world to fulfill all life expectations. What is good for the goose is equally good for the gander.

The African masses must make their cultural presence felt. They must not let others make them feel like outsiders. Because the European "encounter" with the indigenous people of the Americas 'without Africa would have had a different historical reality for neither the European conquerors nor the indigenous Americans possessed the physical labor power necessary for the massive exploitation of the dazzling wealth before them. No history of the Western civilization, as we know it, would be complete without an understanding of the tremendous impact Africans had on the European Industrial Revolution and capitalism which were developed as a result of the triangular encounters of Africans, Europeans and native Americans.[6] Though enslaved, brutalized, and used as "beast of burden", the African's impact has only begun to unfold. Undauntedly, they should carry themselves with pride and dignity, educating their detractors that without the price paid by Africans, capitalism and its parent Industrial Revolution would have had a different fate. Thus it was 'by means of the involuntary labor of the captured Africans that sugar and tobacco were produced; and it was by the production of these goods that commerce and arts of capitalist culture were developed. The rapid growth and unparalleled prosperity of Europe are partly owing to the sugar and cotton plantations in the Americas which could not have arisen to such importance without the captive labor of the Africans'.[7]

The problem compounded by the isolation of Africa must be tackled whether from the Diaspora or from the Motherland. This is another aspect of the African's problems. The majority of the people are still ignorant to the fact that the world today consists of only one general entity. My deduction drew its conclusion on the reality that most Africans instead of perceiving their existence in a more global mutual inter-dependence, rather tend to envision their survival narrowly, only on their immediate environment. By doing so, the competitive ability becomes dormant—due partly to the fact that the inability to compete stems from isolation, making it impossible to catch up with new ideas and evolving trends.

II. SKIN COLOR AND RELIGIOUS BELIEFS

The developments of cultures and traditions have a direct correlation with climatic environment and geography. The Europeans had a considerable idea of the necessity to explore and migrate to other parts of the world with promising economic opportunities, even before the inhuman Slave Trade began. Thus, the role geography played was of great importance in the environmental context. They lived in different degrees of harsh weather, in scattered islands divided by oceans and rivers. Isolated therefore, survival became the utmost objective. This isolation endowed and nurtured in them the ability to recognize their strengths and weaknesses; and this subsequently, made it possible for them to manipulate others to their advantage. The Muslim control of the Mediterranean ocean compounded and escalated the European's desire to gain access to the Mediterranean ocean. The Christian Crusade became important not only because it unified all the European principalities into one Christendom, but also because it provided the opportunity for Europeans to gain control of the Mediterranean ocean.

However, the dominant European attitude beginning from the fifteenth century, towards all non-Europeans, can only be characterized from the standpoint of their historical existence before the fifteenth century. The impact of isolation, and the resultant effect of minimal interaction with other cultures in the world made them to develop a unique world view that is centered on their conception of man, God and the universe—with a lot of emphasis on property acquisition. Two aspects of the European's ordered view of the world manifested themselves in their understanding of skin color and religious beliefs. Henceforth, the myopic understanding of skin color and religion would become the basis for justifying the alleged European superiority. By the same logic, they forgot that Christianity was not founded in Europe. Instead, the Christian religion was developed in Africa (in the Nile Valley) from where it spread to Europe.

In the first place, when Europeans accepted Christianity, greater emphasis was laid on the ancient Africa's mystical and astronomical symbols (which were historicized and humanized) than on the spiritual tenets of the Religion. Spiritualism which has been the underlying divine verity of the African God-concept of spirituality was rejected by the founding fathers of Euro-Christianity.[8] As a result, the ancient African's cosmological cue was desacralized and rationalized into the European politics of the time period. Consequently, religion and politics were intertwined. Henceforth, this led to the emergence of Christendom as the dominant force in Europe. The birth of Christendom not only regulated and socialized Europeans, it also aided in the creation of the European man. Moreover, the political nature of this religious relationship buttressed the elevation of astute political figures, contrary to spiritual conscious personalities, to serve as popes and cardinals within the Roman Catholic Church. This underscored the supremacy of the Roman Catholic Church in every vital aspect of the European life.[9] In other words, the acceptance of the Christian Faith in Europe, thereafter, affected and influenced the development of a European culture. It was Europeanized to be responsive to everyday life demands; and it later became the major element that helped in the unification of the European personality.

Conversely, the Europeans saw the African spirituality as paganistic and defective. The early European Christian missionaries, who came to Africa to conquer the so-called heathens and bring them to their God, were all educated about the misunderstood versions of the African God-concept spirituality. So they undermined the original God-concept of spirituality and the traditions of the Africans, resulting in the suppression of an African cultural identity. But the African understanding of human nature and the universe is deeply rooted in the African God-concept of spirituality which has no doubt been the prototype of all religions.

In the second place, skin color formed the basis of the European concept of the "White Man's Burden". This was the enunciation of the belief that God created the European people in His image, and chose them as the people capable of redeeming humanity from "unrighteousness". So it was their God-given duty to liberate the entire human race from the so-called "forces of darkness". This was expanded to include their economic and political adventurism—bringing civilization to the backward peoples of the world. The French version of this concept is found in the principle behind the policies of "Assimilation" and the doctrine of "Association".

Again, the importance of religion comes into play because to the European mind religion has been seen as being political. But the supposition that politics transcend religion was entrenched ever since the first council of Nicaea in 325 C.E.[10] Let it then be said that the justification for converting the so-called "heathens" of Africa to Christianity, and their supposed acculturation into the ways of the white man were politically and economically motivated. Consequently, it is the will of power and economic opportunities that have been the goal of Europe's missionary activities in Africa as opposed to the rhetorical meaning of the concept: White Man's Burden.

III. THEORY AND PRACTICE OF RACISM

One of the common Igbo maxims teaches us that, *"Onye n'atu madu otu aka, amaro na nkpuru aka ito ya n'atukwa ya onwe ya"*. Or, it can be understood as the riddle of the three fingers pointing back at the accuser. The meaning is that a person pointing one accusing finger at another person is not always aware that his other three fingers are equally pointing at himself. It implies that a typical fool only sees the foolishness of others, but always fails to see his own foolishness. This Igbo maxim draws a parallel with the issues of race and this would become clear as the drama unfolds itself.

When economic expansion became an integral part of the liberal notions of free trade, the struggle to dominate the global market resulted into slave trade, slavery, colonialism, and imperialism. The Europeans emerged as a dominant force in the world. According to Felix Gilbert, "this…represented a violation of the liberal notion of equality, or equal dignity of rational man. It was unavoidable that a rationalization of this elitist attitude was undertaken. The crucial elements in the process of rationalization were Social Darwinism and racism. Darwin was interpreted to have suggested that it was not only natural but almost desirable that the stronger rules over the weaker. Racism provided the justification for the rule of white Europeans over the black, brown, and yellow populations of the globe."[11] No doubt, it also laid the foundation for Nazism and Fascism. This attitude became the fundamental principle behind the emergence of phenotypical hierarchy; and "also underlay the acceptance of the notion that birth or race made one segment of society superior to others".[12] Likewise, racism became the major element employed consciously and unconsciously in the definition of the social strata. Felix Gilbert goes on to explain, "that differences in social status were believed to follow from natural selection, from having 'better blood'".[13] A "better blood" indeed as

Rudyard Kipling defined it in his concept, "White Man's Burden". It was no surprise that an intellectual justification of this prevailing attitude was undertaken in Europe and the Americas. Thus theories like the "Natural Selection" and the "Curse of Canaan" (Hamitic myth) were rationalized and bent to suit the political, economic, and intellectual objectives of the European.

From the foregoing, it is clear that the victimization of Africans became important not only for the Eurocentric moral gimmick, but also to ensure a permanent psychological inferiority complex on them. Great effort was therefore made to explain away this approach by excluding Africans within the Homosapien community. Africans were portrayed as part human and part beast. People who did not fully evolve into full human beings—that they were "half-monkeys and half-men". One of its manifestations has been the truncated view of the black male's super sexual mythos. Hitherto the whole gamut of the black man's image has been consistently portrayed in such a manner as to suggest that he is a hedonistic beast: a sexual animal with an horrific penis. No doubt, they conjured up the image of the black male as animalistic and used it as the justification for many of the atrocious lynch murders and other violent crimes committed against Africans in the United States. The absurdity inherent in this symbolism is deeply rooted in the implied uneasy feelings about the genetic melanin dominance of Africans; and this has been buttressed by the supposed fear of possible genetic annihilation, as a result. This sense of inadequacy or fear of genetic annihilation amongst Europeans has been amplified by Frances Cress Welsing. When she wrote: "That there should be myriad behaviors in the white supremacy behavior system that reflect a deep desire to counteract and compensate for the perceived genetic deficiency of white skin should not be at all suprising".[14]

Overall, this absurd confusion and its ramifications have created a world order where the African has become the "beast of burden" and an object of caricature for the amusement of the Establishment. Indeed, Herbert Spencer the proponent of Social Darwinism and Adolf Hitler the arch Nazi were all products of their environment. They had one thing in common. They both believed in the Darwin's theory of *Evolution by*

Means of Natural Selection, and bent it to suit their respective purposes. In other words, Adolf Hitler and Herbert Spencer were not the European anomaly. In fact, they personified what the European historically evolving ideology has come to epitomize.

"The cry for freedom of man's spirit became a shriek for freedom in trade and profit. The rise and expansion of the liberal spirit were arrested and diverted by the theory of race, so that black men became black devils or imbeciles to be consumed like cotton and sugar and tobacco, so as to make whiter and nobler men happier".[15] The justification of actions or the socio-economic development through cultural, political, social and religious demagoguery destroyed the chance humanity had for a uniform universal brotherhood. It has destroyed the moral fabric that holds humanity together. For the African people, it has become the one thing that had made them "invisible" amongst other biological or social groups. In this respect, W.E.B. Du Bois noted that 'before the enslavement of Africans became the foundation of a new and world-wide economic development, the trend of human thought had been toward recognizing the essential equality of all men, despite obvious physiognomic differences. But with the recognition of the value of the African captive labor, came a premeditated effort to prove scientifically the inherent inferiority of Africans and the innate superiority of Europeans'.[16] Make no mistake about it, when a society is blinded by the pedantry of race prejudice, the word fairness becomes a moral gimmick.

Was it an irony that the rationale behind racism was what gave birth to Nazism? The justification of racism contaminated the minds of most Europeans. And the principles behind the concept of a "better blood", unleashed a monstrous force that dominated the lives of the people. It was accepted and adopted whilst the world awaited its consequent explosion. The Second European War (so-called 2nd World War) was the synthesis of the popular doctrine: White Man's Burden. Was it a coincidence? Or was it part of the plan of the European God? Or was it the optimization of the European ideology? As Du Bois stated, "There was no Nazi atrocity—concentration camps, wholesale maiming and murder, defilement of women or ghastly blasphemy of childhood—which the Christian civilizations of Europe had not long been practicing against colored folk in all parts of the world in the name of and for the defense of a Superior Race born to rule the world."[17] Moreover, the facts remain that racism which was nurtured and encouraged in Europe, came close to being the one thing that could have destroyed the European continent. The impact the War left on the minds of people is unimaginable. It shook the world and left clusters of its demoralizing ugly self scattered all over the entire world.

Hitler developed his Nazi philosophy from the pseudo-intellectual theories on race. However, he narrowed his understanding of race to ethnic groups or nationalities to fit his psycho-cultural objectives. Nevertheless, his was not an isolated case, because the theories which nurtured racism were in most part equally used as political ideology of first degree all over Europe: The survival of the fittest. Hitler's belief was that "the whole work of nature is a mighty struggle between strength and weakness—an eternal victory of the strong over the weak", as was illustrated in his book *Mein Kampf.* [18] Thereupon the idea that the elimination of the assumed weak by the assumed strong has been the basis of human development was adopted by Hitler. And this became the foundation stone for his justification of the superiority of the Germanic race; the principle behind his anti-Semitic atrocities; and the moving force behind the genesis of a masqueraded "Aryan race" supremacy. Hitler's Aryan race was centered on all Germanic people, and was developed to flourish on the notion that the Germanic people were superior to all peoples of the world—the rest of Europe included. It is this exclusion of many Europeans from the Aryan supremacy that is the basis of Hitler's condemnation. For his "condemnation" was not that he committed inhuman atrocities, but that these atrocities were committed on fellow Europeans.

This Aryan supremacy was founded on the belief that amongst Europeans the Germanic people were the "purest", with blond (e) hair and blue eyes, i.e., the whitest of the whites. There was a strong precedent; and the Nazis borrowed from it, to justify their own theory. Because Nazism was an amalgamated product of the European historical, cultural, economic, intellectual and political manipulations; it was a perfect example of the incongruous nature of racism. In other words, the Nazis borrowed extensively from the European race theorists. The popular French race theorist, Arthur de Gobineau, must have inspired the Nazis, directly or indirectly. In *The Inequality of Human Races,* Gobineau made it explicitly clear "that a single race, the Aryans, had created all past civilization, he presumed a correlation between racial characteristics and potential for civilization and further presumed that Aryans alone were capable of creating or maintaining civilization in the future". [19] Also, Houston S. Chamberlain, an English man who migrated to Germany, took the Gobineau's idea of inequality and expounded it much further in his book, *The Foundation of the Nineteenth Century.* Joseph E. Harris noted that, "he [Chamberlain] combined the ideas on the evolutionary struggle with the will for power and presented a doctrine of the master race, later adopted by Hitler". [20] On the whole, however, the rationale behind the doctrine of "survival of the fittest" provided the Nazis with the rationalization they needed to win popular support from the German middle class.

The primary rationale behind the Social Dawinists concept of the Survival of the Fittest was physical attribute. Not surprisingly, the Nazis equally emphasized human phenotypical attributes. But, of course, they knew that they had to depart from the skin color; hence, they concentrated on the color of hair and eyes. On the contrary, the ideas behind the concept "survival of the fittest" and the emphasis on phenotypical attributes such as skin color were formulated to have European consensus, unlike the "Aryan race" theory which was focused on the German speaking people in Europe.

The skin color or skin pinkness provided the unifying force for the Europeans; because except from that, there was no other rational variable common between all Europeans that could have provided a European consensus. The European consensus race politics was built upon the myth of the European skin whiteness and superiority. Moreover, the Christian religion mostly was also used to support the argument of racial superiority, but had not been used exclusively for three reasons. Firstly, it is a fact that all Europeans were not Christians. Secondly, the Christian religion was not traditionally practiced only in Europe. The Amhara people of modern Ethiopia had adopted and practiced the Christian Faith for almost two millennia. In fact, they are one of the oldest practicing Christians in the world. Thirdly, the European Slave Trade was initially rationalized with the notion that the Africans were "heathens" who did not know God—heathens in need of the "white" salvation. Therefore, one of the rationales behind the barbaric European Slave Trade was to bring the African heathens to Jesus Christ. Nevertheless, when the issue of whether the Africans would be made free if they became Christian arose, there was a scramble to rationalize again the African enslavement. This occurred in the mid-seventeenth century until the issue was legally put to rest. This was when a Virginia court amongst others in the United States ruled that "baptisme of slaves doth not exempt them from bondage." [21] It was then that they realized that the use of the Christian Faith as a yardstick for bondage was less persuasive and could not be coherent. However, the skin color provided the rationale they needed backed by the fabricated biblical "curse of Ham", gave the Europeans the pseudo-intellectual argument to systematically condition and brainwash the defenseless Africans, constantly telling them that they were inferior to the Europeans. But the idea was that the African must be made to lose his identity, in order to "escape the doom which according to their amiable theology hangs over him—a curse which so far as he is concerned never had any existence—a miserable fiction, a wild phantasy of exploded commentators".[22]

The Nazis went a little further within the established understanding of racial superiority to develop their own concept. The obvious thing is that the meaning and the understanding of the word or concept race is vague and ambiguous, and will always stand the chance of being used by extremists to advance their own beliefs, ideologies, and ambitions. Its vagueness stems from the fact that racism was first founded and adopted on the basis of skin color using the pink European as the model. Du Bois noted that 'skin pigmentation has been the conventional criterion by which Europeans divided the main masses of humanity to suit the dogmatic beliefs of the racist theorists'. [23] On the contrary, Hitler's understanding of race attached little importance to skin color. Hence, the Nazis mostly based their theory on language, culture, religion, and color of hair and eyes. This cannot be dismissed as unfounded because it leads to three important conclusions. First, that the concept of race is vague and misleading.

Secondly, that the idea of race is just a concept used by the Establishment to solidify and entrench their position. Third and finally, that race is a state of mind, used and abused to the detriment of the underdog.

Racism is a system of power monopolization and social control. It feeds on the human weaknesses of ego, greed, jealousy, fear, envy, hate, anguish and power hunger. It was founded on the confrontational premises of superiority versus inferiority, strong versus weak, dominance versus subordination, control versus submission, white versus black, Christian materialism versus African spiritualism, etc. It can go on and on, until the entire humanity is one way or the other entangled. Kovel articulated this somewhat differently, when he wrote: "For race prejudice—which is, whatever its roots, clearly a causal agent in racism—entails a certain kind of person in a certain kind of setting, holding on to some peculiar beliefs about another who is designated as belonging to something called a different race". [24] Nevertheless, racism in the Western hemisphere is intertwined as an integral part of the organic structure of the modern world. Since the West still dominates the entire world in many aspects of the human endeavor, racism therefore is the moving force behind the dynamics of decision making in the global interaction of people. On the other hand, Na'im Akbar insisted that "racism is a strange phenomenon that blocks human opportunity, that destroys human potential, that is predicated on the destruction of people on the basis of physical racial characteristics".[25]

The "inner" working of the mind of a racist is based on fantasies. It is based neither on factual nor objective evidence or reasoning. However, the problem underlying racism is that, consciously and unconsciously, the contamination of people's minds would change form, if the culture was built on these beliefs. The culture then would become the organ used to nourish and perpetuate the fantasies. These fantasies which are based upon wish and desire could even come true because culture is an organic force in human development. The role played by the dominant beliefs in the evolution of a culture therefore becomes the blueprint and the backbone in the efficacy of symbols and their understanding. Accordingly, Kovel noted that "racist psychology is a prerequisite of racist institutions, and racist institutions engender a racist psychology".[26] The Nazis, most of all, understood the intricacies of this phenomenon and knew damn well how to use it to change the psychological make-up of the Germans when they came to power on January 30th, 1933. They knew that the psychology of the German culture "is to a great extent a symbolic precipitate of the kinds of experience forced upon" their people by their turbulent history.[27]

The obvious vagueness found in the concept of race makes it inherently controversial. The arbitrary use of this concept by eminent Eurocentric historians like Voltaire, Rousseau, Hume and their contemporaries as the basis for interpreting cultural ranking made the understanding of race to become explicitly "racial" classifications of the humankind using Europeans as the model for humanity. On the other hand, men like Gobineau used language to analyze and define "the races of man". In his "great chain of being", Gobineau argued that languages must be placed in the same hierarchy, precisely within the hierarchy of races. This was because he believed that since their Eurocentric notion of race has categories, from top to bottom, that languages were equally an inherent part of this chain of superiority and inferiority categorization.

It was Dr. Robert Knox who, in the nineteenth century, contended the idea of a "transcendental anatomy" in his book *The Races of Man.* He concluded that "race is everything; literature, science, art—[inferring that] in a word, civilization depends on it". [28] The implication of such assertion in the nineteenth century is not only academic, but also underlies the interpretations or misinterpretations of every reasonable human phenomenon. Not only was Charles Darwin noted to have been influenced by Dr. Knox in his intellectual development and on the theory of the "Natural Selection of Species", but that the foundation of Social Darwinism was laid by its Chief proponent, Herbert Spencer, based on the intellectual blueprints of Dr. Knox and Charles Darwin. There is, therefore, no gainsaying the fact that Social Darwinism provided the stimulant for the works of such men like Count Arthur de Gobineau's *Essay on the Inequality of Races* and Houston Stewart Chamberlain's *Foundations of the Nineteenth Century,* amongst others. These works, clearly borrowed extensively from many of the peculiar assumptions of Social Darwinism to justify the alleged inherent inferiority of Africans on the one hand, and the supposedly innate superiority of Europeans of "Nordic" or "Aryan" ancestry on the other.

Undauntedly, however, this conundrum has not escaped the attention of scholars, who are inspired not because of vested interest but are genuinely moved by the juxtaposition of instilling an intellectual and ethical imperative. This is reflected essentially in the following insightful statement:

"The concept of race as a biological category does not coincide with the concept of ethnos (or nation) as a sociological category, yet many communities that are racial in their origins (e.g., Negroes in the U.S.A. or the Colored people in South Africa) prove to be social categories in almost the same degree as ethnic communities. ... The concept of language as a linguistic category does not coincide with the concept of ethnos either, yet we know how important the role played by languages is on the formation and existence of ethnic communities".[29]

IV. BIBLICAL AGENT OF RACISM

If human nature is human consciousness, if all human beings were created by their Faith in one God, and this one God created man in His own image, then all groups must be equal for the theory or concept of one God to stand.[30] There should be no superiority or inferiority of any kind if the Faith in one God is for real. But to the contrary, the concept of one God exists only in theory and yet contradicts itself in practice. From the perspective of the Bible, the Christian God created Adam and Eve, in the beginning, from whom all Christians presumably can trace their ancestry and origin. Theoretically, Adam and Eve, therefore, qualified from its allegorical point of view as the father and mother of humanity respectively, from the point of view of the Bible. After the biblical great flood, it was only Noah's family that survived the biblical flood. So the survival of Noah and his family, subsequently, constituted what is actually considered as the different biological groups, languages, and ethnic groups of the Christian world for those who accept the Christian perspective.

But the Christians created the myth of Ham despite their notion of one God. The Hamitic myth was created to lend credence to the alleged inferiority of the African people, from the "curse of Canaan" in the Old Testament of the Bible, *Genesis 9:20-27*. The Ham doctrine was erroneous, but shows how far the Europeans can go to distort the truth. According to the Bible, Ham was Noah's son, but Noah never cursed Ham; rather Noah cursed his grandson Canaan: "a servant of servants shall he be to this brethren" (*Genesis,9:25-27)*.[31] This has been used for centuries to prove not only the biblical justification, but also the biological justification of the African's enslavement and inferiority. Hence, T. B. Mason noted the doctrine as follows:

"The curse of Canaan, frequently erroneously referred to as "the curse of Ham" was used in the past to justify slavery. It is being used by some today to defend the status quo in race relations. They interpret the curse to mean that the Negro, as a descendant of Ham is destined by God to fill permanently a subservient place in society, that he should never be considered as an equal by the white man. On the basis of the curse, some contend that the Negro is innately inferior and that he can never lift himself or be lifted to the intellectual, cultural or even moral level of other races".[32]

The fundamental problem created since the European Slave Trade was imposed on Africans is that the goal of the Establishment has been to keep the African people permanently dependent. This state of dependency, ultimately, was channeled to make Africans incapable of ascertaining their self-determination, thereby ensuring a perpetuation of their exploitation and condition. The fraudulent distortion of ancient historical documents and the Biblical scriptures was an orchestrated ploy to subordinate Africans to an inferior constitution (hierarchy) within the human family. For their so-called "God did not measure out the heart and the brain according to the color of a man's skin.... That statement is but a salve to the white conscience".[33] Therefore, the creation and conditioning of phenotypical hierarchy by the European to suit some imbecilic notions is at the bottom an attestation of a depraved savage-barbarity. Behold, isn't it "a savagery unparalleled in history?"[34.]

Unfortunately, the problem with labeling or stigmatizing people as inferior is that once a group is labeled as inferior, in most cases—

especially if they had been politically and economically circumvented—is that they assume that role of an inferior group. In addition, the effect of the pernicious stigma of inferiority could evolve and become internalized by the majority of the group, not only in their cultural outlook but also in their intellectual expectations.

V. THE CONCEPT OF RACE

The concept of race has been the fundamental element used to justify the subjugation and subordination of the African people. It has been one of the major elements used in the shaping and the molding of the might of the Western culture. This idea of race was devised and introduced to the world by Europeans to divide and compartmentalize humanity according to the color of their skins. Never in the history of humanity had people ever been so subjected to a cruel category of color-based human worthiness. The ancients never attached serious discriminatory significance to the skin color. Hence, skin color was never used by the ancients to define the status or the intellectual capability of any member of the human family. Rather, "the ancients…identified people according to their national or tribal names. They used such names as Visigoths, Vandals, Saxons, Ethiopians, Carthagians, Jews, Arabs, Persians, Babylonians, Egyptians and Moors".[35] However, with the emergence of the European Slave Trade and the subsequent dehumanization of Africans as chattel slaves, the Europeans deemed it necessary to create phenotypical hierarchy to justify the extreme brutality employed in turning Africans from rational men to beasts of burden, to distort the truth in order to ensure a common European consensus.

The first historically recorded explicit classification of humanity was carried out by Johann F. Blumenbach, a German (1752-1840), when he divided humanity on the qualifying criterion of skin color—the color line. It was based on this first theory that the concept of race evolved to become an intrinsic organ of the European economic, intellectual, political and cultural ideologies.

In other words, the concept of race was a desperate effort to rationalize the vicious European aggression on Africans and other non-

Europeans; and this effort was not only economically motivated, but was also motivated by the political, intellectual and cultural objectives of the Europeans to dominate and build a "master race"—to create a sense of inadequacy on all non-Europeans and to ensure their continued exploitation. Naturally, since the pink Europeans were the protagonists of the racial theory, it was not a surprise that they elevated themselves as the model of humanity. But they did not stop there; for to ensure a lack of unity or cohesion amongst the rest of humanity, they subsequently divided all non-Europeans into categories (beginning with "half-civilized" to "savage" or "barbaric"). They degraded "science" with their futile attempts to give scientific justification to their false theory of race. Also, they tried to be consistent. Backed by the best intellectual minds Europe could muster, they put all the people they have historically oppressed the most into the "savage" or "barbaric" category; and justified their undoing by calling them "half–man and half-monkey". One of its manifestations can be seen in the adulterate and consistent use of the word "Tribe" to describe both the African and Native American's ethnic or national groups. This alteration has affected the contemporary meaning of the word tribe; and subsequently, it has become synonymous with the definition of such words as primitive, backward, wild and savage. So the word "tribe" is now reserved for such groups the Establishment plans to destroy or those already destroyed.

But this materialistic extremity was bedeviled with contradictions which made the architects to become desperate and insecure fostering their moral gimmick. So, they pacified those they oppressed less and defined them as "half-civilized", to win them over to their side, to appease their anger and to ensure their own survival. Thus, most Asiatic peoples inadvertently may have accepted this doctrine especially the aspect that dealt with the damnation and the alleged inherent inferiority of the African people. It is not a surprise that many Asians have been noted to despise and demean blackness.

Nevertheless, the implicit and explicit questions are: What have been the responses of Africans when confronted by the powerfully stimulated myths of racial politics? What were the forces that made it possible for the Establishment to fool the entire world with this racial hypothesis for many years? On the one hand, the African's response to this White Magic has created, to a large degree, the African's contemporary ambivalent view of the world, amongst others. On the other hand, the answer to the later question would be found in the cause and effect of the Europeans Slave Trade and the subsequent enslavement of Africans as chattel slaves for involuntary labor. In fact, these are the factors that led to the European's global domination. Moreover, this immense acceptance and conformity was heightened by the "Gutenberg Revolution"—beginning from the print media, and later was enhanced through television and motion picture. Conclusively, Paul Bohannan described rather powerfully that amongst other things:

"The whole subject of race has been torn asunder and "exposed" by modern genetics, yet the very term has encapsulated connotations from false scientific claims and ethical judgments of centuries. The word "race" means, to geneticists, an interbreeding population with distinct and heritable characteristics. The difficulty comes in properly delimiting the relevant characteristics. For a century and more, race and language were confused—race and culture are still being confused. Language is often a characteristic of an interbreeding population, but it is not a biotic characteristic, and therefore has nothing to do with 'race'".[36].

In short, the concept of race is a European devise. It is a Eurocentric construction of human worthiness used to justify the extreme materialism of the European.

VI. THE DYNAMICS OF RACE

The important thing about life is life itself. Life is not material; rather, life is spiritual. This has fundamentally made morality essential to human existence. Although the universe is material, but the essence of the universe is spiritual. Certainly the biological aspect of the human being is equally considered to be important. Nevertheless, the state of mind of the human being is the most important. That is, what the human being thinks with regards to what it means to be human. This is because the mind controls and influences the individual actions of people. In the words of Dr.

Carter G. Woodson, "If you can control a man's thinking you do not have to worry about his action. When you determine what a man shall think you do not have to concern yourself about what he will do. If you make a man feel that he is inferior, you do not have to compel him to accept an inferior status. For, he will seek it himself. If you make a man think that he is justly an outcast, you do not have to order him to the back door. He will go without being told; and if there is no back door, his very nature will demand one".[37] Thus the understanding, that the human spirit cannot be a human being par excellence until he seeks and finds himself; until he removes himself from the physical plane (material plane) and searches for his spiritual being. It is only then can he be able to comprehend the frustrations, envy, greed, and injustice that constitute what is today called the modern world. It is upon this self-realization then can the pain and anguish of living in this extreme materialistic world become bearable and he may fulfill his entrusted destiny.

"RACE"

The European's assertion of superiority was supported with a polar contrast—the African inferiority. Basically, the bone of contention in the concept of Race is this hierarchical structure of the European superiority and African inferiority. Whilst the concept of Race acknowledges the diametrical opposites of the skin color variations between the African phenotype and the European phenotype, it denies their biological relationship of high level of melanin and low level of melanin pigmentations. This has been one of the pitfalls found in the European's concept of Race. As a result, many European race theorists had strived unsuccessfully to deny the humanity of Africans by using the low level of melanin pigmentation as the standard for humanity. Similarly, this flawed racist framework has influenced the development of many outrageous theories regarding Africa and Africans. Hence, it was based on this premise of the African's skin color being diametrically the opposite of the European standard of low level of melanin pigmentation, that the blackness of the skin was politicized as being an inferior attribute.

Tracing the origin of man, by evolution, most Social Darwinists basically went out of their way to find the origin of Homo Sapiens in the Caucasus Mountain region. Based on this ideological position, Europe was seen by the race propagandists as the cradle of the "thinking" man. Thus, the Europeans were initially rationalized to have different ancestry than the Africans; whilst the African was alleged to be the "missing link" between Darwin's apelike ancestors and themselves—the pink skinned Europeans. The ramification of this idea of Europe as being the original home of the "thinking" man is that Europeans began to measure humanity based on their avowed invidious criteria of what constitutes the characteristics and attributes of humans, i.e., thin nose, thin lips, straight hair, pink skin, blue eyes, etc.

Despite the dynamics of race, if one must rank biological groups, then the original ancestor of humanity offers the qualifying nexus from which one can trace the evolution of genotypes. The original genotype must be the group that possesses the biological properties to produce other groups naturally. If the most distinguishable characteristics between various fairly common phenotypical groups is the differentiation in skin pigmentation, then the group that has the capability to produce independently both high level melanin pigment and low level melanin pigment gives us some clue as to what the original human stock was like. Nature (biology) has shown us that skin pigmentation is the normal and natural physiology of humanity. This biological truth attests to the fact that the black (highest state of skin melanin pigment) genetic material is dominant; whilst the pink (lowest state of skin melanin pigment except for albinos) genetic material is recessive and more susceptible to be affected harshly by the sun which is the life blood on the planet. Insofar as we are concerned, the superiority of the original group makes more sense than any other form of social construction or hierarchy. Biological groupings however must not be based on any form of superiority or inferiority categorization because all human genetic materials complement each other. Biological groupings, therefore, must be based on "a fairly common gene pool which produces people with similar physical characteristics".[38] Indeed, bimolecular markers have been identified in the three primary stocks of humanity: "the *Diego* factor among yellows, the K*ell* factor among whites, the *Sutter* and *Gm6* factor among blacks".[39] Generally, these differences manifest in varying degrees in these respective groups.

VII. THE POLITICS OF RACE

The politics of race have been used to propagate the idea of an "accursed African blood". Yet by historical, anthropological, and biological definitions the alleged "accursed African blood" (dominant black genetic material) flows in the veins of the entire humanity. This is to say, that the possession of the African blood is the qualifying factor amongst all human beings. The evidence has begun to unfold that all peoples of the world shared a common ancestry to one human stock. The idea of the original Great Mother is gaining momentum around many circles. The recent confirmation of the "African Origin Theory" by a team of U.S. research scientists underscored this idea. As indicated in Chapter One, these researchers are believed to have found a new significant evidence to support the theory that all human beings descended from an African woman about 200,000 years ago. Essentially, the rediscovery and re-authentication of the ancient world's intellectual recognition of the continent of Kemet as the 'Land of Gods' is indeed part of the process by which Africa's rightful place in the world can be restored.

Historically, the continent of Africa is the humanity's first cultural universe. Africans so to speak were the original people created by the Hidden One Creator of the universe. In other words, black people were the tree from which its branches spread to cover the entire world. But the propaganda of the African's accursed blood had been "drummed" into the minds of many people, consciously and unconsciously. It has assumed a "scientific" negative connotation and consequently has been passed down from generation to generation, thus perpetuating the eighteenth and nineteenth centuries' racist hangovers. The victims of this vicious human degradation not only believed and sanctified these pseudo-intellectual assumptions, they also resorted to build a "wall" of escape from the stigma attached to the alleged accursed African blood. And thereby they have condescended to the baseless assumptions of the alleged "Nordic" or "Aryan" superiority.

The African American culture therefore is an objective mirror upon which the image of the racial assaults on the African people can be seen clearly. So, many of them adopted a self protective measure of a countervailing nature. The mythical dilution of the alleged accursed African blood became necessary not only for its social significance but also for the psychological satisfaction of being a mixed blooded African of some sort. Thus, it became a prevailing tradition to adopt other "bloods" for the glorification of self, whether real or unreal. When asked, the average African American would then without mincing words tell anybody willing to listen that he or she has an Indian or European "blood" in them. So what? Obviously, the reason they over stressed the other bloods in them is to escape the black negativity. Majority of these folks cannot scientifically trace these other bloods from their ancestors. The evidence of phenotypical attribute is either not outstanding or none at all. However, this attitude is not only ingrained in the inferiority complex conditioned in black people over the years of incessant Eurocentric indoctrinations, it is also the resultant effect of the politics of race.

But the belief from the blacks to have less African blood in their genes perpetuates the environmental inferior conditioning of the politics of race. Why? This is because this myth of having mixed ancestry makes the goal of black unity worst. This, of course, has no doubt encouraged the "identity crisis" frequently associated with black people. Some of this could be attributed to the mental and cultural colonialism conditioned on the minds of black people from generation to generation.

Nevertheless, the people of modern Ethiopia are equally noted to have fallen victims to this racial politics. Many of them denounced their African heritage, and rejected their blackness. However, they were entrapped by the racist tradition of defining any African ethnic or national group that failed short of fitting into the deep-seated stereotype of black folks as either "Caucasoids", "Mixed breeds", "Hamites" or "Semites". Thus, misled by the false theories of race, some of the modern Ethiopians made it clear that they were not black people. Whilst they call themselves

Ethiopians, they rejected the term black, which is a very strong contradiction because the word *Ethiopia* was originally used in the ancient times by the Greeks to describe the Black world or blacks. Precisely, the word Ethiopia came into usage first as the ancient Greek's word for Cush or Kush. Secondly, it also was a geographical expression used to describe the African world by the Greeks. Ethiopia was a particular terminology used to describe the African people by the ancient European writers and the biblical writers. Its historical importance lies primary in its usage in many passages in the 'Old Testament' of the Hebrew *Torah* and the Christian *Bible*. Indeed by rejecting the term black and adopting one of the ancient names of the black folks (Ethiopian), it is important to note that the modern Ethiopians did in fact suffer from identity crises. Perhaps, this may be because of the negative impact the European's politics of race have had on them. As this search of an identity by the modern Ethiopians continues, it must not be made to confuse people from distinguishing between ancient Ethiopia which had represented one of the glories of blackness and the modern Ethiopia.

Moreover, the current day peoples of northern Sudan, Libya, northern Mauritania, Somalia, southern Egypt, etc., because of their religious indoctrinations thought of themselves as being Arabs or closer to the Arabs than Africans. For that reason, the myth that they are not black or African became an issue that was also reinforced by the politics of race. In the memory of Edward W. Blyden, I will echo his timely and prophetic word as a reminder to every African whose intention has been to submerge the biological self into the ideological flood of those who have built their legacies by degrading the African heritage. He writes as follows: *"...Let us do away with the sentiment of Race. Let us do away with our African personality and be lost, if possible, in another Race. This is as wise or as philosophical as to say, let us do away with gravitation, with heat and cold and sunshine and rain. Of course the Race in which these persons would be absorbed is the dominant race, before which in cringing self surrender and ignoble self-suppression they lie in prostrate admiration".*[40]

VIII. THE IMPACT OF COLOR CASTE DURING SLAVERY

The European imposition of chattel slavery on Africans led to the creation of a social caste that was in the most part based on the color-line and was made to be in conjunction with a divide and conquer psychological warfare methodology. In the southern United States, for example, the white slave holders divided the enslaved Africans into two "breeds". The moderate melanin pigmented blacks, were very often regarded as the "House Servants", and the high melanin pigmented blacks were mostly the "Field Servants". This categorization and its underpinnings reinforced the already created myth that the highly melanin pigmented African is at the bottom within the human family. The Field Servants mostly were treated differently in many aspects than the House Servants.

On the one hand, the House Servants were not only encouraged to remain apart from the other enslaved Africans, but also to identify themselves with the interests of the master.[41] As a result, they ate better food, were dressed in better clothes; and certainly, they mostly loved their white master. On the other hand, the Field Servants had nothing to lose. They were the epitome of the term "beast of burden". Therefore, they hated their master and lived a life characterized in either sabotage on the master's property or continuous attempt to rebel from their bondage. The Field Servants spent their time in cotton or plantation fields working from dawn to dusk, whereas the House Servants were assigned with domestic chores within the house. This was part of the divide and rule policy enforced in all aspects to keep the enslaved in their place. According to Chancellor Williams: "*This scheme of weakening the blacks by turning their half white brothers against them cannot be overemphasized because it began in the early time, became the universal practice of whites, and is still one of the corner-stone in the edifice of white power*".[42]

Relatively, the House Servants were treated "humanly"; therefore, they became voluntary informants to their master, informing the master and helping in all possible ways to ensure the survival of the enslavement of Africans as an institution for more than two centuries. That apart, it is easy to imagine what kind of impact this color stratification must have had on the Field Servants. In fact, this created and nurtured an inferiority complex on some of the Field Servants, who began to see their melanin enriched dark skin as the underlying factor for their oppression. This manifested a system where a correlation between skin color and social status was defined. Henceforth, this created the diatribe of skin-color vendetta even within the black community. That is, the association of high level of melanin pigmentation and other African features with an inferior social status.

The mulatto hypothesis consequently was not only inevitable but certainly was desirable in the chain of this phenotypical hierarchy. Since the African's high level of skin melanism (blackness) was supposed to be a sign of the curse of God and of his inferiority to the European, therefore a moderate level of melanin pigmentation resulting from mixed ancestry raised the individual above the level of the African.[43] Consequently, as this fixation was nurtured and complimented, it created two classes of black people in the Americas. Indeed, it created a discriminate pattern that is even more or less visible today. It equally enshrined the belief that left its scars around the present generation. The predominant idea began to take roots. The moderately melanin pigmented blacks developed a superiority complex towards the highly melanin pigmented blacks and treated them with contempt. As E. Franklin Frazier described it, the black people of mixed ancestry thought of themselves as being superior to the Africans. He went further to explain, that to the moderately melanin pigmented blacks their moderate level of melanin complexion became their most precious possessions.[44] It became the passport for social upward mobility in the Eurocentric social construction of human worthiness. Thus, it became a social paraphernalia, bestowed by the magic and might of the European global domination, and blessed by the power the society had imposed on the pinkness of the skin as the ideal color and as the "universal" model for humanity.

However, why some of these moderately melanin pigmented blacks thought of themselves as being better than their highly melanin pigmented black counterparts is within bound with the racist theory of low level of melanin pigmentation being the ideal color. This attitude, nonetheless, had been a conditional environmental phenomenon—the effect of the European global economic, political, and cultural manipulations. Evidently, this hierarchical order benefitted the moderately melanin pigmented blacks politically, socially, and economically, not only in North and South Americas but also in Africa and the Caribbean as well. (In South Africa and Brazil, the moderately melanin complexioned Africans are called "Colored" and are treated better than the highly melanin complexioned Africans.) Many of these moderately pigmented blacks want to preserve the status quo. They loved their "kinship" connection with white people, and hated the vestiges or semblance of blackness in them.

To a considerable degree, many Eurafricans actually have been noted to champion the propaganda of the alleged inferiority of the African people. However, one must be careful of succumbing to poor judgment or undue generalization before taking such an ominous stand. Therefore, to bring this generalization into proper focus and to illustrate this understanding, it is pertinent to first consider both the implicit and explicit rationale behind the propaganda of many mixed blooded blacks, which is rooted in the idea that the redemption of Africans in the Diaspora can only suffice when they are white-washed and bleached through intermingling with non-Africans. In other words, that it is unconditional for Africans not to imbibe and submerge the African biological and cultural vehicle in order to make themselves non-Africans. Why a collective death-wish? This is because many of the so-called mulattoes have historically exonerated the low level of melanin pigmentation along-side the European racists as the legitimate standard upon which the African's progress vis-à-vis predicament must be measured. This testimony is found in their popular phrase: ***'whiten the race to save the race'***.

For decades, perhaps centuries, we have neglected the color factor in the interpretation of many African realities. This color factor is in fact not the historical white supremacist racial bigotry, but the color differentiations between the mixed and full-blooded Africans. This has been the long overlooked factor: That within the black community, the white supremacy system favors the less African-looking blacks in all spheres of the global economic and political endeavors. Thus, the all-pervading Euro-color consciousness within the black community impregnated by the white supremacist's bigotry may have in the past been overlooked in the academic circles. Therefore, we must not overlook the impact of this pathology in the world, even within the historical black community. In fact, most of the "black-white" persons seemingly tend to lack a very deep understanding of the conditions of the African people. Tokenly, they may consider themselves as being black. Nevertheless, many of them often think that they are doing the African people a great favor by acknowledging themselves as black people. To them, their vision or justification for acquiescence is implicitly to improve the race—"To whiten the race."

Given the philosophical premise of this notion, most of the "black-white" persons consider themselves essentially better than the saliently characterized Africans. Subsequently, their fantasy would always dwell on integrating as much as possible with the European people. They live a life of contradiction and ambivalence; they are only black when something good is coming out of being black, for instance, economic, social and political opportunities. Hitherto, some of the Euro-African's identification with blackness is, perceived by the author to be mostly when such identification suited their interests. So, when something happened, for example, a negative thing that drew a public outcry, and within the scenario a highly melanin complexioned black is fingered as the perpetrator, some of them would distance themselves from black people. Not that they all viewed bonafide Africans with contempt; but most of them have found it hard to transcend the ramifications of the Eurocentric color stratification. Thus, they were often heard making derogatory remarks about African people. It is an attitude that is borne out of their beliefs that they are different from the general perceptions of blackness. This whole attitude is not really influenced by ignorance or apathy; but rather may have been influenced by their general understanding of themselves as a distinct group (Multi-racial or Mixed race people). The ongoing agitation by people of mixed-parentage to be classified as a distinct group in the U.S. Census is indicative and equally lends ample credence to my contention.*[45] Perhaps, this disdainful relationship between mixed-parented blacks is only echoing the fragile and volatile nature of tagging everybody with a drop of African "blood" in them as black—a delicate balance. It could be contended that many of these people may not have been interested in advocating a distinct classification if Africa was not part of their mixed ancestry. This undercurrent depicts something akin to the Age old racist belief, about the stigma of blackness, which endorses the notion of the so-called mulatto hypothesis.

On the contrary, many mixed-parented blacks often are driven by legitimate moral purpose to harness their social positions in uplifting and regenerating the deprived African people—to render genuine service to their fellow oppressed African people. Still because many of them, deep down in their soul, think that they are better than the Africans on the account of the magic of their part-European ancestry, their effort occasionally failed short of achieving its original purpose. This could be mostly as a result of the shaky ground upon which such program was founded. One of the fundamental reasons behind such outcome is the logic behind their alleged superiority which is covertly in parallel with the European's self-deluded superiority complex over other members of the human family (targeted mostly at Africans). Nevertheless, by their acquiescence or acceptance to the mulatto hypothesis, to the notion that their mixed ancestry has placed them higher than the Africans and has made them superior to the highly melanin complexioned blacks, many mixed-parented blacks have accordingly accepted their own inferiority to the European people. Hence their acceptance of the European color-line, by implication, warranted their inordinate acceptance of their superiority over bonafide Africans.

In superficial terms, some of the mixed blacks constituted what could be considered the diabolical adversaries of the African image and integrity. It has been suggested that a mixed person "had two souls, two temperaments, two sets of opinions, and was unable to think or act strongly and consistently in any direction. Mentally and spiritually he was attuned to the traditions of neither race, and his soul was the scene of perpetual conflict of inharmonious tendencies". [46] In fact, a cursory retrospective look at the fall of Marcus Garvey's movement can give us an invaluable insight to the true nature of this relationship between Africans and their assumed mixed-parented brethren. (The Late Marcus Garvey founded the Universal Negro Improvement Association in New York in 1917, and became the President-General.) Undauntedly, it has now been unequivocally revealed that the imprisonment of Marcus Garvey was plotted and carried out by a clique of some educated moderately melanin pigmented African Americans. In order to implement and orchestrate the plot, clandestine means were used to infiltrate and disrupt the most formidable mass movement in Black America. Bernard Makhoszwe Magubane in the following commentary suggested what might be some of the reasons behind the disruption of Garvey's movement. He writes:

"The black middle class who also happened to be mulatto were made very uncomfortable by Garvey and feuds developed with them which earned Garvey the epithet of a "hater". To be a mulatto in the time of Garvey was to be better than being pure black; and because Garvey rightly or wrongly rejected these assumptions and preached a black God as opposed to a white God, and a black Empire as opposed to a white Empire, he became in liberal circles an exponent of race hatred".[47]

Of course, this fact may precipitate and provoke a multiplicity of responses, but the common denominator was that many of the moderately pigmented blacks deemed themselves the sole liberators of the African people, following the same line of thinking of the European bigots. There is indeed ample evidence that the clique of the moderately melanin complexioned blacks who masterminded the *coup de grace* on Marcus Garvey's Universal Negro Improvement Association (UNIA) were more concerned on preserving the privileges and their monopoly of the intellectual, political, economic and social life of Black America which had been maintained and sanctioned by the status quo. In other words, they were afraid of losing their privileged status, which the Eurocentric social construction had prescribed. The underlying factors therefore were, first of all, that they felt threatened by the psychological impact of Garvey's magic slogans: "Up, You Mighty Race", "Africa for Africans", "Renaissance of the Black Race", "I'm Black and Proud", Black and Beautiful", and "Buy

Black, Think Black, Look Black" movement on the greater proportion of the African Americans, who were by ancestral descent genuine Africans. Secondly, that this clique of the educated African Americans and their radical communist African Caribbean counterparts did not accept Marcus Garvey's Black Nationalism because of their readily adoption and practice of the Eurocentric views and values. In order to ensure their privileged status (petty-bourgeois interest), they used their intellectual and social positions to influence the black integrationist attitude—an attitude deeply ingrained in slavish imitation of Eurocentrists and adopting their ideal. By so doing, they moved the discussion of African heritage, African pride and black image—my main concerns--into what I consider a new institutional nexus.

This concern of mine is grounded upon the understanding that the African American's response to the Eurocentric culture and the acceptance of the white perspective during enslavement was not only gradual but was necessitated by the exigencies of the institution of slavery. Although the enslaved Africans were mentally and culturally deracinated, they were able to survive the atrocities meted to them because they evolved a unique culture correspondingly, as a countervailing force. In other words, despite the efforts of the slave holder to destroy the African sense of kinship in the Americas, most enslaved Africans almost consistently developed a new conception of family, which imposed a new structure to the meaning of life. Thus, during the era of chattel slavery and immediately after its demise, the African American's family pattern was close–knit and community (black) based. It was from this community foundation that "the rhythmic, spiritual and psychic piles that bottomed the new synthesis called Black America" evolved.[48]

However, after Emancipation the first generation of the petty-bourgeoisie, beginning from the late nineteenth century and up to the middle of this century, departed essentially from the foundation laid down by the enslaved Africans and found themselves increasingly imitating and depending upon the European culture more than it is necessary for their mental and cultural survival. This has exceedingly affected the contemporary general culture of Black America. Despite Garvey's shortcomings, it is my belief that if the Garvey movement of the nineteen twenties was not maliciously disrupted, the story of Black America specifically and that of all African people in general would have been different today.[49]

There are many examples (of a general nature) of these contemptuous relationships between the moderately melanin complexioned blacks and the highly melanin complexioned blacks (particularly in the U.S.A.). A typical example could be found in Anne Moody's autobiography: *The Coming of Age in Mississippi.* In this book, Anne Moody, female and black recounted what it takes to be black in Mississippi before and during the Civil Rights Movements. Anne used her family background to portray and recreate the images and realities of an average black family in Mississippi specifically and the South at that time in general. After reading her book, I came to the conclusion that she was destined to succeed against all the encompassing odds. If not, one might argue that the background she came from was quite the opposite of what she had become. In other words, I saw a courageous young lady who was intelligent enough to use her personal experiences as the vehicle to make the best out of her life. There are two things that stood out, which gave her the courage and the determination to become the very best. First, it was the relationship between her mother, a highly melanin complexioned lady and Raymond, a moderately melanin complexioned black man. The attitude of Raymond's mother Miss Pearl, also, a moderately melanin pigmented black lady, was the bone of contention in this relationship. For Anne Moody expressed her frustration when she wrote, "then I began to think about Miss Pearl and Raymond's people and how they hated Mama and for no reason at all, than the fact that she was a couple of shades darker than the other members of their family. Yet they were Negroes and we are also Negroes. I just didn't see Negroes hating each other so much."[50]

Anne was aware of the pain and frustration her mother was going through, knowing that she was not accepted by Raymond's family, because of the color of her skin. This feeling supposedly later developed into hatred towards Raymond. This is perhaps because he was unable to make his people to accept Anne's mother on what she was and not on the basis of her skin complexion. Anne later moved out of the house; hence, she found it hard to reconcile within herself. Secondly, her competition with Darlene, Raymond's sister (also moderately complexioned) in school, instigated by her (Anne) mother, gave a better picture of how deep this color discrimination between two black families had gone. Anne's mother would always say, "y'all goto do good in school. Y'all can't let Darlene and Cherie be smarter than y'all. They already think they is better than y'all' cause they is yellow."[51]

This color discrimination amongst people of African ancestry has been, in fact, a manifestation of the "duality" existing within the African American (also evident in the Brazilian and South African) subculture. In other words, it will be hard to understand the whole picture of this duality without looking at the leadership pattern coupled with the factors that facilitated the individual rise of people to positions of leadership in Black America, before the Civil Rights Era (1954-1965). Some notable examples could be seen when one takes a step back to two generations, and assesses all the renowned black political leaders (specifically before the Civil Rights Movement in the United States). In this distinct pattern, the Establishment whenever necessary maximizes the utility of the buffer class by imposing the mostly moderately melanin complexioned blacks on the black community as the go-between—the intermediary between the white status quo and the African masses. It was based on these paternalistic maneuvers that the tradition of lower pigmented blacks dominating the political scene within the black community was founded. Not until the 1960s Civil Rights Movement, did highly complexioned blacks become visible in both local and national body politic.

IX. THE GUIDING PRINCIPLE OF WHITE MAGIC

White Magic not only undermines the humanity of all Africans, but also it has ingrained the anti-African myopia which seems to have become endemic to the cultural identity of most people. The impact of White Magic on the African people is seen as an unfortunate catastrophe that has degraded all facets of the African existence. Its transmission has subsequently affected the attitudes, images and expectations of most black people. The understanding of beauty has hitherto been made myopic and parochial as a result. From thence the Eurocentric terms of aesthetics became predominant and have often been reinforced by the dichotomy between wish and reality. Now that is White Magic; but the guiding principle of White Magic is self-hatred. Maulana Karenga summed up the dynamics of this principle when he noted as follows:

"The pathology of self-hatred... the self-mutilation in psychological and physical sense, evolved in great part from ignorance and disappreciation of one's history. So, when the European cultivated historical amnesia in black people, they at the same time set up the basis for psychological and physical mutilation by Blacks of themselves in order to seem white or more human".[52]

Here is the phenomenon that dislocates individuals and mocks the eternal Truth of the One Creator of the universe, whilst depreciating human possibilities. White Magic gave birth to the self-destructive idea that the lower melanin pigmented an African looks the better he/she becomes. As this self-hate idea was intensified, it became acceptable within many black communities. Skin bleaches and other related products emerged in the cosmetic industries, providing the needs of many desperate blacks who wanted to look as much lowly melanin pigmented as possible. Also, hair strengtheners became important because of many roles they have played in the development of a black cultural outlook. They were used to make African hair become what many blacks have termed "manageable" to suit the Eurocentric ideal of beauty. Many creative entrepreneurs cashed in on this black "integrationist" attitude and made considerable fortune in the process. Madam C.J. Walker was the first African American female millionaire who built a business empire that raked a fortune out of "Conk" mixtures. The African natural or kinky hair, therefore, was not only despised and looked down upon, it was also considered uncivilized for anybody to reject the prevailing attitude of pseudo-Eurocentric spectacle. Hence, this cultural dislocation is at the bottom a manifestation of the black self-hate attitude towards their natural physiognomy. Charles Silberman pointed out, that "self-hatred is manifested in a number of ways. The most obvious is the use of hair strengtheners, skin bleaches, and the like in the desperate but futile attempt to come close to the white ideal".[53] Indeed, it seemingly conveys a total submission to all the physical attributes traditionally used by the racist to categorize people.

Because the racist dogma of labeling everything African as inferior was widely accepted, it was expected that the African phenotypical characteristics would be rationalized as the root of the alleged black inferiority. The black skin most of all was depicted as the manifestation of the supposedly innate inferiority of the African people, as an attribute of evil. On the other hand, the European phenotypical characteristics were paraded as the standard of excellence or virtuous qualities; and since it was obvious that most Africans generally diverged from this "standard", they were contemptuously chastised for such European anomaly. Implicitly, if the lowest level of skin pigmentation, the melanin deficiency, is the standard of human beauty and intelligence, then the three-fourth of humanity would be damned immutably.

Nevertheless, it was foreseeable that this White Magic would pollute the minds of many blacks whose understanding of their degradation was perennially justified on the assumptions of race. In other words, it will be an understatement to contend that modern racism, a product of the African enslavement and colonization, has not affected the cultural outlook of most black communities. Its overall impact on African people is the rejection of self. Thus, it is not uncommon to see many blacks who have negative attitude towards their blackness. Many a time, this attitude could be an unconscious behavior that is deeply ingrained in the pervasive nature of black negativity. However, the evident distortion of personal appearance by many blacks echoes the resultant mixed-feelings towards their individual dignity. Thus, in their pretentions they claim to be proud of being black; and at the same time, they ridicule most African physical characteristics and seek to modify or efface them as much as possible.[54] Hence, they systematically try to distort their appearances, in order to look more European and less African.

Against the backdrop of the monomaniac dogma of white racism, lay however the deepening cultural and mental crisis between many descendants of Africans and their mixed brethren. The emotional frenzy and the struggle for an identity began to affect the senses for self-dignity and self-preservation. The idea of good and bad became distorted and once again many Africans were deceived and were made to see their natural attributes as "bad", "ugly", and "uncivilized". This radical round-about turn was influenced by many factors. However, one of the primary influences was the role of the mixed blacks in the Black community, which was encouraged by the status quo to lend credible justification to the mulatto hypothesis. The less-African-looking persons were consequently elevated as the standard of beauty and attractiveness within the black community.

Thus, the less African-looking persons were not only portrayed as the archetypes of the "New World" Africans, but also as the standard for acceptance, or the criterion for the improvement of the alleged African people's goddamned and devilish physical attributes. Amongst other things, the belief that straight hair was the "good hair" and woolly or kinky hair was the "bad hair" became accepted, as a result, amongst many blacks in the African world. It then became necessary for most of these blacks to strive through artificial means to acquire the so-called good hair. The new resurgence of surgically thinning the broad nose and clipping the full-lips to fit into the general outlook equally cannot be overemphasized. However, this conscious and unconscious effort by the African people to imitate and pattern their image from the Eurocentric notions of beauty underlies the black sense of inadequacy and is evident in the overall annual black expenditure in cosmetic and chemical industries.

The ramification inherent in this attitude is that disappreciation and unacceptance of one's natural phenotypical attributes becomes a blatant affirmation to the idea that Africans are a "Lost Race". That they are a "lost" biological group whose lack of cultural identity has become an exemplification of their mental and cultural inferiority. The enthronement of this idea was justified with the argument, that the white man's attempt to destroy the African people's ability to think for themselves was relatively an astounding success. So that although Africans are considered physically free, their mind is still subjected to the forces that have made their mental enslavement inextricable. This point is further emphasized by Walter Rodney:

"The language which is used by black people in describing ourselves shows how we despise our African appearance. "Good hair" means European hair, "good nose" means a straight nose, "good complexion" means a light complexion. Everybody recognizes how incongruous and ridiculous such terms are, but we continue to use them and express our support of the assumption that white Europeans have the monopoly of beauty, and that black is the incarnation of ugliness".[55]

X. THE SYMBOLISM OF RACE

The politics of "blood" (genetic material) and the issue of whether one has "Indian" or European blood must not be explored any longer. We have already had our own fair share of destructive negative myths. We must strive to create positive myths about ourselves. Positive myths are good, for there is a better chance that they can give people a perspective relative to understanding life better, and so making it possible for people to live a harmonious existence. On the whole, however, there are dangers with myths especially when people begin to confuse myths with reality. As Doris Dakwah puts it, "A myth can become misleading propaganda when people seek to transform fantasy into actual history, and encourage the followers of an ideology to submit to myths as facts".[56]

We all are aware that many captured female Africans were "raped" during enslavement; also that some enslaved Africans had very close relationships with Native Americans; but we must not forget that amongst the autochthonous Africans there are different shades of color or skin color variations and varied physical attributes.[57] That this biological fact has nothing to do with intermingling between Africans and other biological groups. This notion of course underlies the idea that the Eurocentric notion of race is an ideology of domination, and that the African people have been subjected to the Establishment's instigated action-reaction syndrome: depending on the moods, whims and prejudices of the European for existence. This effort to undermine the humanity of the African spirit is at the bottom the root of racism—the virus of racial intolerance

In fact, 'it is impossible in Africa or in the Diaspora to fix with any certainty the limits of "racial" variation due to heredity, to climate and to intermingling. In the past, when European anthropologists assumed one distinct African type, every variation from that type was interpreted as meaning mixture of blood. Today, we have begun to recognize and appreciate a broader normal African type'.[58] Of course, this justifies the fact that the African biological vehicle possesses the properties necessary in producing other biological groups. But that notwithstanding, the understanding of "race" is still based on physical attributes. The characteristics are skin pigmentation, hair type, eyes, nose, lips, but most of all the attitudinal frame of mind—education, economic class, etc.

Above all, the main thrust of the Eurocentric construction of race is in its symbolic apparatus, and how it facilitates and reinforces the polar dichotomy of white superiority and black inferiority. But this cultural symbolism is indeed a fantasy that is short of stereotypical impression. That is why, when an African person succeeds in the United States, his/her acceptance into the European culture (status quo) is usually explained away: "Oh, he is different" (honorary white). In this instance, one is bound to the conclusion that "race" is a value system equated with material acquisitionism; hence, the racist attitude of depicting "white" as the paragon of light, beauty, success and life; whilst black is portrayed as the symbol reminiscent with evil, failure, backwardness and ugliness. Therefore, black people are presumed and treated as poor, unfit, bad and evil until they prove to be otherwise. On the other hand, white people are perceived and also are given the benefit of doubt to be rich, good and honest, until they prove to be the opposite. Africans are presumed to be sinners and immoral; whilst Europeans are supposed to be virtuous and righteous. The African is overtly depicted as the symbol of evil, failure, poverty, death and ugliness—as the symbol of "dirt". This symbolic aspect of racism consequently overshadows its inherent cultural structure. It then becomes difficult to see how the organized structures of this symbolism have devalued the humanity of all Africans.

In the final analysis, it is the duty of the African people to not only repudiate the use of blackness as a symbol of "dirt" or evil by the

Europeans but Africans also must insist that the Europeans find some other symbol for their sadistic fantasies. More so, since the pink Europeans have associated the human feces with blackness, they must equally be reminded that the human feces and/or urine can be closely related in color to the melanin deficient pink color. Insofar as the human bodily wastes are concerned, nature has shown that the urine and feces come out in varied colors. African people must not let the European neurotic drives, to control and dominate others, intimidate and suppress their human aspirations for self-preservation. Since the unattainable fantasy for whiteness has dominated the European psychopathic drives, one must not fall into this trap of human reductionism. *For, whilst human blackness is real, human whiteness to the contrary is a fantastic lie.*

Indeed, this way of abstracting and conceptualizing human low melanin pigmentation as white underlies the force of White Magic. It is evident that this idea of whiteness has been part of the motivation for the European's abstraction of blackness as dirt and evil. But the pink color of the Europeans is the lowest pigmentation of skin melanism within the human family. Just as the illusions of skin whiteness is an unattainable goal, so skin whiteness in itself also represents a form of abnormality, an absence of life or the epitome of death and evil. It is given, that perceptions guide behaviors more than reality. Therefore, the European's idea of the supremacy of human whiteness is an abstraction that they superimposed on themselves for a collective mental and cultural identity which has become an illusion of a superior race. Nevertheless, it is an abstraction that negates nature!

XI. THE QUESTION OF GENETICS

The question of genetic inheritance with reference to the intelligent Quotient (IQ) tests contradicts the idea that all humans are created equal. According to Theodosius Dobzhansky, "equality is confused with identity, and diversity with inequality".[59] He went further to infer that, "inequality is also not biologically given but is rather a socially imposed prescription".[60] The use of Intelligence Quotient (IQ) tests to measure the intelligence of blacks and whites is a mockery to science. There was desperation within the Establishment to prove the alleged inherent inferiority of the African people with Intelligence Quotient tests that were definitely biased against Black people and their culture in the United States. So they skewed the evaluation criteria and procedures to favor whites, giving them undue advantage. The late W.E.B. Du Bois elucidated this argument, when he pointed out the inherent discrepancy found within the procedure used to implement the Intelligence Quotient test. He noted thus: "A review of intelligence tests in the United States shows that, first, in most of these investigations the fundamental conditions of measurement and experimentation have not been observed; and secondly, the tests used have been standardized upon whites in the northern part of the United States while most of the Negroes measured have been from the South".[61]

Given the historical record of racism, one can aptly conclude that this Test (IQ) was initiated to lend credence to the five hundred years of the African degradation, which was based and justified on the reasoning that "inferiority necessitates dominance". They (the racists) were conditioned to believe in the fantasy that Africans in general were genetically inferior. So they turned to heredity; however, "heredity is not a status but a process. Genetic traits are not performed in the … cells, but emerge in the course of development, when potentialities determined by the genes are realized in the process of development in certain environments".[62] Therefore "every person is unique and non-recurrent. No two individuals, except monozygotic twins, have the same genes; not even monozygotic twins have the same environment".[63]

The protagonist blinded by racist prejudice could not see the irrelevance of determining the differences in intelligence between the African and European peoples. But their own interest had been to strive by any means possible to maintain the status quo—the five century-old tradition of excluding blacks from the human family must continue. Theodosius Dobzhansky's deduction is a testament to my analysis. He concluded that "the idea that intelligence and other socially significant human traits may be hereditary is repugnant to many people, largely because of confusion of heredity with fate or predestination. A genetic conditioning of the variations in intelligence does not necessarily mean that the intelligence of a person is irremediably fixed by the genes".[64]

The inadequacy of the Intelligence Quotient tests notwithstanding, the impact of intensive care and tutoring of children may have remarkable bearing on a child's potentials and invariably could alter his or her genetic makeup. For an analogy, "nature determines the kind of tree, environments determine the quality and quantity of the fruit".[65] No doubt, the proponents of the Intelligence Quotient tests knew this phenomenon, but chose to overlook it. Conversely, the distortion of scientific facts, obviously targeted at defenseless blacks, is more important than upholding the professional ethical imperative.[66] In spite of the political ramifications of these tests, 'the bolstering up of the alleged European superiority by reference to the IQ tests has been concluded by eminent Geneticists and Bio-chemists to be false and misleading'.[67] Not only were the "Intelligent tests" derived merely from the Eurocentric cultural baggages, but they were predisposed on the dogmatic assumptions of the European cultural "universalism".

XII. OBTUSE PHILISTINISM

Institutional and individual racism is counterproductive—in intellectual, economic, social and other aspects of human endeavor. Therefore, it is a painful fact that men who consider themselves 'professional' would stoop so low, just for a simple reason—to perpetuate the alleged inferiority of the African people. A typical example is the Henry F. Osborn's article "The Evolution of Human Races" republished in the *Journal of Natural History* in April 1980. He stated thus: "The standard of intelligence of the average adult Negro is similar to that of the eleven-year old youth of the species Homosapiens."[68] But paradoxical as the European model of biological determinism may seem to appear presently, the fact remains that the African people have been defined for centuries as happy savages, compared and treated like children who would never grow up beyond the age of twelve. This studious evasion of the truth gained an incredible acceptance within the confines of the Eurocentric ideology. Thus as Basil Davidson noted: "Africans, it would be commonly said, simply lacked the faculty for growing up".[69]

The nature of this obtuse philistinism is, in my view, psychopathic. It is not only irrationally anti-African, it is also an abasement on the self-respect and the intellectual dignity of all African people. On the contrary, this foolhardy in itself depicts something that smacks of childish fantasies on the part of the traducers. Hence, "it merely indicates an imperious determination to skirt around the facts, to hold on to what one wants to believe".[70] As far as I am concerned the issue of ethical or moral conduct has never been applied in anything that relates to Africa and black people all over the world.[71] Whenever it seems like it, it is usually for a different motive. Essentially, it is mostly geared towards assuaging the embittered black rage or agitation. It is hypocritical and amoral, when anti-African ideology fosters a total disregard to the humanity of Africans.

Mired by racist prejudice, the Establishment has consistently, in all human endeavors, proven that there is a conspiracy to cloud and muddle the African image. There is no explanation whatsoever to justify the overwhelming myths created to keep Africa and Africans isolated from the entire human family. It is no gainsaying the fact that these methods of psychological intimidation and dehumanization were highly successful during slavery and colonialism in the Americas and Africa respectively. As Charles Silberman correctly stated: "The system of slavery was administered so as to make the Negroes behave as if they were inferiors—to distort their personalities and suppress their mentalities in such a way as to make them in fact incapable of utilizing the "freedom" that finally became theirs after two and a half centuries of enslavement".[72] On the other hand, during colonialism in Africa, the European colonial conquerors "prodded by their own neurotic drives, waded in and wrecked an entire philosophy of existence of a people without replacing it, without even knowing really what they had been doing".[73] But the intention was to create a species that would be happy to be subservient to Europeans. This conditioning did not start in the Americas, rather it started in 1441 when the pugnacious and avaricious Portuguese came to the West African coast, and began the kidnap and plunder of Africans and Africa respectively.

This anti-African hysteria could be understood, when one takes a critical look at the method used to isolate not only the enslaved Africans but also the freedmen from the outside world. After the Emancipation Proclamation of 1863, effort was made in many aspects during Reconstruction (1865-1877) to limit the human rights Africans had fought for and deserved. Thus began "the conjunction of racism with reformism".[74] For, we know that the problem with American reform for blacks is that it is white-led, white-defined and fundamentally racist. The South where the greater proportions of the "freed" Africans lived began to move towards segregating the descendants of Africans from participating in the political and socio-economic life of the nation. Conversely, in 1896, 'a legalized system of racial segregation was established which stigmatized the African as unfit for human association, and every type of propaganda was employed to prove that the African was morally degenerate and intellectually incapable of being educated. Living constantly under the domination and contempt of the European, many of the Africans came to believe in their inferiority'.[75] So, many Africans accepted White Magic as a way of life, as sacrosanctly bestowed upon the white man by his white God. Subsequently, a racist fantasy founds legitimacy only upon the black man's acceptance of such notion; and thus White Magic having been condoned and sanctioned by Africans has become the European functional reality.

CHAPTER THREE
NOTES

1A. W.E.B. Du Bois, *Dusk Of Dawn,* New York: Harcourt Brace, 1940, p. 58.

1. Eknath Easwaran, *Gandhi the Man.* Berkeley, California: The Blue Mountain Center of Meditation Inc., 1972, p. 49.
2. Ibid, p. 49.
3. I.K. Sundiata, "Creolization on Fernando Po", *The African Diaspora,* Cambridge, Massachusetts: Harvard University Press, 1976, p. 413.
4. R.N. Egudu noted that Igbo names reveal the philosophical basis of the Igbo people's conceptions of the natural and the supernatural worlds and their roles in them. The significance of names in expressing the worldview of the people is demonstrated in this book. In his words, "They... defy the world by saying and believing that the world does not belong to any one person: "Uwa bu nke onye?" (To whom does the world belong?), which is a personal name in the form of a rhetorical question. The fact that the world does not belong to and should therefore not be controlled by any one person encourages the Igbo to make the best out of it". Romanus N. Egudu, *African Poetry of the Living Dead: Igbo Masquerade Poetry.* Lewiston, New York: The Edwin Mellen Press, 1992, p. 4.
5. Karl Marx's theory and concept of "surplus-value" is important for understanding the role of the captive African labor-power in the transformation of European feudalism into mercantilism, mercantilism into capitalism or African human both as a commodity and as a laborer into capital. This basic theoretical premise of "surplus-value" was later amplified and grounded with precise historical facts of the European Slave Trade by Eric Williams. Thus Williams wrote: "The triangular trade thereby gave a triple stimulus to British industry. The Negroes were purchased with British manufactures; transported to the plantations, they produced sugar, cotton, indigo, molasses and other tropical products, the processing of which created new industries in England; while the maintenance of the Negroes and their owners on the plantation provided another market for British industry, New England agriculture and the Newfoundland fisheries. By 1750

there was hardly a trading or a manufacturing town in England which was not in some way connected with the triangular or direct colonial trade. The profits obtained provided one of the main streams of that accumulation of capital in England which financed the Industrial Revolution". Eric Williams, *Capitalism and Slavery.* London: Andre' Deutsch Limited, 1964, p. 52; also read Karl Marx, *Capital, Vol. II.* Moscow: Progress Publishers, 1971; W.E.B. Du Bois, *The World and Africa,* New York: International Publishers Co. Inc., 1965; Walter Rodney, *How Europe Undeveloped Africa.* Washington D.C.: Howard University Press, 1982.

6. P. Olisanwuche Esedebe, *Pan-Africanism: The Idea and Movement.* 1776-1963, Washington, D.C.: Howard University Press, 1982. pp. 34-35.
7. Quoted in P. Olisanwuche Esedebe *Pan-Africanism,* p. 35; see also, Edward Wilmot Blyden, *African Repository (October,* 1881), pp. 114-115. *The Journal of the American Colonization Society,* Vol. I-LXVIIL March, 1825-January, 1892, Washington D.C. (Fourah Bay College, University of Sierra Leone) contains most of the tracts of Dr. E. W. Blyden.
8. Gerald Massey, *Gnostic And Historic Christianity,* Edmonds, WA: Sure Fire Press, 1985, pp. 20-27.
9. Dean Dudley, *History of the First Council Of Nice.* Chesapeake. Virginia: EGA Associates, 1990, pp. 29-120.
10. IBid, pp. 62-97.
11. Felix Gilbert, *The End of the European Era, 1890 to the Present,* New York: Norton & Co, 3rd edition, 1984, pp. 31-34.
12. IBid, pp. 34.
13. IBid, p. 34.
14. Frances Cress Welsing, *The Isis Papers: The Keys To The Colors,* Chicago: Third World Press, 1991, p. 78.
15. W. E. B. Du Bois, *Black Folk: Then and Now,* New York: H. Holt, 1939, p. 127.
16. IBid, p. 119.
17. W.E.B. Du Bois, *The World And Africa,* New York: International Publishers Co. Inc., 1965, p. 23.
18. Quoted in Felix Gilbert, *End of the European Era.* 1890 to the Present, New York: Norton & Co, 3rd edition, 1984, p. 280.
19. I.A. Newby, *Jim Crow's Defence: Anti-Negro Thought In America*

1900-1930, Westport, Connecticut: Greenwood Press, Publishers, 1980(C. 1965 by Louisiana State University Press), p. 9.

20. Joseph E. Harris, *Africans And Their History,* New York: Penguin Books USA Inc. (Mentor),-1987, p. 23.
21. Quoted in William L. Katz, *Breaking The Chains,* New York: Atheneum, 1990, p. 69.
22. Quoted in P. Olisanwuche Esedebe, *Pan-Africanism,* p. 35; see E.W. Blyden. *The Sierra Leone Weekly News* (9 April, 1892), p. 3.
23. W. E. B. Du Bois, *Black Folk: Then and Now,* New York: H. Holt, 193 9, p. 1.
24. Joel Kovel, *White Racism: A Psychohistory,* New York: Vintage Books, 1971, p. 40-41.
25. Na'im Akbar, *Visions For Black Men,* Nashville, Tennessee: Winston-Derek Publishers Inc., 1991, p. 28.
26. Joel Kovel, *White Racism: A psychohistory,* New York: Vintage Books, 1971, p. 44.
27. IBid, p. 44.
28. Quoted in Paul Bohannan, *Africa & Africans,* Garden City, New York: The Natural History Press, 1964, p. 75.
29. Quoted in Rupert Lewis *Marcus Garvey: Anti-Colonial Champion,* Trenton, N. J: Africa World Press Inc., 1988, pp. 125-126.
30. In *The Cultural Unity of Black Africa,* Cheikh Anta Diop postulated the "Two Cradle Theory" of human cultural evolution. He contended that because of climatic and environmental isolation of a group of the original human stock, they underwent both biological and cultural changes that differed from the original human norm, for example low melanin pigmentation, individualistic, xenophobic, and aggressive personality. So one may, in fact, argue that human nature is not universal in its cultural evolution and consciousness.
31. Charles E. Silberman, *Crisis in Black and White,* New York: Vintage Books, 1964, p. 173.
32. T.B. Mason, *The Bible and Race,* Nashville: Broadman Press, 1959, p. 104.
33. Wulf Sachs, *Black Anger,* Westport. Connecticut: Greenwood Press, Publishers, 1968, p. 161.
34. Quoted in Frantz Fanon, *Black Skin, White Masks,* New York: Grove Press Inc., 1967. Evergreen edition 1982(translated by Charles Lam Markmann), p. 130.

35. Rudolph R. Windsor, *From Babylon to Timbuktu: A History of The Ancient Black Races Including The Black Hebrews,* Smithtown, New York: Exposition Press. Inc., (C) 1969. 5th edition, 1981, p. 20.
36. Paul Bohannan, *Africa & Africans,* Garden City, New York: The Natural History Press, 1964. pp. 6-7.
37. Carter G. Woodson, *The Mis-education Of The Negro,* Philadelphia, PA: Hakim's Publications, 1933, pp. 84-85.
38. Molefi Kete Asante, *Kemet, Afrocentricity And Knowledge,* Trenton, New Jersey: Africa World Press, Inc., 1990, p. 17.
39. Cheikh Anta Diop, *Civilization Or Barbarism,* Brooklyn, New York: Lawrence Hill Books (translated from the French by Yaa-Lengi Meema Ngemi, edited by Harold J. Salemson and Marjolijn de Jager), 1981, p. 67.
40. Quoted in P. Olisanwuche Esedebe, *Pan-Africanism,* p. 36. See Edward W. Blyden, "Study and Race", *Sierra Leone Weekly News,* (May 27, 1893), p. 2-4.
41. Lerone Bennett, *Before The Mayflower: A History of the Negro in America.* 1619-1962, Chicago : Johnson Pub. Co., 1962, p. 79.
42. Chancellor Williams. *The Destruction Of Black Civilization,* Chicago, Illinois: Third World Press, 1976, p. 64
43. E. Franklin Frazier. *The Black Bourgeoisie,* New York: Collier Books-Macmillan Publishing Company. 1962, p. 116; see Frances A. Kemble, *Journal of a Residence on a Georgian Plantation in 1838-1839,* New York: Harper, 1863, pp. 193-194.
44. IBid, p. 116.
45. See *Essence* September 1991, Itabari Njeri, "Who Is Black", pp. 64, 66, 115-16; and Robert Anthony Watts, *The Atlanta Journal Constitution,* Sunday edition, December 1, 1991, "Not Black, Not White, But Biracial", p.1A. In these two articles and other related articles, the agitations for a distinct grouping, in my opinion, were inflamed by two basic factors. Firstly, the introduction of the name African American by the Rev. Jesse Jackson spurred the undercurrent movement by some group who do not want to associate their identity with the name Africa. Secondly, it is doubtless that the relative success of the Civil Rights Movement in the 1960s, has diminished significantly the role these "Biracial" persons play in dominating all the major sectors of Black America. For many high melanin pigmented African Americans are now competing effectively with these relatively lower melanin

pigmented folks; and these agitations shade an incredible light on how the effect of this phenomenon is affecting the psychology and the understanding of what constitute their heritage. This has permeated and no doubt will affect in the shaping of the political landmark of not only Black America but also the whole American spectrum itself. Heritage is not purely biological ancestry, it is a phenomenology that is entrenched in the collective historical and material conditions of a specific group. We shall see what the dimensions of the future cultural goal of Pan-Africanism will engender when the cultural unity of Africans all over the world is achieved. And when the world mission of Nzoputa Uwa is enthroned as the fundamental basis of interpreting and addressing many of the problems of the African people.

46. I.A. Newby, *Jim Crow's Defence: Anti-Negro Thought In America,* 1900-1930. Westport, Connecticut: Greenwood Press, Publishers. 1980. p. 134; see also, Ray Stannard Baker, *Following The Color Line,* New York: Doubleday, Page and Co., 1908, pp. 582-98.

47. Bernard Makhosezwe Magubane, *The Ties That Bind: African American Consciousness of Africa,* Trenton, New Jersey: Africa World Press, Inc., 1989, pp. 92-93.

48. Lerone Bennett, Jr. *Before The Mayflower: A History Of Black America,* Chicago: Johnson Publishing Company, Inc., 6th edition, 1987, p. 96.

49. Read, E. Franklin Frazier, "Inferiority Complex and Quest for Status", *The Black Bourgeoisie,* New York: Collier Book-Macmillan Publishing Co., 1962, pp. 112-126. He noted very significant historical and sociological facts when he wrote *The Black Bourgeosie.* Not only did he emphasize the fact that the moderately melanin pigmented blacks constituted the bulk of the so-called "Black Bourgeosie", but he succinctly recorded the impact of this fact on the overall cultural perspectives of the contemporary African American culture. He went into detail to state that from the outset, the "mulattoes" were in fact anti-black, thus went at any length to impede on the cultural development and advancement of the unique African American culture. This was because they were seemingly obsessed in assimilating into the Euro-American culture. As a result, they failed to steer the African population into the dynamism of mental and cultural emancipation.

His emphatic affirmation to the notion that because many Eurafricans were given more opportunities than the bonafide Africans, and also the fact that many of them were already freed before the American Civil War, made them to become the mouthpiece of Black America. They equally became the movers and shakers of the Black Community. He went further to note that they constituted, relative to their low numerical proportion, the majority of the black skilled men and women and artisans, because the dynamics of racism was geared towards given more opportunities to the "least African-looking" persons in the community. The outcome, according to E. Franklin Frazier, was that they became the majority of the "Black Bourgeoisie". Subsequently, they resorted to Europeanizing themselves and thus influenced the overall Black community by their actions.

50. Anne Moody. *Coming of Age in Mississippi,* New York: Dell Publishing Co. Inc., 1968, p. 60.
51. IBid, p. 52.
52. Akyaaba Addai-Sebo and Ansel Wong, (eds.) *Our Story,* London: Hansib Printing Ltd, 1988, p. 20.
53. Charles E. Silberman. *Crisis in Black and White.* New York: Vintage Books, 1964, p. 119.
54. E. Franklin Frazier, *The Black Bourgeoisie,* New York: Collier Books-Macmillan Publishing Co., 1962, p. 186.
55. Walter Rodney. *The Groundings with My Brothers,* Chicago: Research Associates School Times Publications, 1990, (Copyright, 1969), p. 33.
56. Doris Darkwah, "The Role of Africa in the Rise of Judaism", *Black Books Bulletin Vol. 5, No. 4,* (Winter 1977) p. 6. I used this quote which was primary intended for the Jews bearing in mind the implications of certain myths. There is sufficient reason to believe that many of the myths in the Bible were originated by the African people. Nevertheless many of the same myths have been used later by the pink Jews and Europeans to justify their oppression of Africans.
57. There is no doubt that the European Americans and Native Americans have contributed to the African American gene pool. So also have the African Americans contributed to the European and Native American's gene pools. This is normally suppressed for various reasons. According to E. Franklin Frazer, in 1850 the

"mixed-bloods" constituted only 8 percent of the slave population. This implies that whilst there have been continuous genetic interbreeding in the United States, the African element is still in overwhelming predominance within the African American's gene pool.

58. W.E.B. Du Bois, *Black Folk: Then and Now,* New York: H. Holt, 1939, p. 4.
59. Theodosius Dobzhansky, *Genetic Diversity and Human Equality,* New York: Basic Books Inc., Publishers, 1973, p. 3.
60. IBid, p. 4.
61. W. E. B. Du Bois, *Black Folk: Then and Now,* New York: H. Holt, 1939, p. 119.
62. Theodosius Dobzhansky, *Genetic Diversity and Human Equality,* New York: Basic Books me, 1973, p. 9.
63. IBid, p. 9.
64. IBid, p. 9.
65. Quoted in P. Olisanwuche Esedebe, *Pan-Africanism,* p. 37; see E.W. Blyden. *The African Repository* (January, 1879), pp. 3-4.
66. One of the first noted efforts to use IQ tests to measure the African-European intellectual differences in the United States was conducted by G.R. Stetson in 1897 when he tested 500 black and 500 white children in the city of Washington, D.C., public school. In this initial test, not yet perfected by the racists, black children exhibited higher intellectual capacity than their white counterparts. The racists thus were forced to find a different approach for measuring the black and white intelligence that would be used to support their assertion of superiority. Currently, Dr. Arthur Jensen, a professor of educational psychology at the University of California at Berkeley, and Dr. William Shockley, a physicist and Nobel Prize Laureate from Stanford University, have renewed the Age old assertion of European genetic superiority over Africans based on skewed data.
67. Nnamdi Azikiwe. *Renascent Africa,* London: Frank Cass And Company Limited, reprint 1968, p. 62.
68. Henry Fairfield Osborn. "The Evolution of Human Races", (first published January 1926) *Natural History,* Vol. 89 (April 1980), p. 129.
69. Basil Davidson, *The African Slave Trade,* Boston: Atlantic-Little, Brown Books. 1961, p. 7.
70. Cheikh Anta Diop. *The African Origin of Civilization: Myth or*

Reality? Brooklyn. New York: Lawrence Hill & Co. 1974. p. 234.

71. Any time a group of human beings decide to reduce another fellow human beings to the status of "less human" or sub human, they have concurrently removed the moral or ethical responsibility to treat the particular "dehumanized" group as fellow human beings. Thus, most Europeans recognize no morality above their interest. They exist in deceit and falsehood, and have no ability for truthfulness when dealing with Africans. This is the crux of the matter and the basis of their total disregard to the humanity of all Africans. It is amoral for one cultural group to have too much power over the destiny of another group.
72. Charles Silberman, *Crisis in Black and White,* New York: Vintage Books, 1964, p. 87.
73. Richard Wright, *Black Power,* Westport, Connecticut: Greenwood Press, Publishers, 1976, p. 152.
74. Joel Kovel, *White Racism: A Psychohistry,* New York: Vintage Books, 1971, p. 31.
75. E. Franklin Frazier, *The Black Bourgeoisie,* New York: Collier Books-Macmillan Publishing Company, 1962, p. 112.

CHAPTER FOUR
EUROPEAN SLAVE TRADE: AFRICAN MAAFA*

"Africa has, for generations now, been viewed through a web of myth so pervasive and so glib that understanding it becomes a twofold task: the task of clarifying the myth and the separate task of examining whatever reality has been hidden in it. Only as it is stated and told can the myth be stripped away. Only if the myth is stripped away can the reality of Africa emerge." [1b]

---Paul Bohannan

Just as it is now commonly affirmed that the continent of Kemet (Africa) gave "birth" to humanity, Africa equally is recognized to have brooked the shackle that transformed humanity from the ancient to the so-called modern way of life. The modern world is a world driven by the need to accumulate capital, and the role Africa and Europe played in this process of capital accumulation cannot be overemphasized. The capital that the European slave traders accumulated was later reinvested, after the abolition of the Slave Trade, in the African agricultural produce for further accumulation of wealth. So the foundation of the modern world was laid with the blood, sweat, and labor of the Africans, on the one hand. But, on the other hand, the impact of slavery on the mentality of black people is enormous. Was this a coincidence?

Indeed, it is an irony that the Slave Trade that ravaged Africa for many centuries was the lubricating wheel that galvanized and engendered the forces that have transformed the world. But the African who was the victim has not positively been recognized for this outcome; rather, slavery had created an African handicap. It has smeared blackness with an untouchable negative false image. Thus, it began the era where "the [word] "Negro" was used for the first time in the world's history to tie color to race and blackness to slavery and degradation. The white race was pictured as "pure" and superior; the black race as dirty, stupid, and inevitably inferior." [1]

The historical fact of the Slave Trade not only has implanted the idea that Africans are weak and exploitable, but its labyrinthine repercussions will continue to form the basis upon which the rest of humanity interact with Africans. In fact, the Slave Trade has become an organic consequence of the culture and history of the African people. In order to understand the European Slave Trade, many important questions ought to be answered. What made the African in the first place exploitable? What gave the Europeans the audacity to kidnap the African? What made many Africans to sell their own people?

These questions are important because I have often wondered what the world would have been like, if there had been no European Slave Trade across the Atlantic Ocean. What if the Portuguese who first came to the West African coast never indulged themselves in the kidnap and purchase of men as chattels for free labor? The European Slave Trade commonly called the Atlantic Slave Trade is now arousing new interests amongst Africans. The New Africans have begun to study the European Slave Trade from an African perspective, giving new light and fresh meaning into what many have considered the most atrocious savagery ever meted on a people in the history of the world. Thus, Christopher Fyfe accordingly noted, "The Atlantic Slave Trade has now been unequivocally revealed in all its atrocity as a prolonged exploitative device by which millions of Africans were brutalized and dehumanized in order to bring wealth to those who organized it. Most contemporary historians now no longer feel the need to denounce (any more than they would justify) its horrors. They can take them for granted, and concentrate on examining how it worked—how it affected its victims and beneficiaries, how it affected the economics and societies of Africa, America, and Europe and similar lines of enquiry". [2]

Of course, much has been written about this so-called trade in human beings, but because of the lack of many unbiased analyses and syntheses, the average individual has found it difficult to understand. Consequently, this chapter will focus on the overall dynamics that stimulated the trade; and the mechanics employed during the development to enhance the free flow of captured Africans from the African hinterlands to Europe and the Americas.

I. THE IMPETUS OF EUROPEAN COLONIALISM

We have in the previous chapters emphasized the factors that had stimulated the European interest and desire to explore the world. What aroused interest in the European mind was at the bottom commercial incentives and ventures, induced by the desire to live a better life. This was the opportunity to make a living through trade with the outside world. The geographical factor must be emphasized, because environment plays an important ecological role in the desires and aspirations of any species on the planet. For "… this must be sought in the material conditions in which the accident of geography had placed them at the beginning of time".[3] The Europeans were isolated for more than nine centuries from the outside world, as a result of their so-called "Dark Age" period. The celebrated European Renaissance was in actuality the "new light with which Asia and Africa illumined the Dark Ages of Europe".[4] The bitter historical experience of the European Middle Ages (Dark Age) stagnated the European conditions of living and radicalized their mind-set. Thus, the Christian Crusade became to the religious fundamentalists the opportunity to fight for survival. When inflamed by the ideological struggle between the Muslim Moors and Christian Europe, the religious war ensued. The partial defeat of the Muslim Moors set a strong precedent on the European dream for global hegemony. This defeat of the Muslim Moors restored their confidence. (This is because the many centuries of isolation had created feelings of psychological inadequacy, and backwardness—thus the Europeans were at this historic epoch very backward and not very sure of their abilities.)

In addition, the military victory of Christian Europeans over the Muslim Moors equally changed the European way of thinking. It made them overly pugnacious and avaricious. Therefore, the expedition did not wholly begin in a good faith or with a sincere motive for trade. This conclusion is based on historical facts before us, complemented through analysis derived from the understanding of human nature. The indications were clear! For the structural mechanism that underlaid the European exploration set the path for the enslavement of the Africans. That is why, "the rebirth of civilization in Europe began in the fifteenth century. At this time, African and Asiatic civilizations far outstripped that of Europe".[5] The Europeans saw an opportunity not only to secure their future survival, but also to impose their will henceforth on the entire human world.

The access and control of the Mediterranean and Atlantic oceans by the Europeans heralded the end of the Muslim Moorish era. It must be understood that it was the end of the Muslim Moorish era that gave the Europeans the idea of exploring the world. Therefore, this passion to explore the world on the quest for expansionist trade was not only a natural reaction, but also was partly a spontaneous or eclectic reaction fired by religious bigotry and sordid motives. This is evidenced in the European fundamentalist religious background, partly conditioned by many years of fighting on the basis of religion which culminated into economic hardships. First and foremost, they saw the world as either good or evil—the good represented their God and the bad represented a figure that they called devil. All those who did not believe in the Bible, those people who did not follow the Christian's tenets, were the evil people. Secondly, the European religious conceptual view of the devil's image as black would in fact affect the psychology of their relationship with Africans. The figure of the devil is depicted to be black, whilst their God and the angels are portrayed to be white (an absolutist opposite of each other). Finally, equally pertinent was the internal strife that characterized the political conditions of Europe in the fourteenth and fifteenth centuries which inordinately socialized Europeans in a quandary of violence. Consequently, the Europeans were disposed to interpret the nature of their interaction with non-Europeans from a different standpoint. To them, it became a struggle between good and evil, black and white, Christians and non-Christians, loyalty and treachery, hope and disillusion, Europeans and non-Europeans.

Essentially, war affects people's relationship to their environment; it also affects and influences the desires and the aspirations of those who have experienced it, the outcome of the war notwithstanding. The final defeat of the Moors in their last stronghold in Granada during the late fifteenth century was the dawn of a different epoch of human existence. It ended the era of Muslim pre-eminence and ushered in, what many would call, the age of mindless euphemism. The encounter with Africans and other different cultures outside Europe, definitely, had a psychological impact on the Europeans. They were compelled, because of their obvious inadequacies, to base their understanding of culture and traditional values on their own world view—their own understanding of life, man and the universe. However, before delving into the interaction between the Africans and the Europeans one thing needs to be mentioned: The scenario upon which these two distinct and different people would later clash.

On the one hand, the Europeans did have one thing that was missing in the African "theater"—a continent-wide organized religion—Christianity. Its importance lies in the fact that the organized religion brought Europeans together and unified their culture on the periphery through the Greek and Latin languages. Subsequently, Greek and Latin languages would affect and influence the development of the different tribal European languages or tongues. Moreover, to the European mind, to what they called diplomacy and to their understanding of it, war was an inherent part of its mechanism. This must be emphasized, because the European existence from the past two millennia has been characterized by inter-tribal wars between different European tribes. Thus their perception of survival is consistent with this belief in the "Natural Selection". As previously pointed out, the Charles Darwin's theory of the survival of the fittest was a testament and an echo of the prevailing attitude found in the European tradition since the pre-historic time in Europe. In other words, what Darwin did was to give it an intellectual understanding that placed Europe's imperialist goal as a natural phenomenon. Indeed, they called themselves the forerunners of the Christian Faith, the people who supposedly knew and worshipped the "true God"--Jesus the Christ. You can call them the epitome of godliness or the self-righteous and holier-than-thou-people.

On the other hand, the African Spirituality was developed by the specific African national groups based on the doctrines of the classical African God-concept of spirituality. This traditional African religion was an integral part of the traditional and cultural mode of expression of every African ethnic group. Also, some African ethnic groups or individuals were at this time professing the Islamic Faith. A typical example could be seen in the traditional Igbo's, Yoruba's and Akan's religious experiences (to name but few). These traditional African religious creeds, on a closer examination, are very similar because they bear not only similar tenets but also share the same internal dynamism. Just like all religions, also, have those similarities that make religion part of man's reaction to his existence. But the traditional Igbo religious creed, designed and evolved from the Igbo traditional ethos, was meant to be functional particularly to the Igbo speaking people. At the same time, the Akan's religious doctrine, though similar to the Igbo's, or the Yoruba's, is different, because it was meant to be responsive to the Akan speaking people. Ali A. Mazrui amplified this point when he wrote: "These traditional African creeds did not have ambitions to convert the world. They were religions of particular ethnic groups, fundamentally important for those groups, but definitely not intended for export".[6]

Therefore, the lack of a continent-wide organized African "religion" that would have affected the emergence of an African nationalism was the crucial issue. The gap created by this phenomenon can be explained thus: Neither of these ethnic religious creeds was founded on the personality of an individual(s); nor, did an individual rise up to proclaim himself the "Chosen One", thereby helping to spread and consolidate its influence by inculcating a doctrinal zeal and a sense of mission on the followers. However, this uniqueness was a reflection of the importance attached to life after death and the indisputable role ancestors played in the manifestation of the ontological spiritual relationship between their God, deities, and people. Moreover, most Africans did not see the world in "racial" terms—in Africa skin color was politically insignificant, then. This lack of skin color consciousness on the part of the traditional Africans is quite understandable because the Africans themselves come in different shades of color. In other words, they were used to seeing varieties of skin color pigmentations. In addition, the universal principle that undergirds the policies of every political group is indeed relative in analyzing the nature of interaction, between political groups in Africa, which existed before and during the arrival of the Europeans. Fundamentally, all political groups have two types of policies, foreign and domestic. Conversely, because Africa consisted of mostly autonomous states, all of these communities were independent of one another. Consequently, whatever relationship they had must have existed from the standpoint of their respective national interests.

Nevertheless, this lack of an organized traditional African religion would play a significant role in making Africa and Africans exploitable. This is because it seems to be the only element that could have created or encouraged a desire for an African brotherhood that goes beyond the specific needs of individual groups. Thus, it must be emphasized that organized "religion" has played a formidable role, possibly more than any other human social structure, in shaping the attitudes, traditions, and socialization of the human world. This gap created by the lack of an organized African religion was the missing factor. Unlike the case with their European counterpart, who fought a religious war against the Islamic Moors for many centuries. The development of Christendom unified Europeans and facilitated a common attitude and reaction to events outside Europe. This resulted into a competition to dominate and assure the survival of all the European nations from non-Europeans—even though one may not be a member of such nation. These on the whole contradict and put the record straight on the notions that had been put forward by many Eurocentric scholars suggesting that the traditional Africans were by nature gullible. As indicated, it was rather a clash of two diametrically opposed worldviews. It was these opposing worldviews that facilitated the actions of the men who took part in the interaction during the historical period. For the way a man acts is partly a reaction upon his understanding of his world and the universe. Worldviews therefore are influenced by the institutional norms of a larger group. What is believed to be right or wrong. The significance attached to objects, events and human nature, and the overall normative premises and ideas relative to interpreting behaviors, traditions, and customs. This stimulant when shared affects and influences common reaction and the understanding of events.

II. THE GENESIS

The Muslim Moors for a long time served as the middle men between European consumers and the African and Asian traders. For example, the Muslim Moors bought gold from the traditional African societies and sold it to the Jewish merchants in Majorca.[7] The Arab merchants also served as middlemen in the inter-continental trade between East Africa and Asia, mostly India. So, there was little or no direct trading between Europe on the one side and Africa and Asia on the other side. The great demand for spices, Persian silks, Indian cloth, emeralds, rubies, gold, and the subsequent taxes imposed on these products, in Europe, skyrocketed their prices. It therefore became implicit that this condition would infuse or generate serious interest from many people to take advantage of the existing demands for foreign goods—to capitalize on the demand in order to make profits—and to monopolize the supply. In addition, the capture of the strategic city of Ceuta in North Africa in 1415 reinforced this idea and made the Portuguese determined to explore the economic opportunities in Africa.

However, there was the technological obstacle: "The types of ships used in Western Europe from Roman times until the fourteenth century were the oar-driven galley and cog. While both were suitable for calm seas of the Mediterranean, they were helpless in heavy seas and totally unsuitable for long ocean voyages. It was not until the first half of the fifteenth century that, borrowing from the superior technology of Arab sailors, the Portuguese and other Western Europeans were able to devise ship capable of undertaking long-distance voyages. The Caravel, which had both square sails and fore-and-aft-rigged triangular sails, was able to sail into the wind without the help of oars. This revolutionary development in ship design made possible the great voyages that characterized the fifteenth century".[8] The Portuguese found themselves at the forefront of these voyages because they were, at this time, ahead of their European counterparts not only in political development but also in technological advancement.[9] In fact, it was the Portuguese Crown who commissioned the expeditions. Micheal Beaud's description of the European political, economic and social conditions beginning from the fifteenth century is an eye opener. He stated thus, "Monarchs greedy for greatness and wealth, states battling for supremacy, merchants and bankers encouraged to enrich themselves: these are the forces which inspired trade, conquest, and wars; systematized pillage; organized the traffic in slaves; and lock up the vagabonds so as to force them to work".[10] This in part demonstrated the importance attached to these expeditions. Despite this fact, they were very much aware that their control of the supply of these goods wrested on their ability to find the sea route to the continent that they called Africa and India. So when Prince Henry the Navigator was commissioned to find this sea route, he knew the importance of the task ahead—the undertaken task of finding the sea route to Africa and India.

With the blessing of the Portuguese Crown, Prince Henry, although he never did sail, began to organize and sponsor many adventurers and explorers in 1417. These explorers most of all were driven by the desire for wealth, power, glory, and often enough by the adventurer's passions of overcoming the impossible. After many false starts, they found themselves in Madeira in 1418. They continued their journey until "Cape Bojador was rounded by Gil Eanes in 1434, and in 1442 Nuno Tristao and Antao Gonzales reached Cape Blanco on the coast of present-day Mauritania; three years later Dinis Dias explored the mouth of the Senegal River and Cape Verde. The mouth of the Gambia River was reached in 1446, and the coast of Sierra Leone was explored in 1460…."[11]

At first the Portuguese were shocked when they found themselves in the coast of West Africa. This is because they had expected to find a cliff between Cape Blanco and the Gulf of Guinea. This was due to their belief that the earth being the center of the universe is a flat and rigid platform; and as such they were afraid of falling off the cliffy edge of the flat earth. Directly, this observation later would be of immense use to Copernicus, who borrowed from the ancient Kemet's notion of the divination of the sun and backed by the mathematics of the Kemetic Civil Calendar to develop the theory that would later change the European mind. Consequently the Copernicus' Lunar and Planetary Tables would make the understanding of the inhabited earth for the first time to the European mind became more of a "global village". Nevertheless, the arrival on the West

African coast and the subsequent trade and pillage that began was a significant landmark to the Portuguese. In fact, one may acknowledge that "the Portuguese had thus triumphed in one of their main objectives. They had broken the monopoly on African trade that the Muslim states of Mediterranean Africa had possessed for many centuries. They had turned the Muslim flank at last".[12] The first historical impact of the Portuguese achievements on the European continent, was that it began an era which directly influenced the decline of Feudalism in Europe. The decline of Feudalism boosted individual initiatives which stimulated and affected the emergence of "cities". It was a rude awakening.

The European expansions also began an era where the word and the use of language became an effective political machine. The word "discover" became synonymous with the encroachment of Europeans to the lands inhabited by non-Europeans. Names like the following, Sao Jorge da Mina, Gulf of Guinea, Cape Verde, Cape of Goodhope, etc., replaced the indigenous names that must have been given to them by the inhabitants. The European hitherto explorations and discoveries were mere encounters, conquests, or confirmation regarding or available in a particular landmass—there were no fresh or new discoveries. But to the European mind, to their narrow understanding of others, they considered these places to have been "discovered" by them or their so-called "civilized" or Christianized European counterparts. The European understanding of civilization thus became synonymous with the belief in the historic Christianity. It is so because to them all non-Europeans were "Infidels". This Arabic word for non-believers was introduced by the Moors in Europe and was first used to describe Christianized Europe.

In fact, the European expansion was in part the extension of the Christian Crusade and campaign, consciously and unconsciously. In other words, the Europeans carried over with them their state of belligerence with the Muslim Moors. The fall of the strategic city of Constantinople in 1453 to the Ottoman Turk had had a devastating impact on the European belligerency. This city was once the capital of the Graeco-Byzantine Empire. Simply stated, the loss of this city now called Istanbul made Christian Europe overly pugnacious, in many peculiar ways. The result however was that its effect unified Christian Europe against all non-Europeans and non-Christians alike. Thus, the bond of Europeanism was cemented and a new outlook on self-preservation was born.

This pattern of thinking was actually embedded in the whole structure of the expeditions. ***For "following the return of Columbus with reports of the New World the Council of Castille resolved to take possession of a land whose inhabitants were unable to defend themselves".***[13] Thus, the neglect of the indigenous names and the use of the word "discover" marked the beginning of this historical epoch. Equally important in retrospect is that the overall European attitude, nonetheless, gave them the upper hand in the interactions between them and the indigenes. As the first mechanism employed on the indigenes was psychological intimidation through acts of terror and vagabondage, the Portuguese expedition to the coast of West Africa very well could be qualified as the military and economic invasions of Africa.

On the other hand, the autochthonous African's reaction to the European strangers must have been either actions or reactions bent on hostility or shock by the European's appearance. As the historian, Adu Boahen, had noted, that the Africans "naturally… found the new arrivals with their white skin, long hair, and funny looking ships profoundly strange".[14] This is hard to account because there were no detailed written accounts by the Africans themselves, on what had transpired between them and the Europeans. However, looking at it from the African wholistic cultural background, on the importance attached to communal life and the traditional African's concept of ownership, a better understanding will manifest itself. This emphasis on the mundane existence of the African is an attestation to the traditional African ethos. The traditional African society is collectively owned by the entire community. The land belonged to the One Creator of the universe and their ancestors; and therefore, the inheritance of the land was sacred and collective. Moreover, since no one could really own a landmass, I infer that they may have not taken the European explorers very seriously. For the outcome of the African-European interactions made the "African appear to have been even less aware of the portentous nature of the explorations and of the peregrinations of the explorers".[15] Accordingly, however the African wholistic traditions and the European religious bigotry reinforced by their economic imperatives paved the way for the European imposition of the Slave Trade on Africans. The Africans definitely did not take them seriously at the outset of the interaction. They were naïve enough to take them on a face value. They did not judge them from their outside physical appearance; rather, they saw them as part of the different representation of human form.

The third phase of these explorations was began by Vasco da Gama about seven years after Columbus found himself in a landmass across the Atlantic ocean. Vasco da Gamma retraced the already explored course of his predecessors from where he set sail to India. "It is quite evident from the accounts of the Portuguese explorers, particularly those of Alvise da Cadamosto, Pacheco Pereire, Ruy de Pina, and above all, Vasco da Gamma, that they were astounded and elated by the complex, even sophisticated character of the African civilizations they came across, by the extents of political development, and by wealth and splendor of the courts".[16] However, "without the winking of an eye, printing, gun powder, the smelting of iron, the beginning of social organization, not to mention political life and democracy, were attributed exclusively to the white race and to Nordic Europe."[17]

When the Portuguese came in contact with the traditional Africans, their desire was also to establish a trade relationship with them. But this is not a surprise; hence, the expedition was at the outset sponsored and financed for the purpose of commerce. The major commodity the African had at this time was gold, mostly found in the shores of the coastal city they called Elmina or the Gold Coast. In 1482 they built a fort in the coast of Elmina and called it Sao Jorge da Mina—Saint George's Mine. This fort housed about sixty Portuguese soldiers and the occasional use of Africans when necessary to impose their authority on the indigenous people. Moreover, trades in other commodities were equally enhanced. This became feasible because the Portuguese and other European expansionists were a combination of explorers, mercenaries, traders and even monks. Commodities like dried fish, cotton cloth, pepper, ivory, wax, hides, amber, and indigo were equally part of the African products enhanced through this trade. Obviously, this exchange of goods was transacted in a form of "dumb" barter or "silent trade". The barter system therefore was acceptable to both Europeans and the Africans. The understanding of the mechanism involved in this exchange of goods is of utmost importance as it would later form a basis of the African exploitation. The loophole inherent in such an unregulated system would place the Europeans in a favorable position. It would make them to have not only the physical influence on the terms of the trade, but also the psychological influence concerning what aspects of commodities were exchanged. The primary products the Europeans were exchanging with the Africans were textiles, horses, gun powder and intoxicating liquor. Gun powder was invented by the Chinese, but later in the sixteenth century, the invention of the "Crank and Connecting Rod" would help to move Europeans into a more complex industrial development. Hence, the adoption of the Crank and Connecting Rod made possible the advances in Bronze and Iron, and also facilitated the manufacture of firearms, and the basic celestial Navigation Instrument. The manufacture of the gun would later play a decisive role in the overall impact of the European encroachment in Africa, Asia, and the Americas.

Many scholars of African history had contended that the first phase of interaction between Africans and Europeans was marked by legitimate trade, and was wholly controlled by Africans who dictated the terms of trade. This could have been possible if the Europeans had come with good faith or sincere motive for mutual trade. But the Europeans came to plunder and enrich themselves. For an example, when Prince Henry the Navigator sent a special request to the Pope for permission in the rape and plunder of Africa, the Pope willingly consented to this human brutality. When he granted thus: "To all of those who shall be engaged in the said war, complete forgiveness of all of their sins".[18] No doubt, this popish rationale gave them the moral sanction to employ anything within their means—mercenaries, ammunitions, Christian religion and the intoxicating liquor. In my opinion, I think that the Africans definitely did influence the terms of trade; but since the Europeans possessed what the Africans must have considered scarce commodities, the Europeans exercised more influence on the terms of trade than the Africans. The principle of supply and demand comes to mind and must have been applied in a sense, albeit not in a contemporary applicability. Of course, what the Africans gave in exchange, for instance, gold was very valuable and in high demand in Europe. But because there was no unified system or guild on the African side, a system that could have controlled the sale of products to the Europeans, the Europeans cheated and manipulated the African, thus began the many centuries of the African exploitation.

Historically speaking, Europeans controlled and limited the supply of either the obsolete or the ineffective products they sold to Africans. Since the Africans could not control or dictate what the Europeans sold to them, "items like old sheets, cast-off uniforms, technologically outdated firearms, and lots of odds and ends found guaranteed markets in Africa:.[19] As Walter Rodney pointed out, "the whole import-export relationship between Africa and its trading partners is one of unequal exchange and exploitation".[20] Therefore, a system of dependence was not entrenched during Africa's formal colonization, but was enshrined within the attitudes and the structures of the interaction that began when the first Europeans found themselves in the West African coast beginning from 1441. However, the Africans would have recovered from this initial ephemeral dependence if the massive European Slave Trade had not begun. Whether the Portuguese were conscious of the seeds they were planting is open to question. Nonetheless, one thing is certain, that "structural dependence is one of the characteristics of underdevelopment".[21]

Still, this structural dependence had not yet been enhanced to overtake whatever control or influence Africans had on the dictates of the terms of trade. But the involvement of other European nations, for instance, the Spaniards, Dutch, French, and English, intensified the European quests to explore, exploit, plunder and conquer the lands outside Europe and the activities of other European nations thereby aided in perpetuating it. As this structural dependence on the part of Africa was enhanced, Europeans came to a total control of the commodities they bought and sold to Africans. The African market therefore began to be influenced tremendously by the European needs and interests. Europe became the center of the triangular trade, and Africa was relegated to the periphery of the market.

The accounts of many of the European explorers used extensively to create the impression that the control of the trade was in the hands of Africans contradict many aspects of the historical reality of the European explorations. One of the most typical examples is usually an account given by Lok an English man, after his voyage to the coast of Guinea in West Africa. He asserted that the Africans were "very wary people in their bargaining, and will not lose sparks of gold of any value. They use weights and measures, and are very circumspect in occupying the same. They that shall have trade with them must use them gently: for they will not traffique or bring in any wares if there be evil used".[22] Indeed, this was one English man's observation at a time when England did not have much need for African labor. No doubt, the political and economic imperatives in England at that point in time influenced his observation.

The implication of using the word "trade" in interpreting the unequal relationship between Africans and Europeans, since 1441, is that it presupposes that a negotiated and mutually beneficial exchange on both sides took place. But it is in fact a European plunder of Africa, not a trade by any means. That is why, Walter Rodney's eloquent statement provides a better understanding to this fact. He stated as follows: "When one tries to measure the effect of European slave trading on the African continent, it is essential to realize that one is measuring the effect of social violence rather than trade in any normal sense of the world".[23] Whichever way one may want to look at this issue, the facts remain that Europe having fought for many centuries during the Christian Crusade began to see war as a legitimate means of achieving one's goals. The European expedition that was pioneered by the Portuguese was not instigated by the Feudal organization of the then European life. Neither was the expedition inspired by any calculated actions in the beginning such as the slave trade, slavery, annexation of foreign lands, decimation of the Native Americans, or colonialism. Nor did the Europeans anticipate all these developments. In short, they were driven by the aftermath of the Crusade, inspired by their dogged religious ferment and fired by their worsening economic conditions. These levels of consciousness had imposed on the Europeans an idealistic view of a better life.

The necessity to survive in conjunction with the warfare contacts with the opposing Muslim enemies forewarned and forestalled a sense of what was then necessary for European survival. In addition, the psychological impact of the Crusade and its historical longevity warranted that the European expedition began as an extension of the political, economic and religious campaigns that have characterized the Christian Crusade against Islam. Thus, it is amply correct to state that Europeans invaded Africa in 1441, and began an atrocious warfare of high proportion. Yet, it is still questionable whether Africans have recognized this statement of fact. Indeed, this warfare is not only economically motivated; it also constitutes religious, biological and cultural imperatives.

III. THE HISTORICAL FACT

It is on record that the Portuguese initiated and began the European Slave Trade. The kidnapping of the Africans for involuntary servitude began as early as 1441 of the Christian Era, when Antonio Gonzales and his gang kidnapped ten Africans on the shores of the West African coast. The European Slave Trade thus launched was later "sanctified" by Pope Nicholas V, with the papal bulls of 1452 (*Dum Diversas*) and 1455 (*Romanus Pontifex*). Once again this demonstrates the intentions and motives of the Portuguese. Why, in fact, I disagreed with the assertion that the first phase of the interactions between Africans and Portuguese was legitimate trade and was wholly dictated by the Africans. It is an historical fact that "at first most of the slaves they took were kidnapped. But by the middle of the fifteenth century the Portuguese government realized that West Africa was a valuable source of labor, and that a steady labor supply could not be permanently maintained by violent means. Instructions were therefore given that slaves henceforth be purchased, not captured. From then on, with occasional exceptions, Europeans obtained slaves in Africa by a willing exchange of commodities with African vendors—human beings exchanged for consumer goods."[24] At this time this European plunder of the African human and natural resources which has been called "trade began to change from a gambler's search for treasures to investment for permanent income; and this income consisted of goods for sale which were in practice found more valuable than treasures for hoarding. To perfect this arrangement slaves and more slaves must be had".[25] Still for the African lords to be willing to participate in this partnership of hideous human degradation, the Europeans knew that they needed to create the need and atmosphere that would inevitably give the African lords no choice but to sell their own people. The need that would make the traditional Africans to lose total control of not only the terms of trade, but the commodities offered in exchange as well.

Another important phase or the second important phase of the European encroachment began with the exploration undertook by Cristobal Colon, popularly known as Christopher Columbus, which brought him to the Americas in 1492 (fifty-two years after the Portuguese found themselves in the West African coast). "The pious purpose of converting them to Christianity [and engaging them in trade] sanctified the injustice of the project. But the hope of finding gold there, was the sole motive which prompted them to undertake it…"[26] The word "discover" was of course applied on the landmass that would later be called the Americas. The two continents of the Americas that were rich and dazzling, inhabited by different Native American communities, who lived in harmony with their environment.

Needless to say that it became a tradition to celebrate the day Christopher Columbus (Cristobal Colon) "discovered" the Americas. But those celebrating the so-called discovery of the Americas and how great it has become either forgot or were not taught that without the Africans the wealth found in the Americas and the subsequent development would have been only a pipe dream—a child's dream. In speaking of the European Slave Trade, Christopher Fyfe stated that: "Although the overseas slave trade began as early as 1441, it still had not become the principle objective of the Portuguese even a hundred year later. It was the exploration of the Americas and the West Indies between 1492 and 1504, and the subsequent commencement of mining activities and the establishment of tobacco and sugar plantations there, that brought the slave trade to its full growth. The Europeans, confronted with an acute labor shortage in their attempts to exploit the natural resources of the New World, at first tried to use Indians to work the mines and plantation but they proved unequal to the task".[27] However, it is important to state that 'the economic magnitude of the Americas was not only the treasure of precious metal it provided, but also the new and widening market and source of supply it offered European manufactured goods. This outcome first helped to raise the mercantile system to glory and splendor'.[28]

The European development had a direct correlation with the Slave Trade, the encounter and conquest of the Americas and the institution of slavery. However, the conquest of the Americas and the subsequent commencement in the exploitation and extraction of the natural minerals found in the landmass were dependent on the viable labor force. The Europeans themselves lacked the human power and wherewithal necessary to exploit these minerals for the benefit of their home country (government). Hence, Basil Davidson commented that "the conquerors began by enslaving the population they found, the "Indians", but death robbed them of these. Next, they turned back again to Europe and attempted to fill the ranks with "indentured" servants or near slave workers from home. When this would not suffice, they applied to Africa; and there at last they saw their problem solved".[29]

When Christopher Columbus found himself, in what is today called Bahamas, the disguised motive was to establish a trade relationship with the Native Americans and to convert them to Christianity. But it is hard to know exactly what transpired between the Europeans and the Native Americans, without taking into account the psychological makeup of the Europeans beginning from the fifteenth century.

The problem encumbered by interpreting the historical interactions from the sources and documents left by the European racial and cultural bigots has been threefold. First, it has led to the distortion of the truth in favor of the European. Secondly, it has helped to justify the European encroachment, plunder, vandalism and murder of either the Native Americans or the Africans. Thirdly, the Europeans in order to maintain control on the spoils of the war, plundered from non-Europeans began to develop and evolve a world order that pays homage and respect to their sordid accomplishments. The immigration laws, citizenship laws, sovereignty rights, international laws and trade tariffs were all developed by the conquerors who were very much aware that in order to preserve the European hegemony these laws must be vehemently enforced in all aspects on every non-European—for absolute control. This obviously was not only to exert control on their movements but to make sure that they will never have a chance to repeat what they themselves had the opportunity to do. Thus to understand the impact of the European Slave Trade, the conquest of the Americas and the subsequent enslavement of Africans for free labor, one has to point at the impact the Oil Boom in the 1970s had on the economies of those member nations of the OPEC Cartel. The Oil Boom which lasted for about ten years transformed the economics, cultures and political behavior of those nations. In addition it partially changed the then prevailing tendency of referring to the present "Third World" countries as "Poor countries", which was a significant change in the adamant and chauvinistic attitude of the Europeans towards these countries. Therefore, one can imagine the effects of the Slave Trade, plunder of Africa, enslavement of Africans for free labor, and the exploitation of the Americas for minerals, for over four hundred years. In other words, it is an historical fact that the "Europeans shipped Africans regularly over the Atlantic as slaves, to Europe or the Americas, for a period of over four hundred years". [30] It is from this example that one can begin to understand what made the Western hemisphere to dominate the forces of human development in this present historical epoch.

IV. WHAT MADE THE AFRICANS SELL THEIR OWN PEOPLE?

Over the years, there has been one consistent question asked by many people who could not grasp the dynamics and the mechanics involved in the European Slave Trade. One of the most consistent question asked, has always been: What made the traditional Africans to sell their own people? The consistency of this question underlies its importance. On the contrary, many scholars and writers have failed to make the understanding of the important question to everybody, Africans and Eurasians alike, feasible. The reason for this muddling of historical fact is not farfetched. Hence, the correct answer to this question bears a fundamental element necessary in understanding what in fact made the European hegemony a force to be reckoned with in the modern world. It is a fact that to tell the truth about what made the Africans to sell their own people can only be done when Africans and their descendants in the Americas are ready to debunk the myth of European superiority. If they are willing to re-write not only history, but also they must be ready to re-interpret the economic, religious, social and political forces involved in the development of the world. As we can see, it would take an EKUMEKU World Revolution to tell the truth about why the traditional Africans sold their sons and daughters to strangers of another land. It would take an EKUMEKU World Revolution, with an impact that would surpass the effect of the European Industrial Revolution. Bearing this in mind, I will attempt to give new understanding to the factors that made it inevitable for the traditional Africans to sell their own people. This is because what happened to the traditional Africans could have happened to any other group given the same circumstances, if not worst.

The continent of Kemet (Africa) in size is the second largest continent on the planet, following after Asia. It is located in-between the East and West (Asia and Europe); it is the bridge connecting East and West and vice versa. The geographical position of Africa is tantamount to many of its problem. Traditionally or originally, the entire continent of Africa was inhabited by black or Africoid people. The first historically recorded armed foreign invasion in Africa was between 1675 and 1600 Before the Common Era, during the 15th dynastic period in ancient Kemet. This was the Hyksos invasion into Kemet about 2,525 years after the indigenous ancient Africans started the Nile Valley dynastic system in about 4200 B.C.E.[31] The history of the dynastic Kemet was recorded by Mer-en-Tehuti (or Manetho) in 242 B.C.E. Mer-en-Tehuti, the ancient Kemetian priest, who was commissioned by Ptolemy Philadelphius, recorded the chronology of historical events in ancient Kemet. Although the original historical document of Mer-en-Tehuti's testimony has been lost, scholars have depended on the fragments and summaries handed down by many ancient writers. His chronology began from the cycle of the previous Great

Year, at 36,766 B.C.E., to the period of the Greek's occupation of ancient Kemet, thereby giving credence to over thirty-six thousand years of the Kemetic cultural experience and glory.[32]

This ancient civilization of the Nile Valley culture complex evolved out of the Southern part of Africa; and following the Nile River course, this great cultural complex naturally culminated in the northern tip of Africa, at the delta of the Nile in Kemet. This is to say that the ancient civilization of Kemet evolved from Southern Africa to Northern Africa, from east Africa's land of Punt (Somalia and Kenya) to northeast Africa. But the odyssey of the African interactions with non-Africans stemmed from the fact that the African after developing the most humane civilization on the face of the planet became the envy of Asians and Europeans who wanted their own share of the wisdom and culture of the African world.

Nevertheless, the decline of the ancient and traditional African cultural experience can be categorized into three primary phases. The first phase was the successful invasion of ancient Kemet in the fourth century, 322 B.C.E. by Alexander of Macedonia and the plunder of the Royal Libraries and temples. The second phase was the advent of Islam and the militant incursions of Arabs on the banner of Islam into Africa, beginning from about 640 C.E.; whilst the third phase was the European exploration and the plunder of Africa that began in 1441C.E.

When the continuous migration of Eurasians to the outskirt of the Royal Empire of Kemet and the subsequent "two-way process of intermingling" created the first demographical problem, it led to the gradual emergence of a different biological and cultural group. These were the "Afroasiatic" people, the so-called Semites. The Islamic religion was founded by Prophet Mohammad Ibn Abdullah, who was an Arab. Consistently, there had been scholars who have argued that the original people of Southwest Asia were part of the Africoid biological stock. Since the Arabian Peninsula had been historically populated by an African biological stock, until the later migration of the "leucoderm" group, the so-called Afroasiatic languages today are actually variant adoptions of the original African language family. So it was consequent to the migration of the low melanin pigmented Leucoderm (Eurasian) group that the Africoid population in the Arabian Peninsula began to fuse with the Leucoderm element which gave into being the so-called "Semitic" people we call Arabs. In fact, the word "Semitic" or "Afroasiatic" by its linguistic definition means a mixture.

Essentially, the Islamic religion was enhanced in most part by the Africans who took their religious campaign to inner Africa and Europe. The religious and political control of most parts of northern Europe and northern Africa beginning from the eighth century C.E. was the machinations of a combination of autochthonous Africans and Arabs. This was the Mohammedan Africans who had their stronghold in the present-day Senegal and Mauritania. Their political campaign into Europe was launched from West Africa, from where they crossed the strait of Gibralter to Spain. These African Muslims not only ruled the Iberian Peninsula for centuries, but their rule also extended throughout the North African perimeter.

The role Africans played in the development of the Islamic religion is enormous—in the military, political, and ecclesiastical foundations of Islam, not only in Africa, but in the Arab world and Europe as well. J.C. DeGraft-Johnson noted that, "The conquest of Spain was an African conquest. They were Mohammedan Africans, not Arabs, who laid low the Gothic Kingdom of Spain".[33]

We also know that 'Hadzrat Bilal ibn Rahab (otherwise referred to simply as Bilal) was the first high priest of the Islamic empire. After Muhammad himself, it may be said that the Islamic religion began with Bilal, who was an autochthonous African'.[34] Not only was Islam developed and enhanced by both Arabs and Africans, but the fact that it bears an Arabic name and has for centuries been channeled for the development of an Arab civilization makes it on the whole an Arab religion. On this basis, it has been very difficult for most Arabs to separate Arabism from Islam or Islam from Arabism.[35]

This Arabs's cultural and political association of Arabism with Islam and Islam with Arabism has made Islam not only a culture-bound religion but also a political identity in itself. Therefore, the conversion of

Africans to Islam follows with the convert's beginning journey of a new cultural and political identity. The first aspect is the change of the indigenous names to Arabic names. The second aspect is with the use of Arabic language in all religious rituals, such as prayer, reading the Qur'an and all other religious activities (e.g. Islamic schools or Arabic schools). The use of the Arabic language by these people demonstrates not only the political aspect of Islam, but also shows the impact of this religion on the overall cultural outlook of its adherents. The effects of this religious attitude would later form one of the catastrophes of the African exploitation. The same mechanism would be employed later by the Europeans to impose mental and cultural colonialism on their African converts. Chukwunyere Kamalu palpably elucidates this viewpoint when he stated the following: "In similar to Christianity, it [Islam] was a religion used by Arab slave traders and soldiers in an attempt not only to subjugate Africans economically and politically, but to mould the African cultural personality into a form passive rather than resistant to cultural domination."[36]

But to understand why the traditional Africans sold their own people is to understand the basic aspect of the history of Africa. In the first place, the African problems on the whole began primarily because they were the first human stock on the planet to develop an advanced spiritually oriented civilization. This was at a time when other peoples of the world were living in barbarism, cannibalism, intellectual emptiness, and backwardness. As Chancellor Williams puts it, "… the Nile in making, upper Ethiopia (Egypt) so rich in food production… became world famous not only as the "Bread Basket of the world" but also for its highly advanced civilization, stirred the envy of Asia and Europe—from which continents migrants began to settle."[37] The geographical factor becomes important because it played a leading role in the conditions of Africa today. The Asians were the first to take advantage of their geographical proximity with Africa. This becomes evident when one looks at the contemporary inhabitants of North Africa.

The demography of North Africa began to change precisely around the early eighth century C.E. The role religion played in the cultural, religious, and political expansion of Arabs in Africa holds one aspect of the key to the mystery that has engulfed the African existence. In about 640 C.E., the Arabs successfully invaded Africa and introduced their new Muslim religion--Islam. But the introduction of this alien religion in the continent of Africa created both cultural and political conflicts with the African culture which was based upon a different worldview. As the invading Arab armies were relatively stronger and better equipped, Africans seemed unable to stop the political and cultural penetrations of the advancing Arab military power. Thus, as many African states were defeated, millions of North and East Africans began their many great migrations. Modern research has shown that most of these Africans either ended up in the interior of West Africa or in the southern part of Africa, closer to nature, to escape the atrocities meted to them by the foreign invaders.

Nevertheless, upon conversion fellow Africans who were fired by the Islamic religious fervent helped to destroy and demolish the backbone of the world's most profound civilization—the blackman's civilization. For instance, Mahammed Ahmed, the self-proclaimed messiah and Abu'I Hussan Ali, the black sultan of Morocco, amongst others, were in fact Africans who were the faithful servants of Islam. After conversion, these new converts were given the swords, spears, machetes or firearms with the promise that if they die fighting on the Jihad, fighting to liberate the "unfaithful", that they would go to paradise. To the contrary, most often these Islamic Jihads seemed to be less motivated by religious fervor, and tended to be influenced more by the incentives derived from conquests and economic gains.[38]

In the second place, the fact of "the racial" intermingling that had existed between Africans and Asians helped to create a "New Breed", that was part-African and part-Asian. No doubt, the problem with this "New Breed" was that for religious reasons they allied with the Arabs ideologically; and subsequently, were the flag bearers of Islamic expansion into Africa, leading to their settlement in all the potential and strategic landmass within the shores of Africa, especially from the northern perimeter: Northern Africa along the coast. The descendants of this "New

Breed" mostly live currently in North Africa; and they consider themselves in all pretensions as Arabs, and seem to be duly committed to the ideals found in the Arab brotherhood. To many of them, Pan-Africanism is irrelevant, never minding the fact that they live within the shores of the continental Africa that we now have renamed Kemet. In fact, their membership with the Organization of African Unity (OAU) is perhaps only to facilitate their control of its programs. But the impact of the Islamic Jihads or the so-called holy wars against Africans led to either the African's acceptance of the Islamic Faith or their being subjugated as prisoners of war. However, many Africans have been noted to resist these raids and on many occasions successfully drove the jihadist into defeat. On the other hand, if they resisted the jihadist and later were conquered, they in order not to face their reprisals either in conversion or in enslavement would decide to flee and migrate to the interior of Africa to begin life afresh.

Thirdly, the humane nature of the traditional African God-concept of spirituality is another important factor in the understanding of why the traditional Africans sold their own people. The traditional Africans by nature were a deeply spiritual people—a superior spiritual conscious people. One of the typical illustrations of this fact can be demonstrated by comparing the traditional African culture with the European culture. Whereas the European understanding of life lay more emphasis on the material nature of man, the African understanding of life underlaid the importance of a balance between the spiritual and the material existence of man.[39] Insofar as the traditional Europeans were concerned, they only saw life from the standpoint of material "progress" and "acquisition". As a result, they strived much harder, in whatever means necessary, than the African to improve their living condition through material progress or material acquisition. Thus, the lack of the worldly things to the European may be perceived as a spell of doom. Consequently, it is no surprise that a person who lost in the race to acquire material goods found life meaningless and a curse to his existence. He might even opt to take his own life to escape the inevitable doom of living in a vacuum of material want.

Conversely, the contemporary European saw the human life as a race. The majority of the Europeans seemingly saw life as a race in acquiring material goods. It therefore becomes easy to understand the cultural and psychological underpinnings that gave birth to the European concept of Race. Thus, the majority of the Europeans lay higher preference or premium on property rights over human rights. This tendentiousness is self evident in the European belief "that the summon bonum of life on earth is the expansion of the self through its acquisition of property".[40] In other words, the bottom line of the European life is motivated by greed and self-serving avarice. The guiding principle of life is thus the "acquisition of property", induced by the ferocious and perhaps rugged individualism. This excessive "acquisition" mentality is the principle that drives men to commit murder, to enslave their fellow men, to distort history, to deny the reality of Truth, and to commit savage atrocities.

On the other hand, the traditional African's mundane world focused more on his spiritual existence, making him to strive less in the sphere of property acquisition. His understanding of life grew out of his passion to understand the forces influencing the world spiritually—to master the spiritual incantations, rituals, magic spells, sacrifices, and dances that embodied the rhythm that underscored the manifestation of the material world—and to improve on his ability to influence the forces of nature through spiritual means. This was to the traditional African a means of achieving the material comfort of life. Thus, most traditional African religious practices just like the classical religion of the ancient "Egyptians aimed at being able to command their gods to work for them, and to compel them to appear at their desire".[41]

In other words, unlike the Europeans, the ancient and traditional Africans laid more emphasis on human rights and human divine potential in the development of their culture and traditions, rather than property rights or property acquisition. On the contrary, whether the Africans departed from the true nature of things is very difficult to say; and this is because the high marks found in the Nile Valley civilization which was built and maintained for many millennia by the ancient Africans eloquently gave adequate clue to this wholistic existence. This becomes meaningful as to why the traditional Africans did not see religion as being political; rather they saw religion as being sacred—as a metaphysical means to link their existence with their ancestors, deities, and Supreme Being. Typically, this manifests itself as to why religious wars and persecution have never been an issue in Africa before the advents of Euro-Christianity and Islam in the continent.

Religion, therefore has been to the ancient and traditional African a continuous ritual—an appeasement of the sacred forces through libation, worship, and other ceremonies as may be required by customs, reinforced by a sense of duty, loyalty, and the quest to understand the governing laws of the universe. The efficacious use of the energizing power of word, of NUMMO, is the centrality found in the diversity and unity of the African God-concept of spirituality. It is enthroned on the 'principle of interaction of opposites' that brings the invisible forces into physical action, whether positive or negative. The correct chanting of specific words of power becomes the Ankh or life force that "produces all life, all sickness, all health, all evil, all good, in the shape of the word. And since man has power over the word, it is he who may direct the life".[42]

In retrospect, this African spiritual doctrine of guiding the permeation of invisible forces or energy into physical action, through the power of the word, to achieve one's desire was used extensively by the mythical Moses in the biblical allegory on his alleged liberation of the Israelites from the land of Kemet. The biblical Saint Stephen recounted in the Acts of Apostles that "Moses was learned in all the wisdom of the Egyptians, and was mighty in words and in deeds."[43] It is no doubt that the mythical Moses in the Bible could be an African, most certainly a priest, who must have been indoctrinated into the African spiritual rituals and practices.[44] As a result, he must have understood the tenets behind the African spiritual use of the Word for libation and incantation.

The enthusiasm Africans have showed in religious practices and philosophy is invariably embodied in the numerous African myths, parables, proverbs, songs, ritual drama, etc. In other words, the nature of the African worldview and their understanding of life made it almost impossible for Africans to see the political dynamics as embedded in

Hebrewism, Christianity and Islam. This factor is deep-rooted as to why, amongst all national groups in traditional Africa, nobody rose up to proclaim himself the "Chosen One" within the same world-view of the African heritage. The absence or lack of the Chosen One in the African God-concept of spirituality or world-view is the key that would unlock the door of understanding to the idiosyncrasies of the traditional African personality. Because of this gap, Africans hitherto lacked a socio-cultural personality who could have provided the political force necessary in bringing most of the different languages into one or two major indigenous language, economic, social, and political foundation.

The Chosen One is usually somebody who has a good understanding of the people's religious heritage. His role is to organize such religious heritage and make it adaptable to his political mission.[45] For, the same reason, in order to create a fellowship or disciples the individual must not depart fundamentally from the already accepted traditions, but must make some distinctions from the general religious culture and the religion he envisioned to develop around his personality. The role of followers becomes the link used to spread the "good tidings". The teachings of the Chosen One thus become the means of converting the unbelievers. His world mission becomes the means to proselytize and preach to the masses about the mission of the Master Teacher and to facilitate an increase on the Master Teacher's following. The religion so founded would begin to acquire moral and political overtone, which would be used to enthrone the propagated religious symbols as sacred. Thus digression from them will not only be offensive to the adherents, but also may incur the wrath of the believers. The ultimate end would be the emergence of a new elite in the society. The emerging elites would begin to redefine the traditional symbols and structures of the society basing them on the principles propagated by the new religion. But the purpose of such religious development is mostly geared towards the political and cultural empowerment of the followers of the Chosen One who founded it. On the contrary, the African God-concept of spirituality was never organized to the extent of it becoming a political machine.

However, because the African God-concept of spirituality was not founded on the personality of an individual, non Africans were unable to understand the undergirded laws of the universe and human potential that gave birth to the original or non-political religion of man. Howbeit, they negatively called it paganism. Moreover, this misunderstanding is manifested in the non-African* belief that the traditional Africans had no conception of one Supreme Being.[46] But the African God-concept of spirituality acknowledges the existence of a Supreme Being and pays tribute to him (her). Chinua Achebe's *Things Fall Apart,* a social document dramatizing the traditional Igbo life in its first encounter with Euro-Christianity, portrayed a perfect example of this view. For instance, the argument between Akunna an African elder and Mr. Brown a Christian missionary helps to justify this impression: "You say that it is one supreme God who made heaven and earth", said Akunna on one of Mr. Brown's visit. "We also believe in him and call him Chukwu. He made all the world and other gods".[47] The Igbo vis-à-vis the traditional African religious concept of one Supreme Being is indeed not questionable. As this was amplified by Akunna's character in the book: "Our fathers knew that Chukwu (God) was the overlord and that is why many of them gave their children the name Chukwuka—'Chukwu is Supreme'".[48]

These illustrations go down to show that the religions of Faith are yet to understand the essential elements of the African God-concept of spirituality—which the Ekwensu people call Religion. Many not only have demonstrated that they lacked the temperament necessary for spiritual growth, but they also have built their mental image of the universe based on their materialistic inclinations. The Aryan mode of thinking can understand the material aspect of life, but it seems incapable of understanding the spiritual aspect of human existence. That is part of the reason why Europeans degraded and distorted the African God-concept of spirituality because they have failed to understand its essentiality to life.

Accordingly, based on the African God-concept of spirituality, the traditional African understood that the All Beneficent Creator may not possibly be reached directly without intermediaries or intercessors. Nevertheless, the African intermediaries were mistaken for false gods by the self-serving religious propagandists. The traditional Africans regarded their ancestors and their deities (cosmic principles or elemental powers that represent the non-human spirits) as their intercessors to the Omnipotent, Omniscient and Omnipresent God configuration—the Creator of the universe. In contrast, it is historically a fact that the politically organized religions of Faith were known to have used their faithful servants whom they called "savior", "prophet", "enlightened", "saints", etc., as their intermediaries. Of course this difference is because the African God-concept of spirituality was neither built upon the personality of an individual(s), nor was it a tool for political and cultural imperialism.

So the other religions that were built on the personalities of individuals use the individuals upon which the religion was founded as their intercessors in conjunction with other faithful servants. But they still have to elevate or deify these people to the level of an environmental extraordinary (or god). Thus, these people usually are called names like the "savior" "prophet", "messenger", "son of God", "saints", "martyrs", etc. In other words, the ancient and traditional Africans created and consecrated oracles out of the cosmic principles, whose manifesting powers cannot be doubted, as their intercessors to the Supreme Being/Force/Energy. This interdependent cosmological system is the cornerstone of the African God-concept of spirituality. The spirits of the departed ancestors also are believed to intercede between the living and their deities. This communion or piety to the ancestors is in fact the recognition of the powerful influence of departed souls in the continuum of human life. These are the testaments that are enshrined in all the ancient and traditional African sacred spiritual practices.

In a nutshell, the African God-concept of spirituality can be interpreted as follows: In thought, the conception of creation is of one Supreme Being, but in practice or symbolically (i.e., pantheistically speaking) God's relationship with human beings can only be apprehended through the harmonious interrelationship of human life with nature, in addition to the manifesting powers of the cosmos. The African doctrine of complementarity` or duality becomes relevant to an apprehension of this higher Truth. Thus, the African cosmos consists of two distinct but inseparable realms: The visible world of living matter and the invisible world of the spirit. The existence of the ancient and traditional Africans, therefore, consists of a dual relationship, even though interrelated, interposing between the material and spiritual, visible and invisible, masculine and feminine, being and becoming, positive and negative, dead and living, living and unborn, known and unknown, etc. The mutual interaction of the dualities is complemented through the regulation of the equilibrium Force/Energy. Take for an example, when a traditional African dies, he is not considered deceased; rather he is believed to have departed to the other world of the spiritual forces. Hence, the ancestral world constitutes the metaphysical link between the living and the dead. This understanding of life is rooted in the role ancestors play in the daily life of the ancient and traditional African communities. Whenever necessary, the African ancestors whose spirits are conceived as life-giving force could be contacted spiritually by their descendants for support and guidance.

Furthermore, the ancient and traditional Africans understood that the Supreme Being created everything, including humans. They regarded the Creator's image so highly that intermediaries or intercessors were indeed important in establishing a functional or quintessential cosmic balance with the Supreme Being/Force. This belief in the ever powerful spirit of the One Creator of the universe was the reason why no traditional African ever declared himself to be a "God", or "Son of God". Indeed, a "true" African only becomes an "Ekwueme" after passing through the threshold of EKUMEKU, or after mastering the inner workings of the universe, and must have attained oneness with the laws of the universe. Thus, the African understanding of the Supreme Being is not compatible with the idea of a corruptible human being elevating himself as a "God" or "Son of God ". So the spirits of their ancestors and other cosmic/elemental forces were regarded as the proper media for reaching the Supreme Being/Force. Until the divine birth of EKUMEKU on the Second year of Nzoputa Uwa, the human family was ignorant of the eternal Truth of the One Creator of the universe.

Thus, what the traditional Africans believed as the Supreme Being was limited to the world of Ekwensu. The Creator of the universe whom they conceived rightly or wrongly as the Supreme Being in turn showers His (Her) love to them (Africans) by not only blessing them with the right to the land and its many bounties, but also confers in them the genuine spirit for transcending the human stage of life. However, the uniqueness of the African God-concept of spirituality is that both the ancient and the traditional Africans believed that whatever blessing they had received came from the Supreme Being. In addition, they also believed that any misuse or abuse of the laws of the universe would attract vigorous reprisals, on the family, community, nature, and the cosmos, from either the ancestors who had passed down the heritage to them or from the deities, which are the eternal Force/Energy of the Supreme Being. The Supreme Being was understood to be always benevolent, but the deities (Neteru (Kemet), Orishas (Yoruba), Alusiuka (Igbo), etc.) were understood to be the forces that bring either blessing or destruction depending on the circumstances and their divine roles. This transcendental belief is nonetheless geared towards the African's eternal elevation to a higher spiritual cultivation of living in harmony with the governing laws of the universe.

The centrality of the ancient and traditional African spiritual consciousness is based on the transcendental belief that all the components of man's existence are part of man's struggle to attain a higher spiritual cultivation—to enable the fulfillment of the human rites of passage to the next life—which is the higher existence as envisioned in the order of the spiritual configuration of forces, both positive and negative. This idealism of striving for spiritual perfection through a transcendental (abstract) and immanent (concrete) understanding of the universe is the heart of the traditional African's struggles to be a human being par excellence. This brings us to the wholistic nature of the African God-concept of spirituality, its inter-connected unity with every aspect of the African culture. Thus, the fundamental difference between the politically organized religions of Faith and the African God-concept of spirituality is that those religions are cultural baggages established to perpetuate imperialist vested interests, through their organized nature; whilst the African God-concept of spirituality focuses on transforming man from overly material dependence and self-serving avarice through a day to day submission to the Creator as the Supreme Being. So the spiritual vibration or vital force that permeates the forces of life in the universe is recognized, by the African God-concept of spirituality, as the manifestation of Chineke, the Omnipresent, and the Supreme Being.

The foundation of the African God-concept of spirituality was made possible when the ancient Africans founded the fundamental moral principles of MAAT and ISFET, or the values of good and evil. As these fundamental moral principles laid down the basis of the ancient African's life, they also became the prototype of all true cultures and civilizations. MAAT is the basis of righteousness, truth and justice. Therefore, MAAT is not only the divine principle of a moral life, but also the fundamental basis of natural and moral law. The advancement of this concept also led to the emergence of the world's first noted universal idealist. Akhenaton.[49] It was because of the proper conditions presented by the Maatian principles of ethics and morality that made possible for such personality like Akhenaton or Amenhotep IV to become the world first noted idealist. Akhenaton was an autochthonous African, a universalist Pharoah, who championed the first recorded campaign for a revived God-concept of spirituality by strengthening the belief in one universal human spirit as the basis for all rituals. Diop noted that "he [Akhenaton] ordered the destruction of all polytheistic symbols, closed the ancient temples, and introduced the worship of a universal God, Aton. He is considered the first monotheist in history."[50] This idea of oneness of Universal Life was then made an absolute approach to the already existed concept of God, as the basis for the intrinsic understanding of the universe and the celestial bodies. It was then no surprise that the notion of one God or one Universal Life had been embraced by most Africans. But Akhenaton did not invent monotheism, for the concept of one God has been the foundation of the African God-concept of spirituality throughout the antiquity of time. The Late E.A. Wallis Budge in the book, *The Egyptian Book Of the Dead,* described in great detail many of the ancient Africa's doctrine of Life, which the author dated back to about 4500 B.C.E. This amongst others clearly reinforces the fact that what Akhenaton popularized was the concept of one Universal

Life Force, which was later distorted with the doctrines of absolutism. That is why the propagandists who have obviously benefitted from this distortion of Universal Life Force have immortalized Akhenaton as "The Prince of Peace".

Notably, many centuries after the death of Akhenaton, the theoretical aspect (transcendental) of a belief in one Universal Life Force was adopted by the Hebrew group, who lived in Africa, when they created the Hebrew Yahweh(Jehovah) (not the One Creator of the Universe). The concept of one Hebrew deity was then made the center-piece of the Hebrew folklores and religious traditions of messianic prophecies, from whence the Torah was written in about 700 B.C.E. in Africa.

In any case, by the fifteenth century C.E., when the European conquerors came to Africa's West coast, the Arabized Muslims were in considerable control of almost all the coastal landmass connecting Africa to the outside world. This is because the Islamic religious penetration in Africa has influenced the history of African migrations coupled with natural disasters such as desertification. Thus, the history of Africa has been replete with migrations. These migrations have affected the historical reality of the African people in many ways. First, they led to the formation of many national groups. Second, in many cases, they became one of the important factors that made many African national groups to partially lose the art of writing. This statement of fact may sound preposterous to some people because of the concerted portrayal of traditional Africans as non-literate people; but Africans were the first human stock to introduce the art of writing. This point has considerably been espoused by C.A. Diop and other prominent scholars. This is what he has to say: 'That it is a typically indigenous African language that has been the oldest written language in the history of humanity. It began 5,300 years ago, in ancient Kemet'.[51]

However, at that time writing was the exclusive preserve of the few. It was also one of the means upon which the secret order of the African priestly schools were regulated and controlled. Therefore, the movement of the East Africans beginning from the Nile region and the North Africans from the North African landmass resulted in a partial loss of the art of writing. This is not historically unique, because political and religious oppression naturally becomes a stepping stone for people to turn inward. Also, during those days it was easier for the art of writing to be lost because it was undertaken by very few people. The political and religious oppression and the movement of these people in splinter groups for survival led to the formations of many different languages; and these dispersions, on the other hand, made writing a lesser priority. This is because these persecuted Africans became more concerned about their survival from the forces of nature and their enemies. Moreover, some of these African migrants lacked the population, environmental growth, and stability to resurrect all their cultural superstructure. Similarly, many of the migrants "retreated to barren areas, and lost their original cultural form".[52]

Ironically, the Sahara desert seemed to have created a barrier for the Arab's political and religious expansionism. It seems to be one of the elements that imposed a serious setback to the Arab hordes' incursion into Africa. Thus, the Sahara desert created a significant impediment to the advancing force of Arabism. Despite this fact, in Africa, in countries like Niger, Mauritania, Mali, Sudan, etc., the Arabized Islamic control has become very visible and in some cases quite imposing. As usual religion and "sexual traffic" became the weapon used to divide and exploit the autochthonous people. So, the fundamental factor underlying the African history of migration is found in the exigencies and imperatives of Islamic expansionism and Slave Trade. However, this factor has like every other African historical reality been distorted. This becomes important because to understand the history of Africa one must understand what were the motivating factors infusing Africans to migrate from one part of the continent to the other.

Nevertheless, the central issue is that these migrations which were forced on Africans due to the imperatives of Arabism have created many nations in Africa; and these nations, therefore, dealt with each other from the standpoint of their national interest. This was the state of affairs in Africa when the Europeans arrived in the middle of the fifteenth century. It did not take the Europeans very long to understand the language fragmentations of the inhabitants. They were initially astounded by what seemed like many different languages. However, they recovered from that astonishment quickly as it became evident that it was to their own advantage. The principle underlying the divide and conquer policy was entrenched; and it set the stage for the African exploitation and enslavement. How this principle was carried out is found on the overall mechanics which developed and evolved during the historical epoch. The role Africans played in its manifestation was partly a natural reaction found within the context of survival ability. But the structural system present on the African side lacked strong fundamental elements necessary to control the cravings of the Europeans for involuntary free laborers. It is important to note once again that the Slave Trade began even before many African nations and ethnic groups understood the nature of this new phenomenon. The fact that the European Slave Trade began through the terrorist system of kidnapping resulted into a struggle by African hordes to have a share of what they must have foreseen as a new trend of commercial transactions. Therefore, a new class of "privileged" African elites began to emerge. An elite composed of raiders, kidnappers, and hoodlums, that were bent on capitalizing on the European need for African human power. These were mostly the greedy vagabonds who inhabited the coast of West Africa.

There are many vantage points comprising the European Slave Trade: the conquest of the Americas, the gun slave circle, the cost effective labor program, and the skin color vantage point. The understanding of the mores of behavior and the attitude of Africans in relation to their participation in this process of the dehumanization of their fellow Africans—in the raiding, kidnapping, and conquering of men to sell as human commodities—will give adequate clues in a conceptual sense to a pattern capable of unfolding this vital historical tragedy. Just so will the activities of the Europeans in their economic objectives and goals of procuring captive African labor deemed necessary for the attainment of their objectives become the underlying factor. The purpose is not only to collect historical facts and behaviors, but also to find meanings in how they have helped to influence upon our world.

So far, what we have stressed in the foregoing historical outline is that, although the European Slave Trade created a bountiful image of the modern world, the Arabs and Arabized Africans were integrally involved.

They participated not only in their religious, economic, and political cleavages, but equally in the destruction of various African civilizations, in the rape of Africa through the Trans-Saharan and Trans-Indian Ocean routes, and in the occupation of strategic and potential landmass in the continental Africa. The Arab question no doubt is not the major focus; however, it was worth mentioning to render a meaningful understanding of why and how Africans came to sell their own people. So that what Ali Mazrui had called a "triple heritage" is what I consider to be a double-edged sword of the alienating and contradicting forces of Arabia and Europe which have rendered the African culture stagnant.

Historically, most scholars have paid little attention to the conditions of Africa before the infamous European Slave Trade began in the fifteenth century C.E. Now we not only know that the Arab Slave Trade on Africans spanned from about the ninth to the early twentieth century C.E.,; whilst the European exploitation and plunder of Africa preceded the era of the European Slave Trade, dating back to the time of the ancient Greek's and Roman's civilizations. The Arab Slave Trade on Africans is presently still shrouded in mysteries, because scholars have not yet begun to give it the attention it deserves. The available information so far gives indication that the Arab Slave raiders were not only merciless but were also abominably cruel. As one historian described it: "… The slave trade has always been an abomination, especially in Africa where the Arab slave raiders, as late as this present century would seize a whole town, murder the old and the babies, castrate the young boys, of whom eighty percent died, and drive the remnant across country with such indifferent cruelty that half would die on the road".[53]

The European encroachment to the Americas resorted in the economic scramble of all the natural endowments found in the landscape. The system of mercantilism at this time, in the late fifteenth and early sixteenth century, was at its embryo stage. The importance of the Americas and its compatible counterpart, the system of mercantilism, became the moving force behind the doctrine of colonial economics. Mercantilism was in Europe the ideological substitution of the feudal economics and organization. Its inception is directly a result of the initial Europeans' expeditions to Africa and their annexation of the Americas which created the opportunity for the capitalization of the captive African labor-power.

The importance of mercantilism lies in its transformation of the concept Money and Wealth, as the basic component of the community. Essentially, as it superceded feudalism, mercantile economics brought these two spheres within an identical threshold of human organization—as a compatible and inseparable force. Therefore, the mercantile system henceforth made money to become the primary organ of the European community. As money became the substitute for the community and every other thing, it also became the central source of the Occidental racism. In short, money was deified as the essence of life; and the ability to make money was made to become the standard for success and the key to status. Thus, money and wealth which have been the symbolic precepts of the community were reduced to one single motivating schema: profit motive. And for somebody to have maximum profit, definitely another person have to be exploited—that is to say, a zero-sum game. So the world became fragmented between the exploited group and the exploiter group. The whole universe henceforth became a market place to the Europeans. Every aspect of nature was valued according to its approximate commercial worth. As a result, the proponents became irrational, inhuman, amoral, and monstrous, resorting from devoting their life for the community to appropriating and exploiting their community for their individual profit motives. Joel Kovel illuminated this phenomenon when he wrote:

"The very process of seeking became the most highly valued part of the activity; what was sought, and even worshipped, became, through the very abstractification that made it attainable, more and more remote, cold, and dead, and more purely quantitative. The world was remade into dead things to be acquired: and what was acquired was the coldest aspect of these things: their money value".[54]

It is this economic agent, money, that is worshipped and has made most Europeans very ignorant of the eternal Truth of the One Creator of the universe. Indeed, the effect of this ideology on the European mind has become an integral part of the modern world. At that historical epoch, this understanding directly set the Europeans apart from other groups around the world. And it made non-Europeans to appear somewhat gullible in what the Europeans had perceived to be an economic race. What Bob Marley the legendary Reggae singer called "The Rat Race". As the Europeans were encouraged and influenced by this belief, they carried out their various interactions with other cultures of the world within the realms of economic exploitation and extraction of precious metal from other lands, for the sole benefit of their mother country. So as they became the profiteers and exploiters, cultures like the Africans became the losers and the exploited.

On the one hand, the dynamic stimulant of the European Slave Trade on Africans was a direct result of an acute need for labor. The need for cost effective labor force initially necessitated the involuntary use of the Native American's labor as the justifiable means of fulfilling the economic scramble, and as the first plausible experimentation. However, due to three contending reasons the cost effective labor did not suffice. Firstly, the Native Americans were in their own environment, i.e., an environment that was very familiar to them. So it was practically easy for them to abscond and run away. Secondly, the Native Americans' livelihood contradicted the European economic view of exploiting and extracting from the landscape anything deemed viable of economic rewards. Therefore, it was not only because the Native Americans were incapable of becoming a viable labor force, but also because the Native Americans themselves saw the European encroachment as a total negation to their harmonious existence. They tended to see the destruction of their land as offensive and abominable. Finally, during the historical epoch the European disease pool infected the "Indians" disastrously to the point of extermination. But the "Indian" diseases did not infect the Europeans as such. However, the Indians were affected by the European diseases because they were made to adopt the European diet, which altered their metabolism and made them susceptible to these diseases.

On the other hand, the lack of control of the "Indian" labor force and their genocidal mortality rate necessitated that an alternative labor force must be recruited or impounded in order to carry on with the demands of the mercantile system. This was because they were well aware that effective labor is the life force of mercantile or colonial economics. The experiment with Africans in the Caribbean and South America had been profoundly successful at this point. Many captured Africans had been used in collaboration with Native Americans in these areas because the Caribbean and South America were not deemed congenial to European settlement, supposedly due to their tropical climatic conditions. However, when it became explicit that the Native Americans could not provide the much needed labor force for the Caribbean, North and South Americas, a new resolution was adopted.

The system of indentured servitude was adopted to facilitate the acute labor demands. Many Native Europeans were thus brought into the mainland of North America as voluntary labor force. Their labor was owned under the stipulation of a contract. But they were considered fundamentally to be free. One of the most common examples of the nature of this contract was a free passage to the Americas which was recompensed by the person through the acceptance, under contractual agreement, to work for a period of years for the financer of the passage.

There were at least three factors which made the program of indentured servitude incompatible with the ferocious urgency needed for the rapid exploitation of the landscape. Firstly, these servants were mostly English, everybody spoke the same language, often have the same religion—Protestantism—and they were generally Anglo-Saxons. To illustrate this common heritage bond, in the beginning, it was a harmonious relationship. Still it changed overtime because of the structure of the economic system. Initially, the indentured servants were well fed, clothed and sheltered. Secondly, overtime the relationship between these European voluntary servants and the managers "tended to pass into a property relation which asserted a control of varying extent over the bodies and liberties of the person during service as if he were a thing".[55] Thus these servants, their skin color notwithstanding, were made to respond to the harsh realities of plantation farming. This unfavorable labor condition created a large number of runaway cases. But since all Europeans were fundamentally considered to be free, the burden of proof falls on the owner to prove that they had contractual agreement together. This burden of proof bestowed on the white farmers, most often, was very hard to prove. Finally, the institution of European servitude lacked a continuous flow of replacement for those whose contracts had expired, and had thus regained their freedom. The absence of the continuous flow of European laborers compounded and heightened the applicability of this labor policy.

Entrenched by the tradition of greed and the urge to accumulate property, it is a fact that the "capital accumulated from one financed the other. White servitude was the historic base upon which Negro slavery was constructed".[56] Some of the following factors were the stark differences that made white servitude less appealing to the white landlords—less profitable. Whereas the white servant's temporary condition of servitude was a limited status, the African's condition of chattel slavery was for life. More so, the indentured servants' limited legal condition did not affect their offspring whether born during the duration of their servitude or not. But the offspring of the enslaved Africans automatically became slaves from birth. Indeed the white servant's rights, although very limited, were not only recognized by law but were protected by the contractual agreement; whilst the African had no rights, not even the right to live. To the Europeans, the African was a beast of burden, an economic tool created by slavery to be responsive to the needs of his master.[57]

Thus, a fresh emphasis was again given to Africa. In other words, the overwhelming need for cost effective labor found within the confines of the mercantile system engendered and later culminated into the massively European imposed Slave Trade on Africans as chattel slaves, even though it was precipitated by the tradition of experimentation. The principle of the centrifugal force will become the harbinger used to analyze the role Africans played in the fulfillment of the European desire for cost effective labor. The cancer of "tribalism" therefore was planted on the African soil, in the process, to guarantee the free flow of Africans to the Americas. There is no denial of the fact that the traditional Africans sold their own people and therefore must share in the blame for this crime against humanity. However, the African's role was part of the symptoms, not the problem, of the atrocious African–European intercourse, beginning from the fifteenth century. The problem is White Magic.

In other words, the prelude of the African's involvement and understanding of this historic tragedy complements the viciousness of the dynamic as entrenched by the mercantile system. This viciousness invoked a fantastic mystique on the traditional African mind who was yet to understand the vitality of this concept behind the European motives—which is the spiritual and economic force of mercantilism. This lack of understanding on the part of the Africans coupled with their beliefs and expectations that the Europeans, though pink in complexion, were no different from them in their general understanding of human nature, ownership, kinship, and relationship with the One Creator of the universe. However, there was nothing to tell these traditional Africans that Europeans because of their cultural differences and subsequent enthronement of the mercantile system had departed essentially from the cooperative, xenophilic and sedentary order of things. In his book, *The Cultural Unity of Black Africa,* Cheikh Anta Diop debunked the notion of "universal humanism"; and instead through systematic analysis proved that human nature so far as kinship patterns, ownership, political philosophy, and relationship with the One Creator of the universe were concerned has been far from being universal.[58]

In the final analysis, the Slave Trade not only marked another phase of the **African Maafa**, but also with the ravages of the "trade" Europe successfully clouded and imposed upon Africa its White Age vampire. The magic and most of the venom that constitute White Magic propelled the injurious activities that took place between Europeans and Africans. Hence, for the Europeans to successfully emerge out of their so-called Dark Ages, it was necessary that Europe belligerently dominate Africa thereby fostering the conditions that gave birth to the African White Age (an ideological twin of the European Dark Age).

Just as the Arab Islamic incursions into Africa precipitated the historical migrations of Africans within and outside the continent. The era of the European imposed Slave Trade on Africans coincided with the period of consolidation and expansion of many African states. So also was the Islamic North Africa's invasion of West Africa in 1591 C.E., the Moorish menace, and its resultant impact in setting the stage for the ravages of human trade in West Africa. The irony of the African enslavement buttressed the fact that the European explorations to Africa and Americas coincided with the many African nations territorial wars of expansion. The implication of this can be illuminated when one pays a close attention to the various means through which the enslaved Africans were procured, i.e., wars, kidnapping and raids.[59] The intensification of conflicts spurred by the European's tactics of supporting one group against the other group gave further impetus to the already volatile condition, and made it easy for Europeans to fulfill their needs for cost effective laborers

In general, the European Slave Trade can be summarized as the triumph of one of the oldest strategies of warfare: divide and conquer. The European economic and military victories over the Africans were as a result of the structure of the interaction between Africans and Europeans. Although, the intensification and the resultant massive Slave Trade was aided by the advantage of superior firearms on the European side, the activities of many Africans within the Continent helped to push the Slave Trade much farther into the hinterlands. In order to create conflicts and wars rival West African states were backed by the Europeans with firearms against the opposing parties. Thus, the defeat of the other party usually led to an insurmountable number of prisoners of wars (POWS). These POWs were normally bartered out to the Europeans as commodity slaves. As this social crisis increased, many peaceful neighbors began to suspect each other. Consequently, the need to survive and the fear of the impending enemy led to a vicious cycle of guns, POWs and wars. The conditional disaster caused by this state of affairs resulted to the over dependence of Africans in their ethnic groups for survival.[60]

In the vicious human drama of turning human beings into human machines, millions of Africans lost their lives. There is no possible way to calculate the human drain Africa suffered as a result of the Slave Trade. Over the years, the need for a working number of the African souls who were murdered or transplanted outside Africa have led to many speculations. Whilst conservative estimates range from ten to fifty million, another group of estimates range from seventy to one hundred and twenty million African people who were either murdered or uprooted from their homelands. In addition to these numbers, I think that the under population of Africa in relation to its continental space is another means Africans can use to measure the evident human drain the African Maafa has been to our beloved continent.

CHAPTER FOUR
NOTES

*. The term "Maafa" is an expression coined by Marimba Ani (Donna Marimba Richards). It means in Kiswahili "disaster" or "calamity". The greatest calamity in human history has been the enslavement of the African people. African Maafa is therefore a phrase that expresses this painful tragedy.

IA. Paul Bohannan, *Africa & Africans,* Garden City, New York: The Natural History Press, 1964, p. I.

1. W.E.B Du Bois, *The World and Africa,* New York: International Publishers Co. Inc., 1965, p. 20.
2. Christopher Fyfe, "The Dynamics of African Dispersal", *The African Diaspora* (edited by Martin Kilson and Robert Rotberg), Cambridge, Massachusetts: Harvard University Press, 1976, p.59.
3. Cheikh Anta Diop, *The African Origin of Civilization: Myth or Reality?* Chicago, Illinois: Lawrence Hill &Co.,1974, p. 230
4. W.E.B Du Bois, *The World and Africa,* New York: International Publishers Co. Inc., 1965, p. 18.
5. IBid, p. 44.
6. Ali A. Mazrui, *The African Condition,* London: Cambridge University Press, 1980, p. 95.
7. W.E.B Du Bois, *The World and Africa,* New York: International Publishers Co. Inc., 1965, p.46.
8. A. Adu Boahen, "The Coming of the Europeans" (1440-1700), *The Horizon History of Africa,* New York: American Heritage Publishing Co. Inc., a subsidiary of Mc Graw-Hill Inc., 1971, p.307.
9. IBid, p. 3017.
10. Micheal Beaud, *A History Of Capitalism 1500-1980* (translated by To, Dickman and Anny Lefebvre), New York: Monthly Review Press, 1983, p.18.
11. A. Adu Boahen, "The Coming of the Europeans" (1440-1700), *The Horizon History of Africa,* New York: American Heritage Publishing Co., Inc., a subsidiary of Mc Graw-Hill, Inc.,
12. Basil Davidson, *The African Slave Trade,* Boston: Atlantic-Little, Brown Co., 1961, p. 38.
13. Micheal Beaud, *A History Of Capitalism 1500-1980*, New York: Monthly Review Press, 1983, p. 18.

14. A. Adu Boahen, "The Coming of the Europeans" (1440-1700), *The Horizon History of Africa*, New York: American Heritage Publishing Co. Inc., a subsidiary of Mc Graw-Hill Inc., 1971, p. 310.
15. Robert I. Rotberg, "Introduction", *Africa and Its Explorers: Motives, Methods and Impact* (Editor), Cambridge, Massachusetts: Harvard University Press, 1970, p. 9.
16. A. Adu Boahen, "The Coming of the Europeans" (1440-1700), *The Horizon History of Africa*, New York: American Heritage Publishing Co. Inc., a subsidiary of Mc Graw-Hill Inc., 1971, p. 308.
17. W.E.B Du Bois, *The World and Africa,* New York: International Publishers Co. Inc., 1965,p. 20
18. Basil Davidson, *The African Slave Trade,* Boston: Atlantic-Little, Brown Co., 1961, p. 36.
19. Walter Rodney, *How Europe underdeveloped Africa,* Washington D.C.: Howard University Press, 1972, p. 77.
20. Ibid, p. 22.
21. Ibid, p. 25.
22. Basil Davidson, *The African Slave Trade,* Boston: Atlantic-Little, Brown Co., 1961, p. 42; see also, Cary Joyce Britain and West Africa, London: Longsman, Green and Co., 1947,p. 9-10.
23. Walter Rodney, *How Europe Underdeveloped Africa,* Washington D.C.: Howard University Press, 1972, p. 95.
24. Christopher Fyfe, "The Dynamics of African Dispersal" *The African Diaspora,* Cambridge, Massachusetts: Harvard University Press, 1976, p. 59.
25. W.E.B Du Bois, *The World and Africa,* New York: International Publishers Co. Inc., 1965, pp. 52-53.
26. Micheal Beaud, *A History Of Capitalism 1500-1980*, New York: Monthly Review Press 1983 p. 18.
27. A. Adu Boahen, "The Coming of the Europeans" (1440-1700), *The Horizon History of Africa*, New York: American Heritage Publishing Co. Inc., a subsidiary of Mc Graw-Hill Inc., a subsidiary of McGraw-Hill, Inc. 1971,p. 315
28. W.E.B Du Bois, *The World and Africa,* New York: International Publishers Co. Inc., 1965, p. 45.
29. Basil Davidson, *The African Slave Trade,* Boston: Atlantic-Little, Brown Co., 1961, p. 45.

30. Christopher Fyfe, "The Dynamics of African Dispersal" *The African Diaspora,* Cambridge, Massachusetts: Harvard University Press, 1976, p. 59.
31. Charles S. Finch III, *Echoes of the Old Darkland: Themes From the African Eden,* Decatur, Georgia: Khenti, Inc., 1991.
32. Pp.123-126. Dr Charles Finch has demonstrated that the traditional use of the year 3,100B.C.E, as the beginning of the dynastic period in ancient Kemet is not only historically wrong but also depicts a conspiracy to confuse the historical reality of Africa. Despite many imposing evidence that the year 3,100B.C.E. is incorrect, many scholars have continued to use it as the standard date for the beginning of the dynastic period in ancient Kemet. Therefore, I have used the lowest possible date of 4,200 B.C.E., according to Finch's study as a tentative date, until African scholars arrive at a consensus on a new date.
33. IBid, p. 123
34. J.C. DeGraft-Johnson, *African Glory: The Story of Vanished Negro Civilizations,* New York: Walker and Company, 1954, pp. 69-70.
35. John Henrik Clarke, "Time of Troubles", *The Horizon History of Africa, II,* New York: American Heritage Publishing Co. Inc., a subsidiary of McGraw-Hill, Inc., 1971, p. 355.
36. Chukwunyere Kamalu, *Foundation of African Thought,* London, Great Britain: Karnak House, 1990, p.19.
37. Chancellor Williams, *The Destruction of Black Civilization,* Chicago, Illimois: Third World Press, 1976, p. 52.
38. Hollis R. Lynch in *Edward Wilmot Blyden: Pan-Negro Patriot,* 1832-1912, London: Oxford University Press, 1970, p. 69. Lynch observed that "it is certain, for instance, that some Muslim leaders, under the pretext of making war against non-believers pursued largely political and economic goals and that their warlike exploits helped in ravaging West Africa and contributed largely to the trans-Saharan slave trade".
39. The ancient civilizations of the Nile Valley, especially that of ancient Kemet, were founded on the divine ordinance of balancing the material world with the spiritual realm. Such goal has been one of the reasons why the ancient civilization of Kemet was able to endure for a long historical period despite the continuous alien invasions. But the traditional African life, on the other hand, has been overly dependent, in my opinion, on the spiritual realm for its

rhythms of life. That is to say that the traditional African life has not been able to balance its existence between the spiritual and the material world. As a result, the traditional African life has been dominated by spiritual strivings. The implication of this type of deep spiritual indulgence is the neglect of the material aspect of life, individuals become vulnerable to external aggressions from outsiders who may be looking at life from a strictly material standpoint. Some aspect of the African experience gives a perfect illustration of this human phenomenon. For example, the external invasions into Africa coupled with many kinds of natural disasters led to the historical migrations of many African groups into different parts of Africa. During the cause of these migrations many African groups lost some of the superstructure of their culture and their creative production. The ability to reconstruct the original culture is not only hampered by the population but also by the uncertainties of the future. Thus spirituality became the basis of fulfilling the yearnings of life, as many of these groups resigned themselves to the conditions and difficulties likened to people under a siege.

40. Joel Kovel, *White Racism: A Psychohistory,* New York Vintage Books, 1971, p.17
41. E.A. Wallis Buldge, *Egyptian Magic,* New York Dover Publications, Inc., 1971 (This is an unbridged republication of the work originally published in London in 1901 by Kegan Paul, Trench, Trubner & Co., Ltd., as volume II in their series books on Egypt and Chaldea), p. 4
42. Jack Mendelson, *God, Allah and JuJu: Religion in Africa Today,* New York: Thomas Nelson & Sons, 1962, p. 84
43. Saint Stephen, *Acts of Apostles,* Chapter VII, Verse 22.
44. The same basic argument was the fundamental thesis in Sigmund Freud, *Moses and Monotheism*, New York: Vintage Books, 1967.
45. It is important to note that the "Chosen One" of Nzoputa Uwa was chosen by the One Creator of the universe through the Almighty Spirit of EKUMEKU
46. * The term non-Africans here denoted all individuals who do not believe in the original African God-concept of spirituality. It includes African "doubters" who adhere to the religious tenets of Hebrewism, Christianity, and Islam—the unbelievers of the African God-concept of spirituality.

47. Chinua Achebe, *Things Fall Apart*, New York: Ballantine Books, 1983, p. 164.
48. IBid,p. 165
49. Maulana Karenga, *The Book of Coming Forth by Day*, Los Angeles, California: University of Sankore Press, 1990, pp. 23-26
50. Cheikh Anta Diop, *Civilization or Barbarism,* Brooklyn, New York: Lawrence Hill Books, 1991, p. 78.
51. Ibid, p. 215
52. Llaila O. Afrika, *African Holistic Health,* Silver Spring, Maryland: Adesegun Johnson, and Koran publishers, 1983, p. 322.
53. Joyce Cary, *Britain And West Africa,* London: Longmans, Green and Co. Ltd, 1947, p. 22
54. Joel Kovel, *White Racism: A Psychohistory,* New York: Vintage Books, 1971, p. 115
55. Eric Williams, *Capitalism and Slavery,* London, England Andre Deutsch limited, tenth impression 1991, (C.) 1944, P.16.
56. IBid, p. 19
57. IBid, pp. 16-20.
58. One of the implications of Diop's "Two Cradle Theory" is that it has highlighted the fact that the Eurasians have been successful in taking whatever they needed from the African ("Southern Cradle") for the advancement of their culture. But Africans have not yet been successful in appropriating what aspects of culture in the Eurasian (Northern Cradle") that may be needed for their cultural survival.
59. We also know that the use of oracles to recruit Africans into servitudes was widely practiced in what is known today as Eastern Nigeria, mostly by the Igbos. This is especially true of the Igbo people of Arochukwu who used the medium of their venerated Oracle, Ebiri-Ukpabi, to recruit their fellow Igbos into servitude. As K. Onwuka Dike puts it, "The Oracle directed by the Aros, was the medium through which the slaves exported from Delta ports were largely recruited. As the highest court of appeal, this deity was supposed to levy fines on convicted individuals and groups. These fines had to be paid in slaves who were believed to be "eaten" by Chukwu (the oracle), although in fact they were sold to the coast middlemen". K. Onwuka Dike, *Trade and Politics in the Niger Delta,*1830-1885, London: Oxford University Press,1956,p. 40

60. P. Peter Ekeh, "Social Anthropology and Two Contrasting Uses of Tribalism in Africa", *Comparative Studies in Society And History* Vol.32, No.4 (Cambridge University Press, October 1990), pp. 660-692.

CHAPTER FIVE
NOMENCLETURE: THE THREE PROVERBIAL PARADOXES

"We understand that as soon as an African man stands up and declares himself to be a man, he has to put himself in absolute and immediate opposition to the European system, which has defined him by their definitions as less than a man or as not a man".[1a]

...Na'im Akbar

I. THE MYTH OF SLAVERY

Slavery is one of the humanity's oldest primordial institutions. It formed part of the economic, cultural, political, and religious evolution of man and his understanding of either his survival or his nature. There is no culture within the human family that was free of this man's exploitation of his fellow man. However, the dynamics of this institution vary from culture to culture, environment to environment. This becomes important because the survival of man has been embedded on his ability to defend his environment and himself from his enemies. The outcome on the whole often manifests itself in different forms of war. War therefore played a leading role not only in the establishment of slavery as an institution, but also in its perpetuation. Slavery in the old order meant the subjugation and enslavement of men captured during wars or raids of other communities. That notwithstanding, this enslavement of men nevertheless does not mean that they were less human or biologically inferior, but rather their treatment usually were based on the social and economic conventions of the culture they found themselves. In addition, the differences between a freeborn and a slave in many cultures might not even manifest themselves in the economic interactions within the community; rather the differences only become visible in the religious practices of which the slaves in many cases were excluded. But in the Americas, most captured Africans were not only defined as chattels, properties or factors of production, they were in reality brutally used involuntarily at the point of production.

On the other hand, the old notion of slavery recognized the enslaved rights as a human being; therefore, this made his conditions to differ essentially from that of a piece of property. For instance, these conditions of servitude existed in Europe until the end of the sixteenth century; and these slaves were called Serfs. The laws of the land accordingly protected and preserved their basic rights as human beings. Moreover, as Finley observed, "it is equally certain,... that all categories of compulsory labor other than chattel slaves possessed, in different degrees, restricted rights of property and usually much wider rights in the sphere of marriage and family law."[1] Consequently, because of this attitude, some slaves sometimes could rise up in the social strata to become prominent members of the society, leaving behind their previous status. Hence, slavery in the old sense does not bear much resemblance to the contextual meaning of the European enslavement of Africans. Instead, the contemporary meaning of slavery had altered the mere understanding of the word "slavery"; and has subsequently impaired the obvious differences between the European enslavement of Africans and the old slavery which was based on an unfortunate environmental outcome that emanated in most cases out of warfare and raids.

The difference between the European enslavement of Africans and the old slavery is likened to the different perceptions human beings have for night and day. The comparison is so unequal that I am surprised that the African enslavement is called slavery. In my opinion, it is appropriate and precise to refer to the wholesale murder, dehumanization and forceful dispersion of millions of Africans from the fifteenth century to the late nineteenth century as the African Maafa (a Kiswahili term introduced and coined by Marimba Ani, aka, Dona Marimba Richards meaning "disaster" or "calamity"). That is to say that the African Maafa is the wholesale crime Eurasians committed against the humanity of Africans. But in order not to confuse the reader, I will be using the word slavery and the term Maafa interchangeably, whilst contrasting the obvious differences between the old notion of slavery and African Maafa in order to explain the brutality and dehumanization that is compatible with the system of Maafa imposed on the African in the Americas, specifically in the United States. This is important for those Africans enslaved in Portugal and Spain were even treated differently; and as a result, some later rose up to become prominent members of the society. There were many instances of intermingling through genuine marriage even in the royal families; and many occasions of formerly enslaved Africans marrying the daughters of their former masters. Whenever this occurred, and in the cases where the female in question was the only child, the African would inherit not only the title of his former master but also his wealth through this marriage arrangement.

However, the enslavement of the African and its justification bears a strong irony. This irony is found on the idea that the African on all plausible account is the original human stock. Because he was the first, or because of the geographical interplay of nature, he created the first high civilization; and the creation of this civilization led to many of his problems. He made Asia and Europe envious and from all sides of his continental space he was ceaselessly attacked. He was pushed into the interior from where he once again created many civilizations—such as the empires of Ghana, Mali, Songhay, Mwanamutapa (or Mutapa), etc. Then, the Europeans and Asians once again came and plundered his sacred possessions, and this time forcefully took him away as a chattel, with no human rights at all. In fact, animals were made to have some vestiges of rights that were not even given to the enslaved Africans; hence, they ranked higher in scale than the African in the eyes of many Europeans. The one "offense" that the African committed was that as the "original man" or as the "father" he defined and founded civilization and was lenient enough to let his "children" from Asia and Europe share the splendor of his accumulated wisdom. However, what helped to destroy him was the religions of ISFET (be it Hebrewism, Christianity or Islam). As has previously shown, Africans are a deeply spiritual people. They are always searching for the continuous spiritual cycle of rebirth and renewal with the Supreme Being. In the ancient times, Africa was known as the Land of God, and the land of spiritual people. So it was no surprise that the Asians would take advantage of this fact. They came on the banner of Islam, conquering, violating the women and converting them to the Islamic religion. Those who refused to let themselves to such debauchery have no choice but to move back into the interior. Nevertheless, there were many centuries of blood mixing between the Asians and Africans. The product of such despicable "sexual traffic" turned against the African and with the help of his enemies stabbed him in the back.

II. NOMENCLATURE

In discussing how the enslavement of the traditional Africans shaped the modern world, certain inherent elements used in a systematic fashion cannot be divorced in the entire revelation of the dehumanization and the malicious degradation of the Africans brought into the Americas as chattels. Therefore, in order to understand the mechanism of the African Maafa and what in fact made this modern slavery different, one must understand the three paradoxes unilaterally used to psychologically impose a sense of servitude on the African. Hence, it is important to note that "slavery was not put into practice because of racial theories; racial theories sprang up in the wake of slavery, to justify it."[2] A detailed historical emphasis therefore is warranted to bring to the reader a full understanding of how these paradoxes cum racial theories evolved and their subsequent interplay on the mentality of the African people. Also relevant is their conditioning effects on the already willing ego and psychological well-being of the majority of the European people. In addition, these paradoxes would be indispensable to the understanding and following of the tide of historical affairs that culminated into the devaluation of the word "Black". Similarly, some consideration must be given to the sphere of language and its usage beginning from the historical period.

Consequently, it must be acknowledged that the emergence of language as a political machine on the avid war on black imagery enhanced the European's desire for taxonomical distinction between Africans and Europeans—black and white. Not surprisingly, the politics of language came into play because it became the tool used in creating negative images for blacks and positive images for whites. Subsequently, it has influenced the development of words that stressed and emphasized the black negativity, especially in English language: for example, blackmail, black maria, black mass, black monday, black-list, black death, black-eye, black market, black sheep, etc.

III. THE DEBASEMENT OF EVERYTHING AFRICAN

Language provided an efficient means for the debasement of everything African. Just as the enslavement of the African captives provided a rationale for their dehumanization, the debasement of everything African correlates with the avid war on black imagery. In order to demonstrably validate the theories (or false propaganda) that the African was inferior, it became necessary to degrade every spectrum of the African existence. This was done through the creation of many concepts or social theories that degraded and dehumanized the African people. The German scholar, Janheinz Jahn, provided a perfect example of this language politics. When he stated that, "simply by applying a certain vocabulary one can easily turn Gods into idols, faces into grimaces, votive images into fetishes, discussions into palavers and distort real objects and matter of fact through bigotry and prejudice".[3] These have been the reality in Africa. For the African people's given symbols and attributes for the one and only Supreme Being of the universe were debased and the spiritual rituals of the African God-concept of spirituality were reduced to the paganistic or heathenistic euphemism by the alien forces on their quests for political and cultural domination of the African personality. By debasing the original or natural religion of man, Europeans and their Arab counterparts almost succeeded in destroying the ethical, and moral, social, philosophical and spiritual bases of MAAT.

It was Dr. Robert Knox, who notably inspired men like Charles Darwin, when he declared that Race was the decisive phenomenon in human life. Dr. Robert Knox made it clear in his ideas that the human life is defined by race. In short, that "race is everything". Evidently, this type of exposition provided Europeans with the logic for the debasement of everything African. For if the African was indeed seen as an inferior biological being, the argument went, naturally everything that was connected with the Africans must be inferior as well. Since inferior beings can only produce inferior culture, Africans having been stigmatized as inferior supposedly could only produce inferior religion, art, music, literature, science, language, social philosophy, etc. Inspired by this rationale or as Wade Nobles has correctly put it "scientific colonialism",

Europeans went out of their way to reduce Africans as nonentities. They reduced all African languages to mumbo-jumbo or dialects. The same process led to the labeling of all African national or ethnic groups as primitive tribal groups or tribes. That undergirded principle of race (i.e., "scientific colonialism") also was applicable to the ancient and traditional African God-concept of spirituality. Since Europeans perniciously stigmatized Africans as inferior biological beings, it was assumed that they can only be capable of producing a defective God-concept of spirituality or religion; therefore, they reasoned, why not call their religion paganism, heathenism, fetishism, magic, animism, or another African hocus-pocus. Furthermore, the African's many century-old medicinal herbs and their applications were twisted and degraded to a phenomenon called witchcraftism. Insofar as the Europeans were concerned, the Africans were a "lesser breed" to the European's self-presumed "better blood". That is why, by a crude figment of the European imaginations, the wholesome base of African customs and institutions were reduced to nothingness. In this context the debasement of everything African was the divine right of every European, who had appointed himself interested in the scheme of putting every African where he or she must belong—within the prescription of White Magic.

But as the effect, the debasement of everything African has made many Africans to reject their cultural heritage, and sought comfort in the adoption of either the European or Arabian cultural heritages. In so doing, they became consumers of ideas as opposed to being producers of ideas, and have been acutely dependent on those who have "colonized" human knowledge. But being consumers of ideas without understanding the underlying cultural processes that led to their development is even more destructive. Thus, these Africans often blindly worship Western technology and science not because of their intrinsic worth but due to the fact that they lack an understanding of the thought patterns and technical processes that are at the foundation of Western materialism. In the final analysis, they are victims of the anti-African hysteria who could not rise above it, and have resigned themselves to being slavish dependents to the conceptions and desires of those who felt the need to debase everything African.

IV. THE POLITICS OF LANGUAGE

The politics of language is the control of the mind. It is the semantic propaganda device of black condemnation. It penetrates to the unconscious mind, settling on the subliminal perspective of the victim's mental universe and aiding in creating a sense of worthlessness, and inadequacy—enslaving the mind. Many of these words were, originally, in many occasions, untainted by this language politics but later developed and acquired a bad reputation from the misconception of race. As a result, their true and original meaning became obscured, allowing for the malign use of the false ideas they expounded. As Cheikh Anta Diop puts it, that amongst other things "it reflects the special state of mind that prompts one to seek secondary meanings for words rather than give them their usual significance, for that is how deeply embedded *a priori* ideas have become".[4] On the other hand, there are words that were developed consciously to serve a specific purpose, to reinforce the black degradation by associating anything relating to agony, human failure or backwardness with blackness. This is to say that 'whatever objects the European mind could conceptualize as bad, the abstract idea of badness itself became coordinated with blackness'.[5] For example, the following words are used as part of the politics of language, denigration, obfuscation, black death, black hand, black sheep and black monday: When the New York stock exchange crashed in October 1987, the unfortunate day of the disaster was named Black Monday.

Similarly, between the fifteenth and seventeenth century, the liberal notion regarding the equality of all men sparked revolutions not only in Europe but also in the Americas as well. At the same time, the European Slave Trade was booming and a lot of fortunes and profits were being accumulated; it therefore became necessary to use language in a political way to connote and denote messages to specific audiences—to insinuate innuendos coded to be detrimental to black people, and to uplift and give moral justification to all their undoing. (This modality was elaborated after the experiences and repercussions of the Haitian Revolution.) This rhetorical dichotomy left a legacy that has altered the whole notion of blackness, and subsequently has created an imbalance and disunited opposition between the two colors—white and black. It is fairly obvious that this abstract construction was not by accident, but has been rather part of the overall European materialistic scheme of good and evil. They thus have seemingly suppressed the fact that the doctrine of *Complementarity* presupposes and necessitates that without darkness there would not be lightness. That dark and light are identical in nature with basically different levels of energy in the universe, and that neither holds the exclusive monopoly of being either good or bad. Nothing is absolute! All aspects of nature are related and dependent on the cosmic law. In this regard, black magic can be defined as excessive spiritualism, whereas white magic can be construed as extreme materialism, thus the African doctrine of *Complementarity* underscores the need for balance and equilibrium between the two forces of nature. But the lack of comprehension of this reification of the two abstract opposites on the part of the mentally colonized African has been a prima facie in the contemporary conditions of Africans.

Insofar as White Magic is the historical agency of the African's mental and cultural alienation, its conceptualization can be visualized from an historical standpoint; but its understanding is deeply rooted in both the economic and political imperatives of the Europeans, beginning from the fifteenth century. The politics of language played a significant role in the conditioning of not only the Africans but also the Europeans in this process of shaping the attitudes of both the enslaved and the master.

In the first place, language very simply is political. For it has the capability to denote and connote specific images. In other words, there are words that we use on a daily basis, that are associated with conflicting interests, influencing our perceptions and attitudes resulting in the inferences of images, for example: (a) "native"*(* When the Dutch East India Company established Cape Town in 1652 as a trade colony, it resulted in the settlement of Dutch people in South Africa. These settlers were the first Europeans noted to have called the Africans "natives", a term meant to deprecate the humanity of the Africans.), (b) "tribes", (c) wild, (d) primitive, (e) cannibalistic, (f) huts, (g) jungle, (h) naked, (i) dirty, (j) illiterate, (k) pagan, (l) witch, etc. The images that are associated with all these words have been used in pejorative terms. As a result, they influence and make us to categorize people into inferior positions. The importance of language and the part it has played as a political machine for the Europeans becomes evident: when one realizes that the continents of Europe, N. America, and Africa, are the same until we get to their names and that was one of the reasons why we have self-defined our beloved continent with the new name, Kemet.

In the second place, the African continent, mostly in the United States, is still perceived as a country. Why this perception exists at all, is part of the resultant effect of the politics of language. Many typical examples can be found in the incoherent comparisons of many Eurocentric authors, journalist, mass media, and editors of many Newsprints. For instance, David Lamb's comparative analysis of the United States and Africa, whilst discussing Africa's economic condition, is an echo of this confusion. Thus, he wrote:

"Imagine what would happen to the American economy if each of the fifty states traded with the world but hardly ever with one another. California and Nevada might not do business, so Nevada would buy lettuce from Mexico and its beef from Australia. Maine would sell fish to Italy and canoes to Brazil and nothing to Massachusetts. New York and North Carolina would buy all their manufactured goods from Europe and Asia.... To break this dependence on foreign markets, each U.S. State would then try to develop its own light industries, but with no regional coordination, would never know what its neighbors were doing".[6]

Inasmuch, as I am concerned, these problems outlined by the author may have merits but the methodology used in the comparison between African countries and states in the United States bears no resemblance, and contradicts the understanding and the differences between a continent and a country. It is confusing to the reader; or else Mr. David Lamb must be implying that the countries in Africa are the same in status with states in the United States of America, their internationally recognized boundaries notwithstanding.

Finally, the European tribes are accorded the respect as nations or ethnic groups, for example Flemish, Walloon, French, English, Italians,

Portuguese, Spanish, Dutch, Serbs, etc. Whilst their counterparts in Africa or North America are uptil today still considered as "tribes". The Bambara, Igbo, Yoruba, Zulu, Gikuyu, Wollof, Akan, Hausa, Baganda, etc., are nations just like their European counterparts; instead they are called "tribes" All these two national groups from two different continents have everything in common except the word used to describe them. The difference in using different word or term to qualify all "tribes" in Europe calling them nations or ethnic groups is the bone of contention. So it is a carefully conceived plan, to use the word "tribe" to describe African nations, to evoke negative and condescending view towards African nations and ethnic groups. In fact, "the tribe was regarded as a more primitive unit, which in time evolved into a civilized one. The tribe was too small and lacked the complex organization and functions of the nation."[7] Therefore, the word "tribe" brings forth images of a primitive and prehistoric group. Indeed, a tribe is a group that has not yet evolved into a complex unit and thus must be very low in the hierarchy of human cultural evolution. As Babs Fafunwa has correctly argued, "How an ethnic group with two or ten million people in East or West Africa, with a … government can be described as a tribe, and not the Irish, the Scots, the Welsh, the French or the English, still baffles the non-European".[8]

V. WHAT ARE THE CHARACTERISTICS OF A NATION?

In the first place, a nation does not mean a political boundary. Most modern nation-states exist within the context of a multi-national basis. Thus, there may be many nations within a political boundary. In the second place, a nation is a group of people or community who share a common culture and language. People who share and acknowledge the same political system and uphold the basic principles of maintaining law and order are qualified to be called a nation. Within this group, there may be an economic system, defined from their traditional ethos, which is acknowledged and respected. Finally, there must be a particular territory considered and accepted as the homeland. In sum, a nation is a group's sense of distinctness and their cultural consciousness of being distinct in identity and cohesion.

VI. THE THREE PARADOXES

White Magic contains many paradoxes, but there are three fundamental paradoxes that have served as the ideological markers of White Magic at one time or the other. In my view, these paradoxes are inherent in the perpetuation of the *African Maafa* and dilemma; and it is because they were used as dehumanizing categories and as social definitions in relation to the Africans. They also represent the constructive beginning from where a re-assessment of the *African Maafa* and its subsequent effect on the modern world could be interpreted to render meaning to the contemporary image of Africa and Africans. Thus, because of the big differences between the old notion of slavery and the system used by Europeans to enslave Africans, it is important that a clear distinction is made. There are many characteristics eminent with regard to the nature of the *African Maafa* inflicted by Europeans. These characteristics formed the nucleus and became part of the evolution of the modern world. The religious, i.e., Euro-Christian ethics, the biological, i.e., the curse of Ham Jeopardy, and cultural, i.e., the concept of Race, ideologies are the three primary paradoxes that evolved, or were founded for rationalization and justification of not only the enslavement of Africans, but also the extreme brutality and dehumanization brought upon them in reducing them to mere chattels.

Insofar, as the enslavement of Africans in the Americas was a unique historical tragedy, its historical ensemble requires more intellectual prodding and explanation. To the extent that religion, biology and culture served as evolutionary ideologies for the justifications of the predicament of Africans, the European ideological goal had been from the outset to distort and retard the mental and cultural development of Africans, as a whole. The explicit formulations of these social theories, henceforth, have been intended to mislead and to create false values and consciousness on the oppressed victims.

In the fifteenth century in Europe, the Roman Catholic Church was not only the dominant force in religious affairs, its influence, to a large extent, also extended even in the political arena and social life of the people. The role and function of the Christian Church is partly a testament to the psychological motivations of the early European explorers, conquistadores, slave hunters or settlers. Therefore, the development and the origin of the European Slave Trade somewhat can be associated with the power and the influence of the Church on the overall European culture and attitude. This becomes important as events began to overtake the Church's grip to power, and its moral, political, religious and social influence on the European people began to wane. The factors underlying these developments have always been attributed narrowly to the European Renaissance and Reformation—the so-called enlightenment period. However, the true historical currents were unmistakably deeper than those phenomena. Since the Church was the overlord and the king maker over all Christendom, the pertinent questions therefore were: First, what was the role of the Church in the European Slave Trade? Second, what was the Church's rationalization of the actions of its subjects in the Slave Trade and plunder of Africa? These probing questions began the dilemma the Church has ever since found itself. The Church found itself on the crossroads of corruption, greed and a struggle to maintain the status quo. Nevertheless, it was inevitable that change was imminent. Therefore, the catalyst that infused a breakdown of the Church's hold on the European people was the effects of the plunder of Africa and the European Slave Trade. The struggle by the Church to justify the Slave Trade became the first paradox inherent in the African Maafa. Suffice it here to mean that Christianity in other words became not only a religion of Faith, but it virtually became a social status. This fact would later manifest itself more clearly in the eighteenth and nineteenth centuries, when the "freed" Africans would begin to associate freedom with Christian baptism. But to understand how religion became the center-piece of the European organ of expansion and repression, one must first understand the hypocritical nature of the European concept of Christianity. As Chapman Cohen puts it:

"It [African Maafa] was created by Christians, it was continued by Christians, it was in some respects more barbarous than anything the world had yet seen, and its worst features were to be witnessed in countries that were most ostentatious in their parade of Christianity. It is this that provides the final and unanswerable indictment of the Christian Church.[9]

In other words, the Roman Catholic Church saw it coming, for the stimulant that triggered the Roman Catholic Reformation was caused by the scandal-ridden life styles of its leading personalities and their involvement with the Slave Trade. To a considerable degree, the role these religious leaders played in the Slave Trade inspired the revolution that led to the reformation of the Catholic Church. However, the Church's reaction was seen in the rationalization that gradually gained acceptance in Europe. As a result, Christianity was doctrinized not only as a socio-political phenomenon, but also as an economic agenda. In order to keep the European society from chaos that was engendered by the Slave Trade and the wealth and splendor it had created, it became urgent to justify slavery, as far as it can keep the European lower classes in their place. The European lower economic classes thus had begun to see the contradictions between what the Church preached and what it practiced. Thus, the rhetorical posture of bringing the so-called heathens of Africa to the Christian God (Jesus the Christ) became the first justification and the first paradox. Why? Because this rhetorical rationalization was undertaken not because the Establishment had any perceived moral obligation outside Europe; rather, it was due to the compelling reason that the contradictions might affect the thinking of the downtrodden classes in Europe. It was on this basis that a religious justification of the European Slave Trade became necessary, in order to pacify the European lower classes and to keep them in their place. This was to enable the continued exploitation of the African captive labor unhindered by unrest and anarchy.

But this religious justification was ladened with imminent problems. If the "heathens" or "pagans" became converted to Christianity and were baptized, what would be their fate, with regards to slavery? It was clear from the outset that this propaganda of bringing the heathens of Africa to the Christian God (Jesus the Christ) could not provide a lasting banner for the continued exploitation of the free involuntary labor of the Africans; however, it was essentially necessary for the purpose of gaining time. And this was demonstrated in the imperative of outlawing the enslaved African's religion vis-à-vis language. This led to the consequent massive conversion of the Africans to the religion of their slave masters—

Euro-Christianity. It is one thing to make the enslaved believe that the slave master's religious book is the "word" of God; but it is something else when the same religious book is used as an instrument to maintain and perpetuate the condition and status of the enslaved. As a result of this ethical and moral depravity, it became a two-edged sword, that is to say a boomerang.

It was therefore upon this background that the moral bankruptcy generated by the massive African's conversions to Christianity left no choice to the European mercantilists except to find a new rationale for the continued justification of the chattel status of the enslaved Africans. John Henrik Clarke explained this economic madness as follows:

"The heavier the slave traffic grew and the more dehumanized its victims became in the years after 1650, the more avidly did Europeans search for ways to justify themselves. The theory that the African was an "infidel" could only suffice for a time, for if the chattel became a Christian, where was the justification then? More useful was the premise upon which the Dutch in Cape Colony defended slavery. Dark-skinned people, it was said, are the sons of Ham. Since Noah had condemned Ham to serve his brothers clearly the whites were only fulfilling a biblical curse"[10]

With an examination of the biblical genealogical myth of Noah and his sons, its mythological content notwithstanding, it is easily perceptible that the Hebrew deity himself did not curse any of his creations. It is indeed palpable that Noah, who also was depicted as an old drunkard, cursed one of his grandsons, Canaan, the son of Ham. In trying to understand the psychology of the European racists, this passage provides a perfect example of the mental condition of many Europeans who had built a doctrine out of the despicable allegorical depiction of an old grandfather who had lost respect for his old age. I found it quite amusing and rabid that such contention would have been taken seriously even by the lowest kind of doctrinal priests. But it helps to open our eyes to question the implicit racial fantasies of the so-called holy books of the religions of ISFET.

Moreover, we must begin to question those that inherited what was stolen from Africa, for the so-called "holy" books of the three dominant religions of ISFET were derived from the mystical and mythical stories of the African people in Kush, Kemet, Canaan, Babylonia, Sumeria, etc. This uncredited borrowing to a large extent made possible the writing of those books. As one commentator noted, the motivating purpose of the Noah's curse as accounted in the biblical scheme was a religious justification and an orchestrated divine ordinance by the ancient Hebrews for their annexation of the land of the black Canaanites. As he puts it, "It always has been plain to all except bigots that the story of Noah's curse was Israel's way of accounting for that which was done to the owners of the land that Israel needed and wanted".[11]

Furthermore, the biblical curse was first codified by the Jewish compilers of the "Old Testament" to justify their goal of usurping the land of Canaan from its original black inhabitants. [12] That is why, Canaan and his descendants were supposed to be servants to the Jewish Semites who wanted to put their political ambition in a religious context. Nevertheless, this "shibboleth" concerning the alleged curse of Africans by the Hebrew patriarch was later doctrinized again to suit the historical needs of the European economic imperatives of exploitation and dehumanization of the African. Its worst case relevance was the fact that many Africans believed such religious parlay as a proof of the divine ordinance regarding their oppression. Thus, the second paradox was created in the midst of an increasing need to keep Africans psychologically and physically subservient to the pale Europeans. But that was not the only motive for such religious vagrancy. If it were, the cost is certainly high on Christianity as a religion. Therefore, it is an inextricably bound conclusion that the Europeans whilst hoping to pacify Africans with the alleged curse of Ham were also hoping to use this doctrinaire justification to engender moral support from the European masses. This was because they were increasingly becoming afraid that the brutality and dehumanization of the enslaved Africans could have an adverse effect on the European masses, especially in the colonial territories of the Americas.

In the final analysis, the "Curse of Ham" protagonists knew that the biblical Noah cursed Canaan and not Ham. Since they were aware that this biblical curse was part of the Jewish plan for their annexation of the land that belonged to the original black inhabitants of Canaan, they had no choice but to call it the curse of Ham. According to the biblical anecdote, Noah never cursed Ham, rather he cursed Canaan, a brother to Cush (Kush), Mizraim (Kmt) and Put (Punt), who were all sons of Ham.

Most biblical genealogists and African historians have confirmed that Ham could represent, allegorically, the progenitor of the Africoid biological group.[13] Indeed, there is an etymological similarity and correspondence between the ancient African's use of the word Kam or Kham (which means blackness) and the biblical Ham (which means blackness). Nevertheless, the quest to justify the alleged African inferiority (for white superiority runs concomitantly with black inferiority) in order to rationalize the enslavement of the Africans led to the elaborate erroneous doctrine of the "Curse of Ham". The need to prove that Africans were inherently inferior, on the account of their high level of melanin pigmentation, left a legacy and a pseudo-intellectual hoax that still dominates the thinking of many people, until the present time. This erroneous theological reflection has come to be known as "The Ham Doctrine".

Looking at the biblical account, it becomes clear that the wondering Jewish Semites upon their settlement in the Land of Canaan used religious drama of such to rationalize their destruction of the black inhabitants of the land that they had settled. Above all, one must not forget that the biblical stories, even though many of them may be rooted in the African teleological system, are narratives of Faith that may have some reflections of history. However, most of them can be attributed to the messianic prophesies of Hebrews who made these folklores the center-piece of their mental and cultural universe. For one thing, their God-concept is not an equivalent to the eternal Truth of the One Creator of the universe and the One Creator of the universe cannot discriminate amongst any of the elements constituting the creation of the universe. To the One Creator of the universe, all creation are equal according to the Divine Plan of AMUN in whom we trust. Therefore, the aversive racist tendencies of those who have used the "chosen people" myth to advance their cause is just another way of showing the depravity of the world of Ekwensu.

The Ham's doctrine began the phase of what we can call the pseudo-intellectual scramble to use twisted data in order to propagandize the alleged biological inferiority of the African people. The paradox of religion as found within the context of Christianity can be subsumed under religious dogma, which is not exclusive to Christianity alone. Although the Ham's doctrine bears some religious fervor, it was really entrenched in the alleged biological beliefs that the African is innately an inferior human stock in relation to the Eurasians. This was not only a serious error of judgment on the part of the Europeans, but also it did intensify the need to dehumanize Africans. In order to reduce the enslaved Africans to the level of the beast or sub-human, various mechanisms were employed and enforced in such a manner as to portray the African as a "thing"—a non-human object.

Consequently, the ideology of racism is the third paradox and can be traced as the culmination of this struggle to use twisted data (pseudo-intellectual data) to lend credence and validity to the European's fantasies of the African as a THING—as sub-human. Thus, they ignored and disregarded any evidence that provides a contrary view to their interests, and dredged up ideological fantasies that were meant to purify European consciences at the expense of the Africans. For in hoping to salve their consciences and to exploit the Africans, Europeans rightly or wrongly have to imagine that the African is a *Thing*. A "thing" to be controlled, abused and exploited

Although racism, as stated, is the culmination of the fantastic false imagery and the justification of the "thingification" of Africans, it is really a cultural ideology that has its root in the antiquity of the European history. In other words, the underlying basis of racism is not primarily skin color, although the pernicious stigma of blackness is part of the schema. This is not to undermine the color factor in racist ideology; however, the problem of racism is cultural. By recognizing racism as being cultural here, we mean that it encompasses every aspect of the European endeavor. Thus, it has assumed a dynamic character without losing its essential root.

What then is the root of racism? We have been conditioned, over the years, to believe that the root virus of racial intolerance, debauchery, bigotry, debasement, degradation, murder, exploitation, and psychological humiliation of Africans is merely because of the color differentiation between Africans and the Eurasians. But it has become increasingly clear that the root of racism is borne out of over two millennia of ideological negation of the African cultural stamp in the world of ideas. For, it is a truism that anti-African thinking has functioned as the ideological rationalization for the emergence of Hebrewism, Christianity, and Islam on the one side; and to the development of the Greaco-Roman, Arab, and Western civilizations on the other side. That is, that these world systems have been by their nature anti-African. Therefore, the problem of skin color arose as a by-product in the course of development of the absolutist anti-African ideologies. And this was first dramatized by the invading Aryans in the Indus Valley and the ancient Hebrews in their religious theology.

Even with a cursory examination of the origins and history of humanity, it becomes clear that for many millennia black people were the only humans on the planet. Being the original people, humanity was for many millennia judged by the dark pigmentation of one's skin (blackness). Blackness of the skin or the high level of melanin pigmentation was the standard of judging the essence of humanity then. Nevertheless, this essentiality of blackness as the criterion for humaneness was not used in a mundane sense; rather, the blackness of the skin represented the metaphysical or sacred nature of the human being vis-à-vis the innate supernatural potentiality of blackness. That is why, sacred icons and every other religious image were reflected in the color black. The ancient Africans used black capstones in most of their monuments, for instance, in Pyramids and Tekhenwy (obelisks). To them, blackness represented the highest state of the spiritual man and the symbol of the "divine realm"; and as a result, it was the essence of worship—black Auset (Isis) and Heru

(Horus), black Ausar, black Ka'bah, etc. Unmistakably blackness then is the mystery and energy of the human life.

How did the ancient Greeks attempt to change the status quo of human cultural evolution? When the Greeks conquered ancient Kemet, they gave a new life to the pinkness of the skin. This they did by using their low level of melanin pigmentation as the standard for what they conceived to be the emerging human paradigm. In the European Middle Ages, most European intellectuals were immensely influenced by the attitude of the ancient Greeks. The Greek's version of the Torah was commissioned in the third century B.C.E. by the Greek invaders in Kemet, and was called the "Septuagint" version. Alongside the Semites "chosen people" myth, the root virus of racism was implanted by this book which was commissioned and compiled by the ancient Greeks. In the Greek version of the Torah, the Jewish translators passed down to the Greeks the logic for their annexation of the land of Canaan from its original black inhabitants and the premise for their religious negation of ancient Kemet (Mizraim). Many passages of the Torah such as the "Exodus" story, "Songs of Songs", etc., were used to portray black people as cultural "undesirables" and "abnormal" for the first time in recorded history. These were later translated into King James Authorized Version which has become the standard bearer of Euro-Christianity. According to King James Authorized Version, the black woman sang to Solomon as follows:

"I am black, but comely, O ye daughters of Jerusalem, as the tents of Kedar, as the curtains of Solomon.

Look not upon me, because I am black, because the sun hath looked upon me the keeper of the vineyards; but mine own vineyard have I not kept (Songs of Songs 1:5-6)".[14]

The contradiction in the foregoing statement is self-evident. In contrast, to the negation of blackness evidenced in the cited biblical folklore, Rudolph R. Windsor noted that "In ancient Israel, when a man has white spot in his skin, or white or yellow hair, or white skin somewhat reddish, he was pronounced unclean. All people who were victims of this shameful disease were isolated outside of the camp or city".[15] This is to say that the white skin at this period is designated as a deficiency. Further, the

Arabian Peninsula was predominantly inhabited by Africoid people, black, i.e., Canaanites, Sumerians, Babylonians, etc. This in fact contradicts the projection of blackness as a cultural "abnormality" by someone of whom herself was part of the black majority. There is no doubt that this biblical woman was black. Then, why would she have sung such a self-negating song when she herself was black and blackness was the predominant color in the Arabian Peninsula at that time in history? Or why would she have sung that song when she herself was black? The only explanation to this contradiction can be explained as follows: The low melanin pigmented settlers or invaders were astounded by the character of black cultures that they came in contact with. So, in the midst of their "reaction-formation", they sought to create their own cultural identity through antipathy towards blackness.

VII. WHY AFRICANS BECAME THINGS

The saga of the enslavement of Africans is one of the greatest drama in the history of humanity. Indeed, it is not just the religious, biological and cultural drama of tremendous proportion but also it does have serious economic implications. In this titanic upheaval, "Africa and Europe were jointly involved. Yet it is also true that Europe dominated the connection, shaped and promoted the slave trade, and continually turned it to European advantage and to African loss."[16] By losing, the African has paid a gruesome price. For more than five hundred years he has paid this price with his blood, sweat, and labor; Africa has therefore waned and Europe has waxed. Essentially, the importance of stressing the historical and cultural evolution of the Africans in the Americas lies in my recognition that it holds a decisive and a fundamental element in the understanding of the nature of the modern world. Hence, it is the micro and macrocosm or the mirror image upon which the path Africans had treaded in the last five centuries can be visualized.

The power derived from labor makes it the most essential commodity in any market economy. The enslavement of the traditional Africans, therefore, made them not only the commodity but also the laborer. In the Americas, 'the enslaved Africans were entirely a class apart, labeled by their color, doomed to accept an absolute servitude, and condemned for life as chattels not more important than any other domesticated animals'.[17] Therefore, the obsession for property acquisition led to the "thingification" of the enslaved Africans reducing them to captive property in the realm of labor and as the beasts of burden—within the demands of labor. So that the 'the African human was reduced to an African thing, virtually the same in certain key respects as the rest of non-human nature—all of which could become property'.[18] The African is thus made to symbolize the objectified otherness. The African was made to become a living object used for the advancement of the material aspirations of the European. As a result, the African became a thing, a fixed instrument necessary for the material and psychological comfort of the Europeans. This "thingification" of the African has not been transcended and it is evident in the fixed and unchanging image of the African amongst whites, never mind the logic of having lived as neighbors, in some cases, with the African, the African remains a "thing" to be controlled, exploited, abused, degraded, and put in his place. This misperception and misrepresentation of the African people has become, very often, an unconscious and adamant struggle for whites in striving to hold on to the myth of the African savagery.

But the myth of the African savagery is a European paradigm. This European paradigm is nothing but a pseudo-intellectual conjecture used as political, moral and economic justifications by those who felt the need to degrade the human qualities of the people that they have brutalized and exploited. In the context of Africa and Africans, it has been used to exalt the Europeans and to debase the Africans. Thus, the extreme desire for property, reinforced by the drive to dominate others and the human tendency to justify actions are the motivating factors that continuously reinvigorate the myth of the African savagery. In this respect, the myth of the African savagery stabilizes Western domination and has become a source for the nourishment of racism. Indeed, it functions as the idealistic gratification on the equation of virtue with power or inherent superiority with material acquisition by absorbing European aggression and facilitating a social universe that is defined by the delusions of "racial" superiority.[19]

In conclusion, the character of the African Maafa constitutes of at least six inherent components: (a) The property status of the enslaved African; (b) the absolute power of the slave holder over him; (c) the destruction or the arrogant disregard of his kinship, language, religion and culture; (d) the trauma of not only his isolation but also the inevitable hopelessness of being uprooted to an hostile environment; (e) and most of all, the cleavages of skin color. With regard to the skin complexion of the enslaved Africans, it was made to become the stamp of distinction and the basis of his inferiority. This distinct attribute of high melanism was then made to qualify every African as a slave until he/she proves to be otherwise. But this supposedly mark of inferiority has been perpetuated through propaganda, coercion, manipulation and the use of biologically mixed blacks as the buffer system for the Establishment.

CHAPTER FIVE
NOTES

IA. Na'im Akbar, *Visions For Black Men,* Nashville, Tennessee: Winston-Derek Publishers, Inc., 1991, p. 27.

1. M.I. Finley, *Ancient Slavery and Modern Ideology,* New York: The Viking Press.1980, p. 71.
2. Richard Wright, *Black Power,* Wesport, Connecticut: Greenwood Press, Publishers, 1976, p. 9.
3. Jeanheinz Jahn, Muntu: *African Culture And The Western World,* New York: Grove Weidenfeld, 1961, p. 20.
4. Cheikh Anta Diop, *The African Origin of Civilization: Myth or Reality?* Chicago: Lawrence Hill & Co., 1974, p. 242.
5. *Joel Kovel, White Racism: A Psychohistory*, New York: Vintage books, 1971, p. 62
6. David Lamb, *The African New York:* Vintage books 1987, pp. 287-289.
7. Joseph E. Haris, *The Africans and their History,* New York: Peniun Books USA Inc., 1987, p.27.
8. Babs Fafunwa, "Race Prejudice in Textbooks", *Africa* No. 43 (March 1975), p.56. The term "tribe" is a Eurocentric ideological statement that undermines the African cultural ability for self-determination. It is imposed on the assumption that the African must be politically subservient to the European. Because of its ideological constitution, Europeans may never stop using it to describe African societies.
9. Chapman Cohen, *Christianity, Slavery and Labour,* London: Pioneer Press, 1931, p. 44
10. John Henrik Clarke "Time of Troubles"—(C. 1492-1828), *The Horizon History of Africa,* (ed.) Alvin Josephy, Jr, et al. New York: American Heritage Publishing Co., Inc., 1971, p. 390.
11. Alfred G. Dunston, *The Black Man in the Old Testament,* New Jersey: African World Press Inc., 1992, pp. 52-53.
12. St, Clair Drake, *Black Folk Here and There,* Vol. 2, Los Angeles:University of California, 1990, p. 17.

13. Cheikh Anta Diop, *The African Origin of Civilization,* Chicago: Lawrence Hill Books, 1974, pp. 7-9; see also Rekhety Wimby, "The Unity of African Languages" in M. Karenga, J.H. Carruthers, (eds.) *Kemet and the African Worldview,* Los Angeles: University of Sankore Press, 1986, pp. 154-155.

14. *The King James Authorized Version* was officially completed in the year 1611C.E. It is based on the Septuagint Version of the Torah, and the Roman Catholic Bible.

15. Rudolph R. Windsor, *From Babylon to Timbuktu,* Smithtown, New York: Exposition Press, 1981, p.25.

16. Basil Davidson, *The African Slave Trade,* Boston: Atlantic-Little Brown Co.1961, p. 24.

17. Ibid, p. 20

18. Joel Kovel, *White Racism: A Psychohistory,* New York: Vintage Books, 1971, p. 18.

19. Read, Dorothy Hammond and Alta Jablow, *The Africa that Never was: Four Centuries of British Writing About Africa,* New York: Twayne Publishers,Inc.,1970

CHAPTER SIX

WHITE MAGIC IS COLONIALISM AND NEO-COLONIALISM

The basis of European colonialism and neo-colonialism in Africa is the motive force of White Magic. As we have already indicated, the roots of White Magic can be traced back to the ancient Greeks, who laid the foundation of European nationalism after they conquered and stole the legacy of the ancient civilization of Africa. When the Nile Valley civilization of ancient Kemet was conquered by Alexander of Macedonia, Europeans for the first time had access to the African doctrines of life that would later lead to their great awakening. The greatness of Alexander (whom Europeans have immortalized as Alexander the Great) lies in this achievement which exposed the Greeks to the gift of knowledge as symbolized by the mysteries of the Great Her-Em-Akhet (Great Sphinx Statue) and the Pyramids. The ancient Greek's contribution to White Magic becomes important because of their devotion to the task of interpreting into the Greek language the vast knowledge of the universe that the ancient Kemites painstakingly recorded during the course of their several millennia of splendor and glory.

The development of the ancient Greece and later Roman civilizations was the direct consequence of the overwhelming impact of the penetration of the ancient Greeks into the land of Kemet. In my opinion, the European people (Aryans) have not yet been able to evolve a civilization on their own without the help of Africans.[1] In fact, to be precise, whatever cultural achievements ancient Europeans (Aryans) had made have been mostly because of their contacts with Africans. This is a fact that any well informed European consciously or unconsciously has always known but hated. This repressed psychic dependence on the continent of Kemet for cultural development has bred hatred and jealousy on Europeans and thus is the backbone of White Magic.

The author of *Black Athena Volume 1,* Martin Bernal, had argued that much of the culture and language of ancient Greece originated from the Nile Valley culture complex especially ancient Kemet.[2] The importance of this argument becomes clear when one realizes that, before the decline of the Nile Valley civilization, what was later called Greece was a product of the ancient Africans' colonization and civilization of the indigenous population, beginning around 1500 B.C.E. The backward state of the entire Europe, then, is evident because Rome became an important town during the early years of the Ptolemaic era (Hellenistic period). During the Greek's occupation of ancient Kemet, the city of Alexandria was developed as the intellectual and political center of the Greek conquerors. Thus, the development of the Greek letters and Greek philosophy was made possible by the African priest-scientists who taught in the Alexandrine school. These Africans not only taught in the Alexandrine school, they also were made to interpret and explain most of the ancient documents that the Greek conquerors looted from the Holy Shrines and Temples in ancient Kemet.

It was based on the role of the ancient Africans in the indoctrination of Greeks into civilization that the Greek civilization developed to play a decisive role in the transformation of Europe. The rise of the Roman Empire in 30 B.C.E. as well could not have taken off, at that historical period, without the Roman's historical incursions into ancient Kemet. After their defeat of the Greeks in ancient Kemet, the Romans came in control of the vast knowledge that had been developed by the ancient Africans. Many African priest-scientists were kidnapped or captured by the Roman conquerors who used them to develop the foundation of what we today call the Roman civilization. The Roman Empire in a sense was an amalgamation of the European, African and Asiatic personalities. That is why, many Africans rose up to become Emperors, military commanders, Roman Catholic Popes, Roman Catholic Saints, Christian martyrs and aristocratic citizens of Rome.

From the foregoing one can easily concede that the Greek and Roman civilization had been the melting pots of many cultural groups and the residual manifestations of the Nile Valley civilization. If not so, how can historians explain why in all Europe that it was only Greece that relatively could be considered "civilized" during the better part of the Hellenistic era. The same question could be applied to the Roman civilization. For the Roman civilization was developed in the midst of different European tribes who lived in caves and often practiced cannibalism. Still historically civilizations have been known to transcend the ethnic or even the so-called racial boundaries and thereby should be celebrated because of the philosophical stamp of distinctness that they may have contributed in the unfolding of the human drama. Therefore, it is a mockery to reason that the classical civilization of Africa which was created and nurtured by ancient Africans and thus bears an African philosophical stamp of distinction (world-view) is constantly being undermined by both non-Africans and culturally dislocated Africans.

In spite of this fact, the relative short durations of both the Greek and Roman civilizations must have given some genuine historians something to think about. Not only were the spans of these civilizations relatively short, but after the decline of the Roman Empire Africans and Arabs dominated a good proportion of Europe for almost seven centuries. This, in fact, suggests to the idea that what we call Greek and Roman civilizations were the residual manifestations of the remarkable civilization of the Nile Valley in its many stages of decline and renewal. Hence, these European civilizations were not internally developed from the outset as most of the ideas that flourished during their fame and glory came from Africa. This external stimulation of the Roman Empire, for an example, and the powerful influence of many ideas from Africa led to the Emperors Theodosius' and Justian's political proscriptions to many African philosophy of life, e.g., Hermeticism and Gnosticism, which are African doctrines cloaked in the garb of Greek letters. The political bans that were imposed on the practice of some of the African philosophical reflections on life, most of all, resulted in the reconciliations of those ideas to suit the European temperament and development. The implications of these bans also resulted in the development of many powerful Secret Societies. Consequently, after the Edicts banned the European public from practicing many of the African doctrines of life, people who insisted on practicing the "mysteries" of the ancient Kemites were forced by the Edicts to go underground. This led to the emergence of such Secret Societies as the Rosicrucian Order (AMORC), Freemasonry, etc. These Societies carried on the practices of the ancient Kemetic "mysteries" as have been handed down to them by their Graeco-Roman progenitors up to this day.

Therefore, it is correct to say that the actual development of Europe began in the European Middle Ages, when the Christian Crusade and other factors gave way to the bitter evolution of what we now call the Western man. In this period, some Europeans began to develop the intellectual capability necessary for defining and mastering some of the doctrines handed down to them from Africa by the ancient Greeks and the Romans. This is how the historical Christianity evolved to become an essential medium for the creation of the Western man. In addition, the European development became attainable after they developed the social theory of "racist humanism" in the fifteenth and sixteenth centuries. This was when they began to adapt the classical works from Africa, Greece, and Rome as models of inspiration. Many of the Europeans of the Renaissance era, unlike their ancestors, sought inspiration from the works of antiquity without attempting to reproduce or ape the past.

The strong precedent created by the ancient Greeks and Romans in their achievements of utilizing many of the African cultural materials, in creating viable civilizations, had a powerful influence in the development of Europe. That is why, immediately Europeans gained access to the Mediterranean and Atlantic oceans in the first half of the fifteenth century, they did not hesitate to begin their historical expeditions to Africa. It was not a mere historical accident that the doctrine of colonial economics became intertwined with the European access to these oceans and their expeditions to Africa. Again, the development of the doctrine of colonial economics was based on the historical antecedents of the Greek and Roman incursions into Africa.

There is no gainsaying the fact that the doctrine of colonial economics was what led to the European economic hegemony. And colonial economics has been the driving force that mobilized and generated capital for the European economic development. Colonialism, within the context of the modern world, is first and foremost, the product of European expeditions to Africa, Asia, and the Americas. Secondly, it is the resultant effect of the cultural, political and economic encroachment of Europeans to other lands inhabited by non-Europeans; and the subjugation, occupation, and monopoly of the resources of a landmass by a European power. This doctrine of colonial economics is not static; rather, it is very dynamic. It takes shapes and forms that change with the context of the different structural stages of capital accumulation of wealth.

It is based on this dynamic character of colonial economics that the system of mercantilism was progenited and transformed to a capitalist structure; whilst the triumph of capitalism has led to the imperialist system of neo-colonialism. The common basic element amongst these evolutionary systems of economic organization is that from their genesis, Europe has capitalized on the exploitation of foreign lands for the nourishment and growth of the above economic structures. This has ever since made Europe the heart or center of capitalist accumulation of wealth.

I. THE ROLE OF HISTORY

History is the umbilical cord that connects an African to the rich repository of cyclical relationships of time, for the harmonization of self with the community and of nature with the Supreme Being. It is a consciousness that characterizes the community and shapes self. Therefore, in African culture, history is not just a chronicle of historical dates and events of the past, it is rather a deep consciousness of one's location in the universe, i.e., a consciousness of space-time. Although history in the African culture provides the transformative force for human development, a distorted African history is also capable of negating human potential. Thus, if the historical consciousness of Africans is disrupted, the transformative force derivative from such consciousness can also be deformed.

Conversely, there is a correlation between the state of African history and African consciousness. For both seemed to be the roots of the myriad of contemporary problems confronting continental Africans. Compounded by this factor, few continental African students have shown genuine interest in the study of the African history, classical civilization, comparative linguistics, ethnography, archaeology, religion, and culture, as they have seemingly done in other disciplines. One might think that given the fact that the African past has been the area where many European expansionists had concentrated dogmatically in their escapades of making

Africans become subservient, that Africans would show greater interest in the study and research of the African past life.

Up until recently, the modern African scholarship and the African-centered studies have failed to lay the groundwork necessary for evaluative, comparative, analytical and synthesis of the forces that have facilitated the African enslavement, colonization, and the continuous decay of the African cultural material within an adaptable scope of a viable African intellectual development. One may also wonder why it has taken the African people this long to develop an epistemological framework for a genuine African intellectual pursuit. As a result of these deficiencies, it is often hard for many Africans to understand that, within the world community, they are one of the oppressed groups that lack a developed ideological superstructure. This lack of development of an African ideology has confined the African struggle for self-preservation merely on the moralistic plane. Therefore, it is my view that the contemporary Africans suffer from a twofold paralysis: The yoke of Western imperialism with its psycho-cultural Euro-Christianity and Arab Islamic domination.

But the visible emergence of individualistic African personalities whose conceptions of the modern world have been flawed by the incessant Western indoctrination of the terms individualism and materialism fosters a different rationalization of their conditions. As the entrenchment of the Western values of "good life" and "perfect society" impair the understanding of the human conditions in Africa, many continental Africans frequently found themselves interpreting the socioeconomic reality of Africans from a European viewpoint. This confusion has stalemated the Africans' relations with other cultural groups and even with themselves.

Moreover, within the African world, it is disturbing to note that a considerable proportion of continental Africans and their various governments have continuously demonstrated their apathy towards the importance of an African world unity and black consciousness. The ideals of Pan-Africanism have not been adequately developed since the supposedly political independence of most modern African states. I propose to explore the origins and ideas of some of these misconceptions, with the understanding that I can shade a different light into this complex theme. Thus, in the discussion of the Africa's colonial Agents the reader is summoned to be open minded, in order to absorb the relatively different arguments contained in this discourse.

Despite decades of formal political independence in most parts of Africa, the effect of colonialism has been the mainstay, the defining structure and the framework of policy making in contemporary Africa. Although the life span of Africa's colonialist political domination was relatively short, its impact has affected every fabric of the African life. What are the factors that necessitated the mechanism of this dynamic force? And to what extent has White Magic altered the African's view of the world?

II. COLONIAL AGENTS IN AFRICA

There are basic features underlying the European formal colonization of Africa. In order for the Europeans to forcefully colonize Africans, they must first attempt to destroy the philosophical basis of the traditional African life. Thus, the traditional Africans themselves did not see anything wrong with their cultural and religious practices, until the Europeans came and impose their rule on them. To justify this imposition, Africans were told by the European imperialists that they were "savages" and "pagans". In this way, the fundamental matrix of formal colonization therefore involved every aspect of the African society and its dealings with the outside world. It reorganized and distorted the traditional modes of production, indigenous social organization, fundamental values, cultural expression, etc., on the one hand.

On the other hand, the formal imposition of colonial rule in Africa brought about the consolidation of the European economic imperatives of integrating the African economies into the European controlled International Capitalist System. For in the quest to strengthen and solidify control, European colonial strategies in Africa entailed not only the disruption of the traditional African way of life but also the creation of a new social structure, the dislocation and destruction of the African self-sufficient economics, the introduction of both forced labor and wage labor; the imposition of a means of exchange that is controlled and regulated by the colonizer, the creation of a new land ownership law that is deemed suitable for the exploitation of the indigenous groups; the suppression of the Africa's modes of production and the retardation of market competition from local industries to enable the provision of goods manufactured from the "mother" country; the creation of a new cultural outlook that not only negated the old forms of expression, but also one that is based on the mother country's norms and values; the introduction of Euro-Christianity alongside racism as colonial agents for socio-psychological indoctrinations and pacifications; and the imposition of a new local elite as the intermediary between the foreign rulers and the local populations

Julius O. Ihonvbere in the following commentary illuminated how colonialism disfigured and distorted the natural process of state and class formation in Nigeria. Typically, the same dynamic stimulant is prevalent in all colonial units within the continent of Africa. He writes:

"Indigenous institutions, values, tastes, and cultures were deformed, stultified, or completely wiped out. A subservient, corrupt, and unproductive class was created and nurtured to depend on vertically integrated trans-national corporations which dominated all sectors. The pattern of production and trade introduced was to ensure the economy's dependence on external stimulus and demand".[3]

The main purpose of this analysis, on the African colonial experience, is to explicate and explain the role of the Africa's local elites of White Magic in the entrenchment and perpetuation of the African economic and social conditions. As previously stated, most of the local elites in Africa are the agents of White Magic. They have worked closely with the European colonizers in imposing the dependency syndrome in Africa. First of all, it has been clear that these Eurocentric elites are the unwitting enemies of Africa. Secondly, the way and manner through which these Eurocentric local elites rose up to dominate most of the state apparatus in Africa equally attest to their inseparable connections with the European and European thought pattern. The Eurocentric elites have never fought for Africa's interest, ever since their formation, and are incapable of defending Africa's interest in the overall scheme of things. Thirdly, they are a non-revolutionary group whose formation and consolidation of the state apparatus have been the direct consequences of European colonialism in Africa. In fact, most contemporary African elites not only lack the direct ownership of the means of production but also the moral and ethical foresight, and therefore have a distorted vision of the world. It is in this particular sense that Chinweizu's observation becomes relevant. In his words:

"A new class of Westernized Africans, petit-bourgeois in outlook, had been produced. Their position was based not on their class origins in traditional Africa, but purely on their possession of western education and skills".[4]

Many have argued with me that the African agents of White Magic secured political independence for most African colonial units. But those who make such argument refused to see that the securing of political independence is as well to the best interests of the designs of this group. As Kwame Nkrumah correctly stated that, "It was partly the restrictions placed on the business outlets of the African bourgeoisie which led it to oppose imperialist rule".[5] Thus, these Eurocentric Africans fought for nominal political independence, not necessarily to change the fundamental contradictions that grew out of the European colonization of Africa but rather to replace or substitute European colonialists with themselves, thereby using the state apparatus as their source of class consolidation. This has been buttressed by the abominable looting, corruption and compromises of national interests against the individual gains.

The local African agents of White Magic having imposed on themselves the European pattern of thinking are incapable of changing the fatalistic logic and overwhelming ignorance prevalent in modern Africa. Their positions in the African nations will continue to be secured and protected as long as the African masses continue to remain ignorant of the essential complicity of their role in Africa's condition. If one has to give this servile class some credit for the nominal political independence of many African countries, they must also be held accountable for their economic mortgage or sabotage of Africa, since nominal political independence. As they did not have the moral, ethical, or economic capability necessary to transform the African countries after independence, they resorted to being pawns of the metropolitan power elites.

Education in Africa is still diametrically opposed to the essential needs of transforming the African society from a colonial set-up to become purposeful, functional, self-sustaining and responsive to the needs and interests of Africa. This perpetuation of the colonial apparatus is not only at variance with Africa's own existence, it is self-destructive to the logic of self-development. Therefore, there are two particular questions the African agents of White Magic have failed to answer: Why are the educational systems in Africa up until the present still Eurocentric? Why are Africa's youths still being taught to look at themselves through the eyes of the Europeans? Of course, I am aware that by the nature of their mental and cultural dislocation, this local group lacks the will to answer these queries. However, I will tell them why they have failed to revolutionize and re-Africanize the educational set-ups in Africa.

Because of the nature of European colonialism in Africa, a group of cultural hybrids had been created. It is a hybrid group who are caught up between two worlds without the accompanying ties of origin to either worlds. In other words, I am of the opinion that these cultural hybrids have failed to radicalize and re-Africanize the colonial system of education in Africa after the attainment of political independence, because they were afraid of being exposed in the process. Thus, the whole systems of education in Africa have mostly remained the same as they were during formal colonization.

The role of the Eurocentric Africans in the underdevelopment of Africa can never be overemphasized. Until the African masses begin to see these cultural-hybrids as colonial agents of White Magic, the economic and social conditions of Africa would never be addressed. Although we recognized the complex nature of this problem, we are nevertheless undaunted that the antagonistic nature of Africa's monumental problem can only be addressed first as an internal problem. That is to say that the fundamental problem confronting Africa is the deeply rooted internal contradictions partly brought upon by the activities of certain groups inside Africa. The European penetration and colonization of Africa would have been an impossible task, if greedy and narrow-minded Africans did not collaborate with the Europeans to sell their motherland to outside strangers. Not only were these Africans the forerunners of White Magic in Africa, but their activities have been inconsistent with the logic of internal development.

III. RECAPTURED AFRICANS WERE TAILOR-MADE FOR WHITE MAGIC

One of the greatest tragedies of the European doctrine of colonial economics was the dehumanization of Africans to become chattel slaves. As we have discussed in the previous chapters, when Europeans gained control of the African market they initiated and defined whatever commodities were deemed important for the European market. The colonization of the Americas by Europeans intensified and dramatized the labor needs of mercantilism. It was then to the best interest of the European mercantilists that this problem of labor shortage must be solved. Through try and error tactics, Europeans became convinced that Africans possessed the survival ability and physical know-how necessary for the exploitation and development of the Americas to suit the mercantilist drives of colonial economics. Between 1503 and 1506, Father Bartholome' de Las Casas, who was a missionary but later became the Catholic Bishop of Chiapas, advised the Spanish Crown and the Roman Catholic Pope about the replacement of the Native Americans with the Africans. In the *History of Indies,* Father Bartholome' de Las Casas recorded how the rapid decimation of Native Americans made him to suggest their replacement with Africans of the Guinea Coast (West Africa). The massive European Slave Trade on the Africans partly began as a result of some of these factors, which were underscored by the need for cost efficient labor force.

The Slave Trade having been engineered by the Europeans was also stopped by them, when it became obvious that the need for markets and sources of stable raw materials overrides the need for the African involuntary free labor.[6] Since the Great Britain was then the indisputable leader of the Triangular Trade, it was not a mere coincidence that the European Industrial Revolution began in Britain. First, the spread of the industrial machines not only added much impetus to the capitalist system of colonial economics, but it also influenced the gradual demise of the captive labor as the backbone for the capitalist accumulation of wealth. Secondly, the emergence of these industries in England, created the need for stable sources of raw materials and more markets for the young industries. Finally, just as the massive European Slave Trade on Africans was influenced by the economic imperatives of that historic epoch, so also would the abolition of the slaving system become influenced by the internal development of capitalism itself. For the same reason, the abolitionist movement would emerge first in Great Britain before it surfaced in any other country. This is because modern industrialization, steam engine, was shaped and molded in England before it spread to Western Europe and the Americas.[7]

After Great Britain abolished its international slave trade on Africans in 1807, it instituted a British Naval Blockade as part of its measure of stopping the transportation of captured Africans to the Americas. Already the establishment of the colony of Sierra Leone by the Sierra Leone Company was made feasible after the repatriation of about twelve hundred freed black Nova Scotians in 1792 and five hundred and fifty black Jamaican 'Maroon' settlers in 1800. But the historical importance of Sierra Leone in West Africa began when in 1808 the British Crown took over the administration of the Colony and made it a haven for the settlement of recaptured Africans.[8] These were recaptured Africans who, instead of being sent to the Americas as commodity slaves, were recaptured by the British Naval Patrol who sent them to its colony in Sierra Leone and set them free. Although the British Naval Blockade in itself was relatively a failure, as far as the European Slave Trade was concerned, the British were able to settle many thousands of recaptured Africans in their Sierra Leone Colony. Needless to say that the British also used the suppression of the Slave Trade to cloak their economic objectives of increasing the supply of raw materials needed for their new industries and in addition to their missionary interest of converting Africans to the Christian Faith.[9]

However, one of the immediate implications of this historical affair has been its effects on those recaptured Africans. To these Africans, the facts were very palpable. Fellow Africans captured and sold them to strangers of another land, but by the benevolence of these British strangers they were saved from the agonies of enslavement. They were so impressed by the British "humanitarian" act that they felt convinced that the British culture and religion had more to offer them than their own traditional African God-concept of spirituality. Then, they became captivated by the religious and cultural traditions of the British people that they stopped at nothing in their goal of making themselves black Englishmen and women. But they could not be Englishmen and women. Not only because they were disparaged by the same people they were seeking to imitate but also due to the fact that they were in a cultural dilemma, torn asunder between two worlds without belonging to either one. It is within this identity crisis that European names, Christianity, English language and dress were symbolically transformed to become the central source of their identity.

To the extent that they adopted every possible English way of life, they in turn refused to identify with Africa in all possible terms. They not only changed their African names and adopted English names, but they in fact saw themselves as a community of 'counterfeit Englishmen and women'. To this group, everything British seemed to be good and all things African seemed to be bad. As they adopted the English thought pattern, they began to see Africa through the eyes of the British. Africa became to this group the "savage backwood" which has not yet known the Jesus Christ of the European. They literally sought and blindly worshipped British Europe to the extent that they became the caricatures of the Victorian society.

Yet the irony of these recaptured Africans' immersions to everything British was the fact that they refused to see that, in reality, it was the European doctrine of colonial economics that initiated to send them into slavery and not Africa. Many of them who studied in the British Institutions were so mesmerized by the capitalist accomplishments of Europe that it was hard for them to see that Africa was only the victim of the European barbaric economic aggressions of capitalism. But the historical role of the recaptured Africans is that they created a powerful precedent which would later become the yardstick for the Eurocentric indoctrinations of Africans through Western education and Euro-Christianity, during the formal colonization of Africa by Western European powers. As subsequent African students of Western education were influenced or even taught by this group, Africa entered a new White Age of preparing her children to be direct agents of White Magic, in detriment of her own future.

The same pattern of thinking has been prevalent in the Republic of Liberia, when some freed African Americans were repatriated to the landmass under the sponsorship of the American Colonization Society. The formerly enslaved Africans on their arrival in Liberia demonstrated the powerful influence White Magic had on their mental image of the universe when they rejected African norms and adopted all the Eurocentric attitudes of what a civilization was supposed to be. The consequences were the brutalization and discriminatory practices enforced on the original indigenous groups within the territorial boundaries of the Republic of Liberia from 1847 to 1980. The case of Liberia is not only a painful legacy but however shows how the destructive force of White Magic operates on the mental universe of most Africans. The role of the Americo-Liberians was somewhat unique. This is because they had been victims of enslavement, and therefore supposed to understand the inherent injustices and repercussions of discrimination and brutality.

Notwithstanding the fact of their unjust enslavement, this group who call themselves Americo-Liberians refused to de-colonize and re-Africanize themselves because they were enchanted with the American aspect of White Magic. Unlike the recaptured Africans who developed the Krio or Creole culture in West Africa, the Americo-Liberians on their settlement in Africa quickly declared their political independence with the election of Joseph Roberts as the first president on 26th July 1847. After independence, they retained most of the attributes of their adopted culture and attempted to impose this culture on the indigenous groups who were there before their arrival. By seeing themselves as the prototype of White Magic, the Americo-Liberians refused to integrate their cultural experiences with the cultures of the original groups within the boundaries of the State of Liberia. Indeed, they attempted to use the machinery of government which they exclusively controlled in perpetuating their infantile mission of "civilizing" the African masses to their avowed Christian State. When the illusion of being more "cultured" and "civilized" overwhelmed them, they abandoned the objective of pursuing a full-blown development program for all Liberians, the entire State of Liberia suffered as a result.

Nonetheless, it is reasonable to suppose that the Republic of Liberia provided the European imperialists with an African model for the neocolonial quasi-independent clientele status of post-colonial Africa. In this particular sense, the contradictions created by the Krios (Creoles) of Sierra Leone along with their Liberian counterparts would be exploited later by the European imperialists. In the words of Robert G. Weisbord, the "Americo-Liberians and the Creoles in Sierra Leone never assimilated into African society. They viewed indigenous Africans with condescension and like European imperialists, had no qualms about exploiting them".[10]

IV. REPERCUSSIONS OF THE SLAVE TRADE IN AFRICA

Although the European Slave Trade successfully suppressed the dialectical development of the African economic independence, within Africa there was a struggle to maintain political and cultural independence. But as the scope of maneuvering became more and more dictated by the powerful influence of the European economic dimensions, the internal economies in Africa became dramatically distorted. In other words, the underlying determinant on the formal colonization of Africa by Europe was the overall mechanism of interactions between the continents of Africa and Europe. The distortion of the economic backbone of Africa was consciously and unconsciously manipulated by the European invaders beginning from their first encounter with Africans in the continent.

The rapid capitalist development of Europe has been proven to be directly related to the retardation and transfer of Africa's factors of production to Europe and its satellite States. Therefore, the impoverished peripheral context of Africa is the logical consequence of the unevenness or inequality that formed the basis of this asymmetrical exchange between Africa and Europe.

Thus, the success of the European exploits in Africa did not begin from the era of formal colonization, but rather it was entrenched in a four century history before the Berlin Conference of 1884-85. This becomes very clear to understand; because the Triangular Trade not only enhanced Europe as the center of the developing world-wide system of international trade, it also relegated Africa as a peripheral landscape made to respond to the needs of Europe—The center. Hence, the massive Slave Trade, slavery, and colonization of Africans were the inextricable outcomes, given the fact that the European's encroachment to the Americas intensified the need for cost efficient labor force. Whilst the maximum use of the Africa's involuntary labor force created a surplus capital value that stimulated and gave birth to the European Industrial Revolution. The European Industrial Revolution, on the other hand, could not have flourished rapidly without the continuous flow of Industrial raw materials. In each case, Africa played the unfathomable role of providing Europe with the features it needed for its further development to the detriment of Africa's own productive development. Plainly, as Europe waged a successful economic warfare that drained the economic resources and potentials necessary for Africa's development, Africa not only became stagnated, it definitely waned dramatically in contrast to Europe, which waxed stronger economically and otherwise.

Given the fact that the European interaction with Africa was initially mostly economically motivated, in the course of the centuries, European aggressive economic extensions began to spread into every sector of the African life. Its underdeveloping impact on the political sphere is indeed important because it prepared the way for the formal colonization of Africa. As we have stated earlier, the framework of the African-European intercourse has been one dimensional. Europeans not only defined the trends of the interaction, but also have continued to control the terms of trade. One of the profound effects of this external control of the terms of trade in Africa has been the devaluation and humiliation of most African elites. They were reduced to the status of middlemen and/or marginal partners in the service of the European center. Since Europe became the center of this relationship in the practical sense of the word, it became the "real" market. Thereupon, European merchants became the "real" merchants. This repugnant pattern of "real" on the part of Europe and "unreal" on the part of Africa trickled down to the superstructures of both continents. The African market became "unreal". That is pseudo, because it was made to be externally stimulated, to service the needs and wants of Europe and not that of Africa. The same thing has been applicable to the African political structures and leaders. The African political structures were as a result not recognized by Europeans when they sat in the Berlin Conference table and shared their "savage" African booty. Also, the African political elites who became "unreal" as a result, began to respond to the music tune of the European political and market demands for their own individual survivals.

There were other African elites and merchants who equally were motivated by the "real" European market. They were inextricably bound to the mystifying spell of White Magic. These human aberrations of high proportions were of course not evidenced in every geographical community in Africa, in the beginning. But it is safe to state that by the late nineteenth century in Africa, the characters of this dependency syndrome have extended directly or indirectly to every sector of the African life. Conclusively, this process of Africa's external economic location has been diametrically opposed to the internal development and enhancement of the productive forces in Africa.

It was this external location of the African economic activities and the European needs for stable sources of raw materials that necessitated and fostered the decisive political or formal colonization of Africa. For as the Europeans became able to penetrate into the hinterlands of Africa, which was dictated by the imperialist or capitalist needs, they realized that the massive African labor and natural resources can effectively be exploited within the framework of formal colonial organizations.

The scramble to control Africa's resources reached yet another turning-point, and later gave birth to the infamous Berlin Conference of 1884-85. The objective of this conference is indeed analogous to the imperialistic designs of the European powers, and their role in the exploitative measures of dismembering the continent of Africa. This meeting which was held in Berlin, Germany, has been historically called the Berlin Conference. And it symbolized or represented the embodiment of many centuries of the European economic imperatives in the continent of Africa. The fourteen nations present on that occasion are as follows: (1)Germany (2) Britain (3) France (4) Austria-Hungary (5) Belgium (6) Portugal (7) Denmark (8) Italy (9) Russia (10) Spain (11) Sweden (12) Norway (13) The Netherlands (14) The United States of America

It was Lord Lugard, the noted architect of "Indirect Rule", who correctly stated that "The partition of Africa was as we all recognize, due to the economic necessity of increasing the supplies of raw material and food to meet the needs of the industrialized nations of Europe".[11] According to Jaja A. Wachuku, "The Berlin Conference sealed the fate of the African continent... by partitioning the whole Africa[n] continent to various European powers' spheres of interest, and regulating their rights of navigation in the Congo and Niger Basins".[12]

From the European viewpoint, the Berlin Conference was a success because it minimized the internal rivalry and bloody struggle for power and wealth that have characterized the European encroachment and plunder of the lands and resources outside Europe. However, the Berlin Treaty only regulated the "imperial depravity" and bloody struggle between European powers for a short period, until the eruption of the First European War (so-called World War I). On the other hand, the Berlin Treaty notwithstanding, the Europeans recognized that the task of establishing control over the portions of Africa that they have shared amongst themselves could not become feasible without the effective utilization of the various willing African elites. These were mostly the Africans living in the continental Africa who had established themselves as the middlemen of the European merchants over the centuries. That is to say, that even though the African agents of White Magic were not present during the sharing of the "savage" African booty on a conference table, their historical role as European middle men had sanctioned by implication the European economic goals for Africa. It was these colonial agents of

White Magic who devoutly supplied the Europeans with the human power and tools they lacked for the exploitative penetration of the interiors and hinterlands of Africa. Walter Rodney penned down this reality, when he wrote: "Africans conducting trade on behalf of Europeans were not merely commercial agents, but also cultural agents, since inevitably they were heavily influenced by European thought and values".[13]

As Europeans moved further into the interiors, their annexation of the African landmass was given legitimate impetus by many African elites who saw the character of the European economic goals in parallel with their individual ambitions. That is not to say that all leaders in Africa supported this arrangement. In fact, many political leaders in Africa recognized that the success of the Europeans in establishing direct political and economic control over Africans would ultimately lead to their loss of sovereignty, for example King Cetshwayo of the Zulu, King Lobengula of the Ndebele, King Jaja of Opobo, the Emperor Menelik of Abyssinia, the Mahdi in the Sudan, the Moro-Naba of Wagadu, the Asantehene Kwaku Dua III who is commonly known as Prempeh I, etc.[14] As a result, these leaders were motivated to resist and fight for their own survival. But the European military technology and power triumphed in the course of events, of course, with the exception of the Emperor Menelik's Empire.

Again, the triumph of the European technology could not have been decisive without the role played by the collaborating African agents of White Magic who helped in the recruitment of the African youths as soldiers who would fight for the European cause. The role of these African agents of White Magic is further underscored as they emerged within the context of the formal colonization of Africa as a powerful class. Thus, they began to derive their elitist character from their support or acquiescence to the European imperialism and their other supportive roles in furthering the goal of the European exploitation of Africa. Far from deriving their identity from the social matrix that is evident within Africa, most African elites thereby derive their socio-cultural identity from outside of Africa, mainly from Europe and Arabia. In other words, it is correct to say that the legitimacy of this elite group of White Magic is dictated by the external needs of Europe which do not put the development of Africa into consideration.

Under the euphoric spell of White Magic, instead of adapting to the cultural identity that is synonymous with the African personality, most African elites began to distinguish themselves from the masses by adopting either European or to some extent Arabian cultural norms, lifestyles, modes of thinking, canons of tastes, mores, beliefs, etc. And as they worship the European organizations, institutions, status symbols, etc., they have used them as means for the perpetuation of the ideological nuances of White Magic in Africa. Similarly, this group's interests are diametrically opposed to the internal development of Africa vis-à-vis the interests of the masses. They are mostly parasites whose roles in Africa have been essentially negative.

Given the structure of the African–European relations, it must be pointed out that the role of these African agents of White Magic was inevitable. Human nature being what it is, it was naturally expected, at least, at the outset that some group might allow themselves to be used in this process of reducing Africa as a continent without an authentic right to development. But the problem lies when such groups succeed in entrenching this self-destructive behavior as a way of life for the entire continent of Africa. Rodney was correct when he stated that, "it is a widespread characteristics of colonialism to find agents of repression from among the colonial victims themselves".[15] Thus the role of Africans in the enhancement of European exploitation of Africa is one irony that Africans have yet to come to terms with.

V. THE QUEST FOR WESTERN EDUCATION: EUROPEAN STATUS.

One of the main features of White Magic is that it always creates mental aberration to the norms of human aspirations i.e., as human beings become dehumanized, they consequently become caricatures, empty vessels, and literally fools. They lose all the senses of self-preservation and creative cultural continuity. Ultimately, they will begin to decay culturally as the manifestation of their mental stagnation becomes clearly distinguishable. One pertinent example of this phenomenon is the absurdity of African lawyers' usage of white wigs as the insignia of their profession. Even if they are spell bound, they should have at least been using black wigs, as opposed to white wigs.

In order to change a society and make it susceptible to exploitation, the manner upon which that society views their world becomes the image window that must be degraded, disfigured and shut down. This can be done through religious, educational, and other psycho-cultural indoctrinations. So that whilst indigenous patterns of thought are deformed, degraded and debased, the exploiter pacifies the exploited group by imposing contradictory norms and values that are logically useless to the environment and condition of the exploited group.

Before the political colonization of Africa, the works of the recaptured Africans in the spheres of Christian evangelism and Western education had begun to have serious implications in Africa. The recaptured Africans played a very significant role in the colonial machinations of the colonialists. They were not only used as economic agents, but equally they became the faithful servants of the colonial master's indoctrination of the African to the agency of White Magic. In West Africa, where the tropical weather conditions were not quite favorable to the low melanin pigmented skins of the Europeans, most recaptured Africans, their descendants and other Africans who had joined the bandwagon of the White Magic agency, became the instruments of the British and French colonialists who depended on them for their colonial quests of exploiting and suppressing the African cultural personality.

As the mission schools and Christian evangelism were one organic unit, they were effective in the goal of creating a group of de-culturalized Africans who derived their frame of reference from the European cultural universe. Western education was made the central key that unlocks the barred gates of the colonialist's haven for the Africans who wanted to pick up the crumbs of European colonialism. This led to the increasingly emergence of a new African elite that is imbibed in the European values. But Western education did not just facilitate the emergence of a new elite in Africa, it became the passport for social mobility—a powerful social paraphernalia within Africa. For this African elite (petty bourgeoisie) from their existence in Africa have been in alliance with the Capitalist West who use them as instruments for the exploitation of the African human and natural resources. In the process, they are usually compensated by the foreign agents of colonialism. Without the compensation by the foreign agents of White Magic and their post-independence consistent looting of the state treasury, their elitism would only have been a superficial imitation of the values of another bio-cultural group—the European group. Chinweizu has pointed out that: "In return for keeping Europe supplied, Africa's elites of today, like their predecessors of slaving times, are still rewarded".[16]

In this manner, the role of the comprador, technocrat or petty-bourgeois Africans has helped to entrench the underpinnings of White Magic as a way of life in most parts of Africa. One of the impacts of this has been the elevation of the European status symbols as the standard of success in Africa. The successful entrenchment of White Magic in Africa has influenced the high utility value contemporary Africans have imposed on the European educational system, which Europe originally garnered from Africa and made responsive to Europe.[17] But the problem with the African's adoption of the second-hand doctrines that came from Africa, is that they failed to re-structure and re-define this educational system to be responsive to Africa and not to Europe. As a result, every aspect of cultural development in Africa that is considered to be "least European" is treated as undesirable. This has been the height of their folly, of which the peril is White Magic: They abandoned the African moral code but have found it impossible to create a new one.[18]

Africa not only gave the world its fundamental basis of human civilization, but the repercussions of this gift have been the causes of the numerous invasions Africa had suffered from envy outsiders who wanted a share of the Africa's accumulated wisdom. These invasions no doubt not only played a significant role in the ethnic fragmentations of Africa, but also they constitute the main reason why many African groups lost what their ancestors gave to the world. These are writing, science, arts, architecture, philosophy, medicine, mathematics, astronomy, law etc.

From the beginning, conquered Africans were taught not only to look at their cultural traditions as backward, heathenistic and primitive, but also to look upon the European or Arabian culture as the key for their admittance into the world of White Age. In other words, they were conditioned from the outset to deride, ridicule or despise authentic African traditions and institutions; whilst at the same time being brainwashed to worship and glorify the social and material conditions of Europeans or Arabs, as the case may be. This has been the crux of the contemporary African condition and the core of the prevailing internal conditions in Africa. It also will be the essential basis of an intense cultural struggle in Africa. Hence, the intensification of the liberation struggle will not be between this group (which I prefer to call Europeanized and Arabianized Africans) and the masses; rather, serious cultural cleavages will emerge between the Euro-centric, Arab-centric and African-centric elites. The Euro-centric and Arab-centric elites will try to use their respective alienating religious and other foreign forces as weapons to pacify and win over the African masses. But in the end, the African-centered elites will triumph because they have MAAT or Truth on their side. Africa will be the battle-ground once again before MAAT shall prevail. Make no mistake about this fact, for there will be a cultural war waged between Africans who want to cling to the wand of White Magic and those who have a complete African vision for the future generation of Africans. Accordingly, we will resurrect the spirit of our ancestors and the battle would begin.

The Africans having adopted the religious paraphernalia of an alien culture, naturally also adopted the ideology that comes with the religion. Thus, frequently one hears many African Muslims and Christians, for example, calling other non-alien indoctrinated Africans names such as "pagans", "heathens", "infidels", "jahiliyya", "onye-nkiti", etc. this fostering of anti-African modes of thought through the influences of Christianity, Islam, etc., has seriously undermined the integrity and self-worth of Africans. But Africans cannot expect to be treated as equals by the world community, when they themselves hold their culture in self-contempt.

It is also a fact that the products of the European-centered cultural indoctrination (and Arab-centered too) have become the most powerful elites in Africa and are factionalized in every major sector of the African political economy: government, military, civil service, educational institutions, etc. But their blindness and mental dislocation lies in their hypocrisy and ignorance to the grand tradition Mother Kemet bequeathed to the human family. They were consistently taught that unless they reject Africa and her traditions that they would never receive the blessings of White Magic. Naively, these Africans believed their European and Arab counterparts, and with all ferocious urgency went out of their way to Europeanize or Arabianize themselves, as much as possible. Their faith in Europe or as the case may be in Arabia and their institutions has been unspeakable. Many have lost their original languages, names and cultures. To them, it is either Europe or Euro-Christianity as the key to African redemption, or Islam as the hope for Africa. But they have always failed to remember the degradation, dehumanization, and murderous history Africa has had with the two phenomena. European or Arabian manners, modes of dressing, languages, modes of thinking, canons of tastes, etc., were copied and adopted in thought and in practice by these Africans. They became bewitched by White Magic, which reduces them to mere human caricatures or apparitions of human integrity. The Eurocentric and Arabcentric thought patterns have permeated, through these Africans, the very fabric of the African life and are being transmitted from generation to generation. The solution to this monumental human anomaly lies in challenging the alien indoctrinated Africans to resolve their dilemma and become "real" Africans. They must be made to explain why they choose to live in Africa without being African. Why they have elevated anti-Africanism as the basis for status allocation? Indeed, Africa is the birthright of all well-meaning Africans. Yet there is no compromise to the future role of the ancient and traditional cultural heritage of Africa in the development of the Continent. For Africa must neither be a cultural "dumping heap" for other Continent, nor must she be allowed to continue playing a secondary role in the global affairs. She must in thought, feeling and action have her own unique personality—an African Personality.

In conclusion, it is a fact that most African elites are driven by external logic. And that the continent of Africa itself has ever since the fifteenth century served as the buffer system for the reconciliation of the inherent contradictions brought about by the rapid development of Europe because of the reactionary role of the African elites. Thus, Africa will remain largely the perpetual provider of raw materials for the capitalist centers, unless the reactionary elements in Africa are displaced by the progressive forces.

CHAPTER SIX
NOTES

IA. Kwame Nkrumah, *Class Struggle in Africa,* London, Great Britain: Panaf Books Ltd, 1970, p. 25.

1. When one takes a deep look at the European history, it is easy to come to the conclusion that Africa has played very important roles in the transformation of Europe. Not surprisingly, the first full-fledged University of Europe, i.e., Salamanka University in Spain, was established by Africans after they had conquered and occupied the Iberian Peninsula in 711 C.E. These Mohammedan Africans and their Arab counterparts who were often called the Moors dominated the Iberian Peninsula for almost seven hundred years.
2. Martin Bernal, *Black Athena, Vol I: The Fabrication of Ancient Greece 1785-1985,* New Brunswick, NJ: Rutgers University Press, 1987.
3. Julius O. Ihonvbere, "A Critical Evaluation of the Failed 1990 Coup in Nigeria", *The Journal of Modern African Studies* 29,4 (1991), p. 603.
4. Chinweizu, *The West and the Rest of Us,* New York: Random House,1975, p. 86
5. Kwame Nkrumah, *Class Struggle in Africa,* London, Great Britain: 1970, p. 56.
6. Read Eric Williams, *Capitalism and Slavery,* London: Andre Deutsch Limited, 1964. Eric Williams' fundamental thesis has no doubt proven that it was the changing economic conditions of colonial economics that primarily necessitated the campaign to abolish the European Slave Trade as opposed to humanitarian ideals. This is important because the concept of race or the idea of human inequality was elaborately developed after the demise of the European Slave Trade. This belief that Africans were innately inferior (less human) to the European became the basis for the justification and rationalization of the inhuman atrocities continuously meted on Africans, at home and abroad.
7. Basil Davidson, *The Black Man's Burden,* New York Times Books, 1992, pp. 23-30.
8. In 1787, the so-called Black Poor were repatriated from London to Sierra Leone, but a considerable proportion of them died. As a result, they were not able to make any lasting contribution except that they constituted the first experiment in Africa. But after the

settlement of about 1,200 black Nova Scotians in 1792 and 550 Jamaican Maroons in 1800 at Freetown, the colony became a viable community. However it was between 1808 and 1864 that the British Naval squadron became able to settle about 150,000 recaptured Africans in Sierra Leone. This was an estimated 10 percent of the human shipping engagement that existed at this period in the west coast of Africa.

9. Chinweizu, *The West and the Rest of Us: White Predators, Black Slavers and the African Elite,* New York: Random House, 1975, pp. 39-40.
10. Robert G. Weisbord, *Ebony Kinship*, Westport, Connecticut: Greenwood Press, Inc., 1974, pp.32-33; see also Melvin Drimmer, "Review Article-Black Exodus", *Journal of American Studies 4,2* (1970), pp. 249-256.
11. Quoted in Chinweizu *The West and the Rest of Us,* p. 55; see also Sir Frederick D. Lugard, The Dual Mandate *in British Tropical Africa,* Edinburgh and London: William Blackwood & Sons, 1923, p. 613.
12. Jaja Anucha Wachuku, *Nigeria, Africa and the World: The Concept of Nigeria's Leadership Role in Africa and the World,* Benin, Nigeria: Lecture Delivered To the Bendel State Civil Service Forum, 26th February, 1988, p. 10.
13. Walter Rodney, *How Europe Underdeveloped Africa,* Washington, D.C.: Howard University Press, 1982, p. 142.
14. Adu Boahen, "The Partition of Africa", *Topics in West African History.* London: Longmans, Green and Co Ltd, 1966, pp. 127-133.
15. Walter Rodney, *How Europe Underdeveloped Africa,* Washington, D.C.: Howard University Press, 1982, p. 144.
16. Chinweizu, *The West and the Rest of Us, New* York: Random House, 1975, p. 32.
17. For example, the creative impulse in Western tradition found in the Greek and Roman letters descended from ancient Africa. Hence, it is from the ancient Kemetic alphabet that the Phoenician alphabet was developed, which was later borrowed by the ancient Greeks. The Greeks modified the consonantal system of the Phoenician alphabet to incorporate a vowel system. Then, the Greek alphabet was adopted by the Etruscans, from whom the Romans got their own alphabet .

18. The European culture has been able to survive to this day, despite its extreme materialistic tendency, because Europeans have managed to direct their internal problems on to non-Europeans. But a Europeanized "African" culture is bound to be self-destructive. Simply because Africans are not Europeans. And as such will not be able to develop a culture that destroys "others" in the name of "progress". Such a Europeanized culture will end up destroying itself.

CHAPTER SEVEN
CONCLUSIONS AND LEGACY OF WHITE MAGIC

"We are so accustomed to base our view of the world and our whole conception of history on the idea of Europe that it is hard for us to realize what the nature of that idea is, Europe is not a natural unity, like Australia or Africa; it is the result of a long process of historical evolution and spiritual development. From the geographical point of view, Europe is simply the north-western promulgation of Asia, and possesses less physical unity than India or China or Siberia; anthropologically it is a medley of races, and the European type of man represents a social rather than a racial identity. And even in culture the unity of Europe is not of the foundation and starting point of European history, but the ultimate and unattained goal, towards which it has striven for more than a thousand years." [1a]

---Christopher Dawson.

"Five hundred years of constant propaganda, cultural exploitation, information distortion, and physical annihilation have left the African world shocked out of its own historical reality and purpose in the world". [1b]

---Molefi Kete Asante.

For the Ekwueme People of Truth, the First year of **Nzoputa Uwa** was the New Beginning from which we reckon the date of all things, beyond which every other event is reckoned according to the historical process of the time of **Oge Nzuzu**. The historical process of **Nzoputa Uwa** would always exist in the wholeness of eternity in disagreement with Nsi that pervaded and embodied the historical process of **Oge Nzuzu**. No doubt, the Ekwueme dispensation is against all forms of agreement with Nsi. Whosoever lives in agreement with Nsi is an imposter, the Ekwensi, an unbeliever.

......The Chosen One

According to the teachings of ***THE HOLY ANKHUWA***, **White Magic is the extreme materialistic tendency that encourages the abuse of human morality and the consequent misapplication of the universal**

principles of life. Because it is through the misapplication of the universal principles of life that we can trace the patterns of the abuse of human morality, the delusions of an effortless virtue and irredeemable vice become the basis for the understanding of the skin color contraption of the religions of ISFET.

In the skin color contraption of the religions of ISFET, there is no human morality. What exists is a delusional contraption of skin color whereby white represents what it means to be fully human, and black represents what is dehumanized or less than human. White Magic and its delusions have excluded those who are not white from the definition of what it means to be fully human. It is a created image of good and evil based on the skin color contraption of the religions of ISFET. Therefore, to follow the religions of ISFET is to worship a created image of the human mind that is white and if the human spirit is not white such a person must occupy mentally (if not socially) an inferior subordinate position in the skin color contraption world scheme. As a result of the skin color contraption of the religions of ISFET, black became the embodiment of what is evil, unclean, impure, ugly, corrupt and doomed; whereas white is glorified as the embodiment of what is good.

To the followers of the religions of ISFET, what is black is what is inferior, what is sinister and evil, what is dirty, wicked and what is indicative of condemnation, abuse and discredit. No doubt, the followers of the religions of ISFET conceive evil as what is black and what is black to them is whatever that is conceived in their mind to be sad, ugly, shameful, gloomy, grotesque, calamitous, grim, or distorted. So, to be black to the followers of the religions of ISFET is to be inferior, nothing of importance. In short, to the followers of the religions of ISFET to be black is to be nobody. To them, black is marked by the occurrence of disaster and inferior conditioning as long as one is a follower of the religions of ISFET. This is to say that to be black is to be cursed as far as the followers of the religions of ISFET are concerned.

In contrast, white is designated in the skin color contraption of the religions of ISFET to mean upright fairness, free from moral impurity, beautiful, considered favorable and fortunate, blessed, clean, free from obstacles, not dark, just, equitable, impartial, not stormy or foul, charming and flawless regardless of character. The followers of the religions of ISFET have made whiteness to be superior in opposition to blackness which is made to become inferior.

Wherefore, in the skin color contraption of the religions of ISFET white is the human being par excellence, the superior being. Not because of character or intelligence; instead it is due to the skin color that one is born with in the world of Ekwensu.

Let it be known that the Truth of the divine birth of EKUMEKU has liberated us from the dead end nature of the world of Ekwensu by bringing the Ekwueme Universal Life that is the new human paradigm of what it means to be fully human. **This new human paradigm of the Ekwueme rejects the skin color contraption of the religions of ISFET by insisting that what defiles a man or woman is neither the whiteness of the skin nor the blackness of the skin.** The eternal Truth of the divine birth of EKUMEKU has revealed that what defiles the human spirit is the unrepentant life of living in agreement with Nsi.

Without any shadow of doubt, this skin color contraption exists because the followers of the religions of ISFET have mistaken metaphor for reality: The metaphor of darkness versus lightness. But there is no real struggle morally speaking between darkness and lightness.

The Ekwueme Universal Life is not defined by skin color; instead, it is defined by the moral character of the human being who has attained the devotion of purpose to the supreme principle of EKUMEKU. The Ekwueme is the universal being who is skillful in thought, speech and action through the voluntary worship of the One Creator of the universe. Therefore, ***Ekwuemeism*** is the moral definition of our conviction to live in disagreement with Nsi.

In other words, to live in agreement with Nsi is to accept that black is the embodiment of evil. It is to accept the skin color contraption of the religions of ISFET, and that is what is called **Ekwensism**. **Let it be known that there is no skin color that possesses the monopoly for beauty, virtue, purity, cleanliness, etc., or ugliness, vice, impurity, dirtiness, etc. Consequently, the Movement of Nzoputa Uwa has defined the Ekwueme as the ideal character of what it means to be fully human and as the new human paradigm.** It has also provided the worldview of the universe which enables the Ekwueme to function effectively.

In conclusion, the yoke of living in agreement with Nsi has made the Ekwensi mind become a terrible thing to be wasted from generation to generation. **But in this time of Nzoputa Uwa, our Savior and Redeemer has come to liberate the human spirit from the yoke of living in**

agreement with Nsi. Without any doubt, the skin color contraption of the religions of ISFET is a death-trap, a monstrous evil.

It is objectionable to the Ekwueme for any group or persons to brand the black image as exclusively and absolutely evil and to condemn the black skinned people to eternal doom without any moral justification. **Let it be known that the skin color contraption of the religions of ISFET is a gutter ideology that would never be tolerated by the Ekwueme People of Truth.** The Ekwueme must never condone the immoral philosophy of the followers of the religions of ISFET, which is steeped in error.

Therefore, the followers of the religions of ISFET are the Ekwensu people who are in the need of EKUMEKU for deliverance and salvation. The Akwunakwuna is confronted with the skin color contraption, with the intolerance of a religious persecution of skin color, depriving the human spirit the dignity and freedom to live a worthy life. However, the divine birth of EKUMEKU on the Second year of Nzoputa Uwa has come to redeem everyone that is dead under the yoke of living in agreement with Nsi. **With *nkuzimatical fervor*, the Ekwueme is ordained to go into the world of Ekwensu to liberate the individual Chi of the Ekwensu people in the Almighty Spirit of EKUMEKU.**

CONCLUSIONS

The history of the modern world constitutes the tragic but also the incredible drama of the African's oppression and the subsequent Europeanization of many African minds or the resultant suppression of the African personality and values. These have affected the endless distortions of the forces of human development and the seeming obliteration of the significant pioneer landmarks of Africa—which indubitably have made possible the development of the modern world. The anti-African hysteria has been the underlying force that has propelled the European people to successfully undermine the African legacy. Therefore, the phenomenon of White Magic is quantitatively and qualitatively the most destructive and frightful chasm ever used by man throughout the history of the human race to inflict an irreparable damage on a people. It is easy to produce examples of how Europeans have vigorously attempted to reduce Africans as imbeciles and buffoons. A typical example is the following contention illuminated by John Henrik Clarke. He writes: "The Africans, upon entering into the slave system of the Americas, became exposed to the most diabolical and consistent application of mental and physical torture the world has ever known."[1]

Historically, the cornerstone of the European expansion after the decline of the Roman Empire began from the middle of the fifteenth century C.E. By the middle of the fifteenth century, the end of the Christian Crusade had dramatized the European living conditions; and the access to the Mediterranean and Atlantic oceans further gave impetus to the European people's desire to live a better life. These led to the trend of phenomenal historical radicalism which began not only with the renowned European expedition to Africa but also with the so-called "discovery" of the Americas in 1492. When Christopher Columbus (Cristobal Colon) found himself in what is now called Bahamas (which he called San Salvador), he heralded a new era in the world. This singular undertaking underscored by the European materialistic mentality would change the world forever.

Conversely, the European encroachment in the Americas and the subsequent commencement of mineral extractions and agricultural developments led to a chain of events. As the interplay of variant forces led to the enslavement of Africans, it helped to fill the void which the annexation of the American landmass had created. Consequently, the need for labor and the initial violent actions meted on the Africans in the West coast of Africa engendered and accentuated the idea of an African involuntary labor force. Thus, the African involuntary captive labor was based not only on agricultural farming but was also used to develop an economic system that has changed the means of production of goods and services. Indeed, there is a strong causal relationship between the Americas and the massive European Slave Trade on Africans and the development of capitalism.

As the accumulation of capital evolved through the Triangular Trade, which Europe dominated and defined, it led to the European Industrial Revolution. But before industrialization became widespread and advanced, millions of Africans had been captured, kidnapped, tortured, conquered, bartered, murdered, and enslaved. The role Africans played in the development of a European economic, political, intellectual and cultural hegemony can never be overemphasized. Nevertheless, the main thrust of this African-European intercourse emerged and became the motivating force of oppression, exploitation and human degradation—White Magic. In this interaction the continent of Africa has waned, whilst Europe has waxed stronger. The theory of human inequality arose. The African people were not only depicted as inferior to the European people, but they were in actuality treated as non-humans--as chattels. Africans they were noted to have said were the "missing link" between man and animals—that they were part-human and part-monkey.

The Charles Darwin's theory of evolution, *On the Origins of Species by Means of Natural Selection (1859),* was rationalized and bent to suit the needs and interests of Social Darwinists. Herbert Spencer, Houston Stewart Chamberlain, Count Arthur de Gobineau, Lothrop Stoddard, and other eminent European race theorists developed various arguments bent on justifying the alleged inferiority of Africans on the one hand; and ramifying the European's self-proclaimed assumption of their superiority amongst other peoples of the world, on the other hand. In this scramble to lend "scientific" validity to these false assumptions, selected passages of the Bible were orchestrated as the justifications of a divine ordinance.

But out of this crucible of the African degradation emerged a problematic reaction by Africans regarding the color black. The psychological imbalance of being dominated and oppressed by those who consider themselves to be superior because of their skin coloration (low melanin pigmentation) and the suppression of human aspirations of a collective group naturally created a warping dependency syndrome on the victims. The outcome has been the near total destruction of the cultural perspectives of the oppressed Africans and thus the creation of group disillusionment and anarchy.[2]

In other words, the underlying dynamics found within the European racist thinking is the need to monopolize power, human knowledge and human development. Insofar as racism is a contagious disease that contaminates and infects anything that the Europeans and their descendants around the world come in contact or are associated with,

White Magic will continue to create false values on its victims. White Magic is the debilitating element, destroying all that it comes in contact with. It is the distorting element, predicated on the destruction of the African perspective. It is the synthesis of several centuries of the European's and Arab's violent aggression on Africans. In a word, White Magic is amoral, a brute force cloaked under the pretexts of "progress". Accordingly, it is the excessive material tendentiousness that undermines the spiritual realm in its quest to conquer nature. It neither recognizes spirituality nor does it have any moral cognition.

There is no phenomenon or calamity in the history of the world more destructive than White Magic. Africans have paid the bloody price of White Magic for too long. The phenomenon of White Magic is the phantom of ignorance. Most Africans are ignorant of their past, especially their history with the Europeans and Arabs. But they have failed to understand that the mistakes of their ancestors, with regard to the European and Arab slave traders, were because of the ancestors' ignorance to the potent force of White Magic.

But the effects of White Magic have no doubt changed the world from what it was known to be, before the euphemistic era called the modern world. The obvious changes in the world, in this present Age, have been mostly negative. And this is to say, that the world has become partly a creation of depraved men. The Eurocentric man in his frailties has dominated the world, not from moral conviction but from greed, from his cultural compulsion to control and exploit the weaknesses of his fellow men. The modern world is a world pregnant with complex problems. In this world, we will live and die. Who knows? May be there is another world. The experiences we have gathered in this world, then, could be put into use in a new world, where man can put into practice what we have learnt from this world. Or unless, the African who has been used as the beast of burden—as the caricature of humanity—has the moral courage to regain his collective humanity and to use it to change the world from this amoral madness, there would be no hope for humanity. Without any doubt, the Ekwueme People of Truth have answered the call to serve humanity by the virtue of the new world order of EKUMEKU through the historical process of Nzoputa Uwa. In fact, as Molefi Kete Asante has argued, "there is no other truth more necessary for the intellectual, political, economic, and cultural advancement of the world than African people immersing themselves in the waters of a cultural rebirth".[3] That is to say that the future hinges on the ability of Africans to regain their collective humanity and reclaim their cultural heritage.

I. THE LEGACY

In this conclusive chapter, my effort will be to summarize some of the themes discussed in this book and to wrap it up for readers to understand the connectedness of these issues as they relate to the African's present state of mind. The history of human existence can be qualified as the history of the continuous migration of peoples. There has always been migration throughout the history of humanity. But the impact of the European expansion has had tremendous effect on the modern world. Thus, the mistakes of our fathers paved the way for the Europeans and Arabs to trade on the African as a commodity. The famous African proverb reminds us that those who do not know their history are bound to repeat the past: 'that a people without the knowledge of their past is like a tree without roots'. Have these new generation Africans learnt how to deal with the world from a position of strength?

In the first place, the dynamics of what we presently call racism is an historically evolving phenomenon, because it changes form ever since its inception. It is entrenched as an amalgamated feature of the European economic, political, religious, intellectual, and cultural global hegemony. Of course, its fantastic mystique has equally affected the development and the relation of other non-Europeans with regards to Africa and Africans. However, it is deeply embedded in the anti-African hysteria of superiority versus inferiority. The origin of racism dates back to ancient Greeks, and was later expanded in the fifteenth century when Africans and Europeans began to have various scopes of interactions. Nevertheless, the birth of the term "racism" in my view was nourished and expanded by an acute need to rationalize the enslavement of Africans by the Christian nations of Europe.

Today, it is universally acknowledged that the European Slave Trade ushered in the so-called modern world; and the subsequent subservient role the Africans played in their partnership with Europeans in the bringing forth of the modern world is the bone of contention. This could very well be qualified as the motivating factor in the eruption of the virus of anti-African hatred and intolerance. The need for Europeans to keep Africans and their descendants subservient manifested itself in the foundation of the concept of Race, as a universal "sham". Thus, the concept of race was founded on the premise that the human stocks were of three different kinds: the civilized (Eurasian), half-civilized (Mongol-Asian), and savage or barbaric (Africoid). These were called the states of man, which were supposed to be absolute, permanent and immutable.

However, the concept of race has been expanded by many of its prominent theorists to incorporate other vital human exigencies. This was done in a futile attempt to make this concept a scientific devise. The core of this concept was focused primarily to enable the subjugation of non-Europeans (mostly Africans), at least psychologically, and to foster a sense of consensus within the European's pillaging and conquering of the entire planet for the global goal of ruling the world supremely. On the whole, the concept of race was deemed inevitable because of the brutal dehumanization of captured Africans brought into the Americas for the sole purpose of exploiting their human labor. Initially, this labor was geared towards the extraction of minerals abound in the Americas. Subsequently, they were later used for a wide variety of chores, ranging from plantation agriculture to domestic housekeeping, and even other complex and non-complex economic undertakings.

Secondly, let us look at the world from another spectrum, "tribalism" or ethnicity is also a phenomenon. However, it is a relatively new phenomenon, in comparison with racism, which sprang from a seedbed tended by the Europeans, beginning from the fifteenth century. Hence, the needs for the Europeans to procure captive labor led to one of the oldest principles of warfare—divide and conquer. This was carried out in many different fashions; but one of the most notable aspects was the European's backing of a specific African nation or ethnic group with firearms against the opposing belligerent party—playing one nation or ethnic group against the other nation. Thus, the defeat of the other party usually led to an insurmountable number of prisoners of war (POWs). These African prisoners of war were normally bartered out to the Europeans as captive laborers. The fear of the impending enemy led to a vicious cycle of guns, prisoners of war and wars. The conditional social crisis that was caused by this state of affairs resulted to over dependence of Africans in their ethnic group for protection and survival. Precisely, this was how the European cancer of "tribalism" was planted on the African soil.

No doubt, during the advent of formal colonization, the European colonial conquerors endeavored to enhance this destructive phenomenon, through their strategies of keeping Africans disunited and weak. But the problem of ethnicity in Africa becomes important due to the role of the African elites in its perpetuation. During the nationalist movements in Africa most African leaders began to adopt the dynamics of ethnicity subtly, sometimes very eloquently, in their shortsighted ideologies. It is no doubt that the political elites fomented ethnic sentiments as the weapon and as political ideology in their lust for power. This has helped to entrench its mechanics into the fabric of the post-independence philosophies of most African countries. The narrow scope and the undue relationship attached to this ethnic fantasy is uncalled for and has stagnated the development of most African countries. Ethnicity, however, becomes relevant only in understanding how the African elites exploit their ethnic heritages for the service of their selfish and opportunistic ambitions.

The effects of these two phenomena, "racism" and "ethnicity", are not only counterproductive but have undeniably affected, perceptibly, the African's understanding of the modern world. Unmistakably, racism has entrenched a contagious legacy, that has defined every aspect of the African modus of existence as inferior. Its impact has contributed immensely to the physical and cultural suicide still witnessed until the present generation amongst African people, both in the Diaspora and in the Continent. Also, the incongruent phenomenon called "tribalism" is not only witnessed in the continental Africa. It is rather a pervasive African elite's maladapted pathology that has gradually grown to affect many of the ideologies of Africans in the Diaspora as well.

Instead of conferring different tags or labels to these counterproductive and self-destructive forces, I have labored, through my understanding in the need for systematization and specification, to bring all these negative forces under one umbrella.[4] This was how my theory of White Magic evolved. This is because I have consistently found that in almost every aspect of the contemporary problems of the African people the common denominator is usually the impact of Eurasian ideologies, attitudes, political, cultural, intellectual, economic, and religious imperatives. These mechanistic manipulations of forces by the Eurasian peoples always prelude the emergence of the respective mental and cultural outlook of Africans.

This magic spell makes us to dislike things and sometimes people that remind us of our selves. It makes us, bluntly, to hate each other; to see each other as potential enemies; to feel uncomfortable about our historic past; to hate our history; to hate each other's development; to work against the common unity of the African people; to discourage unified spirit of cooperation; to work against the common upliftment of the African heritage that has been disremembered by several centuries of tyranny and conspiracy; to come together as one people; to take the destiny of our lives into our own hands; to uplift ourselves; to take positive initiatives; to acknowledge our common ancestry, etc.

Ngugu wa Thiong'o used the term 'cultural bomb" to further describe what he sees as the most devastating "weapon" used in the attempt to destroy the collective human conscience of all African people. This is reflected particularly in the following:

"The effect of a cultural bomb is to annihilate a people's belief in their names, in their languages, in their environment, in their heritage of struggle, in their unity, in their capacities and ultimately in themselves. It makes them see their past as one wasteland of non-achievement and it makes them want to identify with that which is *furthest removed from themselves; for instance, with other people's languages rather than their own. It makes them identify with that which is decadent and reactionary,*

all those forces which would stop their own springs of life. It even plants serious doubts about the moral rightness of struggle. Possibilities of triumph or victory are seen as remote, ridiculous dreams. The intended results are despair, despondency and a collective death-wish. Amidst this wasteland which it has created, imperialism present itself as the cure and demands that the dependent sing hymns of praise with the constant refrain: 'Theft is holy'. Indeed, this refrain sums up the new creed of the neo-colonial bourgeoisie in many 'independent' African states".[5]

Since "racism" was devised and propagated by the Europeans, they in turn will also pay the price or suffer the ultimate consequences of its role in the human development before it can be eradicated. Europeans are by no means capable of eradicating racism. It is the moral obligation of Africans to not only eradicate racism but equally to save humanity from this path to destruction. The African, on the other hand, will be incapable of eradicating racism until he purges himself from the mental and cultural colonialism upon which he has been encumbered. That is to say that the African can eradicate racism, only when he has regained his collective humanity and Africanness. Until then, racism will continue to emasculate the mind of many African people; and the world at large will not be redeemed from this evil. So there will never be peace in the world until Africans collectively regain their human dignity.

Thirdly, the dynamics underlying White Magic is enthroned in the creation of antagonistic contradictions amongst its victims. In other words, White Magic is geared towards the suppression, suffocation and annihilation of the African cultural attributes, the African worldview, in order to facilitate domination. For instance, in economic organization, it distorts reality by making the economic backbone of its victims externally dislocated. In the Diaspora, many Africans like to patronize businesses that are not black-owned even if the black-owned is around the corner. Also in Africa, most continental Africans consider anything that is made outside Africa to be better than the ones made in Africa. The same pattern of behavior is evident in all spheres of human endeavor. Heretofore, the symbolic images of beauty thus far are predominantly whatever that is judged to be less African: The less African one is perceived to be, the more beautiful that person is made to become, especially by the agents of White Magic.

(a) The most decisive impact of White Magic is in the symbolic realm. The Europeans were able to use contrived and sublime images to not only create caricatures of the African people but also to standardize these images based on the European's functional reality. One of the most successful arenas is in the spheres of skin color and hair type. The manifestation is quite visible, both in the Continent and Diaspora, where many African people's understanding of beauty and aesthetic appeal could be said to be quite distorted. It could be said that this aspect indeed portrays the propensity of the European's desire to enthrone Eurocentricity upon the African's worldview.

(b) The ultimate idea of White Magic is to create a sense of inadequacy on the Africans though the manipulation of the media, and also through the use of the less-African looking blacks as the archetypes or models for Africans. It is an unequivocal fact that whilst businesses, black-owned and otherwise, condone this nefarious act by their prevalent use of the less-African-looking models for their advertisements and public relations, they cynically reinforce and implant the idea that the closer one gets to the European model of beauty, the more beautiful one is perceived to become.

(c) The doctrine of White Magic is manifested in the Eurocentric philosophy of the "civilizing mission to uplift the heathens and savages of Africa".[6] But the actual purpose has been the European notion that the African must be made to lose his cultural and mental identity, in order for him to be accepted as a human being.

(d) White Magic is the foundation of an ideology that is grounded on the belief that the African must be mentally and culturally colonized. This is to create an "honorary white" personality out of the African. To create if possible people with "Black Skin" and "White Mask" as Fanon described it, or people with "Double Consciousness" as Du Bois saw it. Or to create people who would become the effigy and ego-trip of the European man, as have been amplified by many of the arguments in this book. These are the invariable issues of identity, authentic vision of the world, cultural continuity, and human potential.

Of course, the European torch-bearers of White Magic were mindful of one of the universal truths governing humanity. This has been what Edward Wilmot Blyden reminded us almost one century ago: That no meaningful people can develop a dignified and moral society without a connection to their historical past. His prophetic enunciation bears strong and adamant testimony to the contemporary plight of Africans all over the world. His deduction was that people have consistently developed a progressive society only when such development is entrenched on their own line of thinking, i.e., their own worldview. When such development is centered on their positive historical and philosophical view of the universe.[7] That is why the control of one's own history is of paramount import; because the role of history in this process of growth cannot be overemphasized.

Therefore, the trans-migration of the African souls to Europe conveys the tenacity of the Europeans, and their ubiquitous struggle to use their extreme materialistic tendencies to put Africa into the White Age. Thus, they understood that "a colonized mind is always on the verge of menticide, the destruction of the minds, the suicide of minds" as Molefi K. Asante puts it.[8]

THE RELIGIOUS FACTOR

The religious aspect of White Magic is the most encompassing–the most traumatic—of the African's catastrophic existence. Consequently, Africans do not need any alienating creed that negates their humanity—that condemns their culture and their natural attributes as unacceptable or unworthy. Such religion(s) would in fact become a colonizing, alienating or brainwashing device used to suppress and thus impose contradicting norms and values to the victims. Therefore, any religion that is not centered on the self-image, self-determination, self-fulfillment, cultural and historical universe of the African people cannot be used to correct the African problem. If it cannot be used to liberate the mentally and culturally colonized minds of the African people, Africans do not need such a religion. This is because it will be incapable of transforming them to the supreme good of human aspiration of becoming the human being par excellence.

It is no mere historical accident that the massively imposed European and Arab Slave Trades on Africans were carried out under the banner of the Christian and Islamic religious experiences. The African day of reckoning will be the day when Africans would wake up to the spell of White Magic. On that day, they would realize that any religion that does not put Africa at the CENTER, that does not recognize Africa as its Holy Land, is invalid and inapplicable. As Chancellor Williams puts it, "But what happened in the process of converting the blacks to Islam and Christianity was the supreme triumph of the white world over the black. Millions of Africans became non-Africans".[9] The implication of this condition is profound. Thus, the powerlessness of the African people is heightened by the fact that the religions practiced by most Africans are essentially controlled from the outside. They are not centered around the people themselves. Consequently, the Ekwueme struggle is to displace ISFET and restore MAAT as the dominant consciousness in the universe of life. In other words, the world mission of Nzoputa Uwa underlies the need to integrate the moral and ethical principles of MAAT into the African's mental and culture universe through the threshold of EKUMEKU. In the words of one ancient Kemetic sage, Ptahhotep, "MAAT—the way of Truth, Justice and Righteousness—is great; its value is lasting and it has remained unchanged and unequaled since the time of its Creator"[10]

II. WHAT IS THE PURPOSE OF RELIGION?

Religion, in a generic sense, is unique because of its contextual differences from other human endeavors. That is why, religion is derived from specific human needs and experiences, and is supposed to function within the scope of transforming man's ability to cope with the more rigorous phases of the worldly or human stage of life. At the same time, religion also is focused on interpreting life after death, spirit and matter, cause and effect, etc., with the ideal goal of imposing a harmonizing balance of morality and ethics amongst the living. So it aspires to deal with the divine challenge of death, resurrection, and transformation.

In seriously seeking to understand the underlying purpose of religion and its practices, it is important from the outset to acknowledge that religion in itself has been a creation of the human mind. This human conception is projected to render meaning and relevance to the visible and invisible forces coexisting in the infinitesimal universe. By the same logic, religion is meant to be functional to the human metaphysical, epistemological and axiological needs of spiritual and mental harmony. If man created religion to suit his yearning and anguish, it is understandable that man did not depart from those forces that have influenced his existence; and these forces could be called supernatural and nature forces. The degree supernatural and natural forces have influenced the development of religion becomes the fundamental element in understanding religion, its practices and its effect on human behavior, individual and group.

The influence of religion upon the human development can be seen from its formative role in the historical exigencies of cultural evolution: in the ontological interpretations of the supernatural and natural orders of the visible and invisible forces and its effects on the chain of priortism and relativism of the believer regarding his various mundane interests. Given the fact that man's innate nature is ritualistic, it is necessary to state that all societies may have been impelled by the normative order to practice religion. In this case, religion becomes the derivative historical influence that gives material and spiritual meaning to human existence. In essence, religion provides for man an undergirded normative basis not only for the cosmological and cosmogonical interpretations of life in the universe, but also for the primal organization of his human desires in order to find comfort and stability on the planet. In other words, religious practice, in any form whatsoever, is a system that men created to give meaning to their existence, with regards to the satisfaction, regulation and protection of their vital interests, in both the symbolic and fantastic realms. Thus, religion is the mirror for understanding the normative value premises of early cultures and how these value premises had helped to shape the evolution of worldviews, institutions and ideologies of humanity.

The purpose of religion in most part becomes the basis for apprehending the nature of the universe. The foundation of the universe is laid by the principle of opposites which shows that all things manifest in duality. Thus, the universe is material; but the essence of the universe is spiritual. That is to say, that it is through the spiritual source of Being that the manifestation of matter is Becoming. Therefore, the universal goal in its divine sanction is to strive for harmony, balance, complementary, etc. For nothing can exist independently without the constant interaction of its pair of opposites. This principle of opposites is the purpose of religion. The purpose can be stated as follows: The human being is part of the divine plan. His ultimate existence in this infinitesimal universe will depend on whether he has the ability and capacity to adhere to the divine plan. That is, whether he has the ability to balance and complement the interrelated opposites.

Although the purpose of religion is to balance the material realm with the spiritual realm, humanity has witnessed both the spiritual and material extremism: black and white magic. For instance, white magic opened the way for the emergence of organized religions of Faith and for their theological absolutism. But the tendency for absolutism in organized religions of Faith is the desire to control and manipulate the known and unknown workings of the universe. In other words, the absolute doctrines of life and the universe are the results of extreme materialistic ontology. They are predicated on the goal of manipulating and controlling what is known and what is unknown in the universe. The implication is White Magic; and thus much of what we call the religions of Faith today is magic.

Conversely, the purpose of religious practice in many of its form is on the whole focused to cultivate "universal consciousness", i.e., to transform man to a higher level of consciousness for the purpose of attaining a state of equilibrium. Again, this universal consciousness expands to its fullest capacity in projecting the highest aspirations for the human being. 'This universal consciousness is not about religion in the popular sense, because it is non-denominational and non-sectarian. Universal consciousness has little to do with going to church, to the mosque or to the synagogue'.[11]

Therefore, the appraisal system for religion must always be seen from the standpoint that the underlying ethical premise of religion is to unify human beings with the spiritual source of Being, i.e., the Universal Life Force. In other words, this universal spiritual principle was thought of as the essence of unity amongst the different biological and cultural variations of the human being. This in fact is the recognition that the human being is part of the divine plan. So, if religion is geared towards the unification of all human elements, within one Universal Principle, such religion must be inclusive and not exclusive to only those that adhere to the particularistic cultural interpretations of the relationship between the One Creator of the universe and the creation of life upon which it was founded. Within this parameter, the purpose of religion thence becomes a concept of Universal Life Force: Balance, Reciprocity, Harmony, Truth, Justice, Order and Propriety. It was to this particular normative premise that the notion of Truth as the divine attribute of MAAT was developed. Thus, the moral principle of MAAT is the foundation for balance, reciprocity, harmony, order, law, righteousness, justice, truth, complementarity, love, unity, etc., on the planet.

There is no gainsaying the fact that the development and advancement of this inner vision was made possible by the ancient Africans who were in the ancient time the noted leaders in human development. For example, the ancient Kemetian Pharaoh Akhenaton has been immortalized for revolutionizing this concept of one Universal Life Force because he used Aton as the central symbol (supreme deity) of Life in the universe. Ironically, over the centuries it has become clear that it is only the Africans who seemed to have truly embraced this notion of the universality of human life/spirit. The contemporary world most organized religions of Faith (Hebrewism, Christianity and Islam) have demonstrated that whilst they accepted the African God-concept of spirituality in theory, they rejected its universal spiritual principle in their practices of the embedded belief—the universality of the human spirit or oneness of life.

This has been disastrous to Africans, for they did not realize that these religions exemplified White Magic in its most characteristic forms.

One of the most noted aspects of the African heritage of oneness of life or the concept of one Universal Life Force has been its impact on the historical reality of interactions between Africans and Eurasians. There are many instances where Africans rightly or wrongly, for better or for worse, have demonstrated that they loved Eurasians more than they love themselves or their fellow Africans. Given the basis of this argument, I will use some typical examples to illustrate this internalized cultural tradition. Firstly, during the era of chattel slavery, many enslaved Africans have been known to love their slave masters to the extent that many seemed willing to die for the sake of their brutal masters' lives. Although these enslaved Africans resented their bondages they nevertheless saw their bondage as a divine test for the redemption of their white masters. But most of the white masters rarely possessed the essential spiritual element necessary for spiritual consciousness, and therefore could not understand or appreciate the attributes of higher spiritual consciousness. Instead, they called the Africans "childlike" pagans who could never grow up into adulthood. Secondly, in the continental Africa, it is important to state that although "ethnicity" may be rampant amongst the elites, the average African's reaction to the European and Asian descendants of those who have stolen, enslaved, colonized, and occupied the African's ancestral inheritance has been cordial and benevolent. This has always puzzled many of these foreigners in Africa or elsewhere; because they failed to understand why many Africans do not bear serious deep-seated grudges against the various atrocities their ancestors (and sometimes themselves) have meted to the Africans. It was to this fact the Arabs who knew that Africans are spiritually superior to them have been taken advantage of this fact. The Asians (Arabs) currently are penetrating more and more into the interior of Africa with the imperative of consolidating their African booty. Thirdly, one of the major factors in the decline of Africa's glory (ancient Kemet) as a major power has been the cross-cultural intermingling between indigenous Africans and other invaders into Africa; but this interbreeding rose to an epidemic proportion because Africans in the Nile Valley wrongly adopted in-toto the principles of the oneness of Life in the universe.

Some may see these historical facts as anachronistic, but the concept of one Universal Life Force has been an ingrained African tradition that most Eurasians never adopted and will never adopt. The African possession of higher spiritual element has not only imbibed him with a higher spiritual consciousness, but also a higher respect for human value. Whilst the African's negations of himself and others that look like him have been explained in many passages of this work as a result of the constant propaganda, devaluation, degradation and humiliation of the African personality, by the enemies of Africa. These have effectively conditioned the African to see himself as being "less than a man". It has been through this process of dehumanization that the average African's perception of himself and others that look like him seems to have become as "a lesser being". So, the average African reacts to himself and others that look like him from the standpoint that they are lesser beings; whilst at the same time, he treats most Eurasians as human beings by unconsciously applying the internalized African doctrines of one Universal Life Force. This is because the African naturally perceives Eurasians as human beings, therefore must be treated accordingly.

Generally, it is a fact that the African God-concept of spirituality is in theory the basis upon which the contemporary world most organized religions of Faith were founded. But in practice, it is clear that these most organized religions of Faith are mere corrupted or profaned versions of the African God-concept of spirituality and are used by the controlling groups to entrench and preserve their respective vested interests. One may thus far argue that because man is a religious man (ritualistic animal) and a political (power conscious) animal, the African God-concept of spirituality has been abused and defiled by mostly Eurasians who have neglected its universal value of one Universal Life. History shows us that these religions of Faith from their genesis were used as socio-political phenomena by those who control them to advance and serve their interests on the one hand, and to suppress other men on the guise of sharing the knowledge of the Truth on the other hand.

Despite these facts, these exclusive and politically organized religions of Faith have the illusion of bringing the One Creator of the universe to the level of man. That is why they created the human personalities they call God, "son of God", "saints", "matyrs", etc. But the eternal Truth of the One Creator of the universe has revealed that there is no other Creator of the universe but AMUN in whom we must trust. The Creator is One. The One is AMUN and the Divine Plan is EKUMEKU. There is no God that is worthy of worship because every God is the created image of the human mind.

In my view, the world will never be a safe place for Africans until they embrace the eternal Truth of the One Creator of the universe and become the devoted followers of the Divine Plan of the One Creator of the universe. The eternal Truth should be understood as an intrinsic organ of humanity's universality, and as an intimate experience of human kind towards the need to exist as seeker of self-knowledge for the purpose of being spiritually one with the Supreme Sprit of Life. The survival of Africans as a distinct biological group with an authentic culture can only suffice if Africans are capable of using the spiritual knowledge of the divine birth of EKUMEKU to commensurate with their quest for liberation and self-determination. This is necessary because the concept of one Universal Life is a spiritual phenomenon that is within us and around us. But when one hates self and his likes, the application of the spiritual principle becomes unattainable because self-hatred breeds spiritual poverty. And this poverty of the spirit is destructive to one's self-interests as a living being. It is in this context that Gerald Massey's statement becomes crucial for the African people. This is expressed in the following statement: "In this world of struggle, this scene of survival for the fittest, the poor in spirit stand no chance, and find no place; there is no victory for those who fight no battle".[12]

Furthermore, spirituality has been the Ankh (Life force) that undergirds and propelled human beings to seek a mystical Netherworld after death within the unknown and the mystery of the supernatural order of life. The eternal Truth of the One Creator of the universe views the world and nature as one intrinsic life force. It is geared towards the transformation of the individual, aiming to develop his individual Chi and mind from the human stage to a higher plane of human possibilities.[13] According to the teachings of ***The Holy Ankhuwa***, the human spirit is born in the world of Ekwensu in agreement with Nsi and the human spirit ought to be born again in the world of Ekumeku through the devotion of purpose to the supreme principle of creation in order to become the human being par excellence. Such a transformation is known as salvation and it makes the Ekwueme to exist in disagreement with every form of Nsi of any kind. Without any doubt, the religions of ISFET are the religions of Faith and they are diametrically opposed to the everlasting Truth of the divine birth of EKUMEKU.[14]

Therefore, the spirituality of EKUMEKU is fundamentally different from the religions of ISFET as many people may have not been opportuned to realize.[15] Conquered Africans having adopted the religions of their conquerors have inescapably helped to perpetuate their powerlessness and oppression by their adoptions of alien religious experiences which are inherently anathema to the spirituality of displaying ISFET and restoring MAAT. The socio-cultural development of the African personality not only has been hampered and stagnated, but can never realistically develop unless most Africans repudiate the alien religions of ISFET that they have been practicing.

III. AFRICAN PEOPLE MUST "THINK".

As a Kemite, I have often pondered about the seemingly exploitable conditions of most African people. I have in many a time asked myself the question: Why are Africans so exploitable? On numerous occasions when I thought about this issue, I have always arrived at one answer: The thought pattern of the African must be distorted. Yes, more than two millennia of external pressure, war, murder, dehumanization and conspiracy have rendered the African mental and cultural image of the universe in shambles. So it may be said that the African's ignorance of Ekumeku—the lack of the knowledge of self—has made this "conceptual incarceration" inescapable. What am I saying here? It appears to me that the thinking faculty of most African people has been their *Greatest Enemy*.

This has been because most Africans seemingly are suffering from cultural and mental amnesia. Thus, the intellectual faculty of a given African, the African's sense of identity or better still his lack of identity, influences and stimulates every decision he undertakes throughout his life span.

The main problem of the African is internal. If the African can overcome the internal contradictions of chronic cultural and mental dislocation that have been inflicted upon the African heritage through the spell of White Magic, he stands a hundred percent chance of overcoming racism and its aspects of human degradation—which are the external problems. The spell of White Magic has degenerated most Africans to the point of view that they have refused to "Think". As a result, most Africans have obviously rejected the human phenomenon of Thinking. It is a fact that the human mind (Akhu) is the most creative element of the human body; because it not only interacts with the six senses, it is located in the brain and spinal cord (central nervous system) that regulate and control the behavior and actions of man. Indeed, it is through "thinking" that the fundamental conceptions of human existence, such as the origin, location, purpose and destiny of ideas, the difference between ideas as things and as signs, the role of abstraction in the attainment of knowledge, etc., can be construed and explained.

In 1937, Dr Nnamdi Azikiwe admonished Africans in his book, *Renascent Africa,* to think. His Zikist philosophy of a 'New Africa' echoed: "Let the Africans think and think and then think".[16] This emphasis on thinking as a creative process was understood by the father of Zikism to be vital for the African's spiritual balance, social regeneration, economic determinism, mental emancipation and national resurgence'. Therefore, there is indeed a need for a multi-faceted revolution that entails the Ekumeku transformation of the contemporary notions of spirituality, economic, cultural and intellectual modes of Thinking. And to "Think" is to be actively engaged in the spiritual and material struggle of the Ekwueme people from all anti-African forces. This task must include the debunking of the Western notion of "progress" (linear or materialistic conception of space-time), "race" (black degradation) and "property acquisition" (self-serving avarice) because these materialistic forces will ultimately lead humanity to ecological and moral destruction.

IV. THE POWER OF BLACKNESS

The heart of the conflicts between Africans and Europeans began in 332 B.C.E. This was after the successful military penetration of the Greeks into North Africa, which was then the seat of the African power vis-a-vis world power. But what began as a military aggression later transformed itself and became a cultural mission as the Greeks plundered and hijacked everything they could lay their hands on. In the process, Africans gradually began to lose control of the monumental achievements they had made in their various intellectual and psychic endeavors. As the Greek conquerors copied and translated every volume of the multi-faceted African doctrines of life, most of them maliciously left out the original sources of the information they copied. What some historians have called the Greek philosophy, from all indications, is the misunderstood and misinterpreted version of the African philosophy of life. The reckless abandon that characterized the Greeks' looting of sacred Temples and holy Shrines of the Nile Valley resulted in their half-baked exposure to the natural or original civilization of humanity. The Greeks not only misunderstood the spiritual basis of the African life, but by their seemingly lack of higher spiritual (cosmic) consciousness they abused the envisioned natural order of human development organized for several millennia by the ancient Africans.

The ancient Greeks saw the world purely in its material configurations and thus laid the foundation for greed as the basis of human development in the modern world. First, the philosophical underpinning of MAAT was replaced by ISFET, the divine opposite of MAAT. The abominations brought upon the world by the Greek's adherence to the doctrine of ISFET manifested in greed, deceit, strife and ignorance, and was called "rational" thinking. But it was in reality the exclusive confinement of knowledge to the objective materiality of the physical plane, which overlooks the moralistic or subjective plane. Accordingly, greed, strife and deceit were elevated to the highest hierarchy of human life and have become the supreme good of life. The ethos of ISFET, chaos and disorder, not only manifested in the development of Greek and Roman civilizations as slaveholding societies, but also have become pandemic in the modern world with the enslavement of Africans for over two centuries as the foundation of the Western civilization.

The African God-concept of knowledge (the Maatian interdependent order of the universe) was replaced by the god-concept of nemeses, deceit, greed, ignorance and strife. Thus, the objectification of knowledge solely to the realm of physical forces have seemingly made might (ISFET) to be right and righteousness and spirituality (MAAT) to be wrong.

With the African God-concept of spirituality (MAAT), knowledge of the governing laws of the universe or the practical facts of nature stood as the foundation for spirituality. In other words, knowledge of the governing laws of the universe is the foundation upon which faith can be built and with faith in this order comes immortality. But the so-called major religions of Faith made faith, belief or fantasy without knowledge of the facts of nature the essence of their religious rituals. The founding fathers of these organized religions of Faith no doubt misunderstood the ancient African's astronomical symbols; and therefore they went out of their way to make them historical facts by humanizing and disguising the mystical symbols as historical facts. Thus far, the human beings ever since have been held for ransom by this fearsome, jealous, ignorant, deceitful, and spooky God. In this process, Africans have suffered dearly; because the legacies left by the Greaco-Roman invaders and their Arab counterparts have left Africa in a cultural crisis she has not yet recovered from. As a result, the culture, science, art, religion and civilization Africa gave to the world began to be defined and controlled by different outsiders who repeatedly fought against each other. In this respect, Africa became the battleground for fame and glory; and generations after generations of Africans saw themselves on the sideline of the world history and as spectators in the global contest for power.

But it is the contest to control the power generated by the mysticism of blackness that led to the foundation of the world's most organized religions of Faith. These religions whilst departing essentially from the spiritual basis of the African God-concept of spirituality, made the most sacred of their religious icons to reflect the black source of power, i.e., Auset (Isis) and Heru (Horus), Kabala, Black Madonna, Ka'bah, Buddha, etc. Also the mythical Christ of the historic Christianity, when its original symbol, the "Lamb of God", was humanized, the human figure's image was depicted as being a high melanin pigmented black man.

The electromagnetic energy of the sun is the producer of the vibration that generated the planet's vital force and cosmic consciousness. Given that the role of the solar radiation of the sun on the planet has been the synthesis of life, most African people are the profound human embodiment of the sun in its relationship with the pineal gland. The pineal gland is an endocrine organ or the 'eye of Heru' that secretes varied chemical elements, for instance, tyrosine and melatonin.[17] According to Carol Barnes, "The manufacture of MELANIN in the skin and various organs throughout the body of the BLACK HUMAN depends on a catalyst (battery) located within the Melanosome. The catalyst or battery provides the necessary energy to convert small chemical units such as tyrosine, serotonin, melatonin etc., to MELANIN".[18]

In addition, the eternal Truth of the One Creator of the universe conforms to the inter-relatedness of every aspect of creation. Without any doubt, the Divine Plan of the One Creator of the universe is the spiritual basis of the human life that encompasses every aspect of creation in the universe. Thus, it is enthroned on the wholistic view of human life, which includes both the spiritual and material, feminine and masculine principles that bring forth a natural balance to the visible and invisible forces of nature. That is why, blackness, both material and immaterial, is the producer of energy and balance on planet. It is the archetypal mystic of the God-concept of knowledge.[19]

Africa's experiences in the last two millennia have been the most virulent nightmares, that have almost crippled the idea of a re-awakened Africa. This ongoing crisis has been directed to enable the destruction of the African cultural material. The destruction of every aspect of the African cultural material, for example the burning of African books in the then world famous library of Alexandria in Kemet in 48 B.C.E., has been the nature of this anti-African hysteria. It is a struggle that has not only demonstrated the resiliency of the African culture, but also has had tremendous impact on the history of Africa. But these excruciating socio-cultural and economic onslaughts suffered by Africa have helped to reduce Africans as second-classed agents of either the European metropolitan powers or the Arab Islamic power structure. Africans therefore have become non-Africans in their struggle to sustain some form of existence.

The power of blackness must be taken seriously by any well meaning African; because the primacy of Africa and Africans in human development will be the basis upon which the New Africans would develop a new human vision that is capable of re-discovering the hitherto lost African glory. Africans as a whole must not let themselves be misled by the European or Arabian interpretations of blackness. (We should not allow people with calcified pineal gland to define what blackness is all about. Not only do they lack the attribute necessary to experience blackness but their cultural traditions evolved out of the ideological negation of Kemet.) This is because history has shown that the hidden power of blackness is the only means by which the erstwhile African virtue can be re-constructed and re-gained. Furthermore, the understanding of blackness is to apprehend the governing laws of the universe for the purpose of attaining equilibrium between the spiritual and material forces of life. Thus, the secret to the African liberation lays in the bosom of Mother Kemet, and not in Europe or Arabia. There is no compromise to this fact. For it is a fact that most Africans have been misled through the European or Arabian indoctrination to reject their rich African heritage. By rejecting their cultural heritage, many Africans have rejected their collective human conscience. It does not take an astute observer to see that the void created by this cultural dislocation is at the bottom of the powerlessness of the African people.

The rejection of the Kemetic cultural material on the part of the contemporary Africans has made Africans incapable of offering anything substantial to the contemporary world. The result has opened many Africans to all kinds of alienating ideas that make the exploitation of Africa inextricable. Similarly, since many of these alienating ideas did not evolve out of the cultural experiential universe of Africans, the best Africans could do with these alien ideas very well have been slavish imitations which contradict and negate the essence of their human potentials. But Africans must have their own human vision of the world to offer the modern world. It has to be the human vision that evolved from the cultural universe of the African people. It is time for somebody to stand up and say that enough is enough for the bandwagon abandonment of the Kemetic cultural heritage. The sooner we re-claim our heritage, the closer we will be in the quest of achieving eternal freedom/liberation for the future generations of Kemites yet unborn.

Insofar as White Magic as an anti-African phenomenon is the obsession with materialism that is predicted on the suppression of blackness, it is very important to at least review the meaning of the color black. For the European imposition of whiteness as the supreme color of life has literally and figuratively attempted to overturn the biological and other scientific meanings of blackness. The question is not whether this has been successfully achieved by the Europeans, but that its implications have indeed traumatized many African people to the extent that some have willingly committed physical and cultural suicide as a way of escape. The imposition of White Magic has also led to the seemingly lack of awareness by many Africans as to the true cultural heritage of Kemet. Conversely, the current potency of White Magic gives a clear indication of how the world has been distorted. But to understand blackness, is to unlock the door that leads to the power of the eternal Truth of the One Creator of the universe. The negative connotations to the symbolic and abstract definitions of blackness and its derivative nuances began clearly to be demonstrative with the temperament and attitudes of the ancient Greaco-Roman invaders into ancient Kemet.

On the other hand, the power inherent in blackness has been one of the critical elements that has sustained African people from the over two millennia of savage brutality. It has been proven scientifically that skin melanism is the unconscious mind that makes it possible for higher spiritual consciousness.[20] That is why, in the ancient time the supremacy of blackness was based on the spiritual transformation of the individual Chi. First of all, it is evident that blackness is not only the vibrational receptor of the cosmic energy, but also the spiritual source and inner vision of love, balance, complementarity, harmony etc. Suffice it here to say that, unlike white magic which is based on extreme materialism, black magic is predisposed on excessive spiritualism. Secondly, human skin blackness is not only the dominance of melanin in the skin, it is in fact a biological phenomenon that links individual descendants of Africa to the rich cultural heritage of "The Holy Land of Kemet". Thirdly, blackness is the mother of all colors. That is to say that everything comes out of blackness. The entire humanity is a product of blackness. Finally, human skin blackness is the highest state of skin melanism, whereas the pinkness of the skin is the lowest state of skin melanism. Thus, human skin blackness is the "archetype" of humanity.

Therefore, the Ekwensu people(unbelievers) of the divine supremacy of the eternal Truth of the One Creator of the universe must pay the price for their ignorance and treachery. We must defend the honor of Kemet without given any apology to anybody: The Kemetic cultural heritage must be rehabilitated, enriched, and propagated to the world. It is then a moral duty for this generation of Africans to embark on an Ekumeku Universal Revolution. And no matter the reason for not facing the facts, the Ekwensu people(doubters) must be reminded and rebuked for their treachery to the truth. For the rich Kemetic heritage is the foundation of the African pride and Ekumeku Universal Revolution; whilst the unity of all African people can only be achieved, when the descendants of Africa have understood the true nature of their oppression and of our Kemetic heritage.

V. THE STRUGGLE BETWEEN FAITH AND TRUTH!

Rooted in the womb of time, the struggle between the notion of Faith and the idea of Truth can be traced back to the beginning of human development. The notion of Faith must first be understood to have an emotional or sentimental content in the human life; and in its heuristic point of view, Faith is based on the sociology of myth. In contrast, the idea of Truth must first be understood to have its foundation on the sobriety of thought, organic and constitutionally based on the sociology of knowledge in its heuristic point of view, without any effort to fit into pre-established categories.

It can be observed in the notion of Faith that the mythological structure remains constant without any deviation, undertaken in order to formulate an outlook of the world devoid of reason, externalizing neurosis in an imitation of thought. Thus, in Faith, the structure is neurotic when it is compared with the organic structure of Truth. The formation and elaboration of the myths upon which organized Faith is based strike us as conflicted clusters formulated to have given rise from a particular time and in a particular environment. But on a closer examination or investigation, it becomes very clear that the myths were formulated to fit into pre-established categories, arising in part from the records of previous cultural forms.

The central idea is that the struggle between Faith and Truth is fundamental in determining the mindset of the individual, thought and behavior. Before the time of **Nzoputa Uwa,** the notion of Faith and the idea of Truth were projected to be inseparable, but were understood to be distinct of each other only by a certain class of people. However, the general masses were mostly made to believe that Faith and Truth were synonymous. No doubt, this confusion between the notion of Faith and the idea of Truth during the time of **Oge Nzuzu** was used to keep the masses of humanity ignorant of their essential nature, that is to say, being ignorant of EKUMEKU.

Underlying all the notions of Faith is a collection of myth that is contrary to the historical fact which is devised and elaborated to serve as a substitute for the Truth. The question may be asked: Why substitute for the Truth instead of asserting the Truth? The answer lies in the processes of the struggle between Faith and Truth. **Faith is not Truth but it is often times disguised to appear as the Truth. That the Truth alone is supreme and eternal is the reason why Faith is often disguised as the Truth in order to gain authority**.

Organized Faith founded on mythology and supported with codified opinion had made serious attempt during the time of **Oge Nzuzu** to subvert the Truth and make the particulars of Faith supreme by compulsion and arbitrary force. The function of conscience has been the obstacle that the particulars of Faith constantly fought against in the vain attempt to use Faith as a substitute for Truth. Until the emergence of the Ekwueme People of Truth into the center stage of world history, the people of Faith had subverted the Truth by dominating the human conscience with myths disguised as historical facts.

Once the notion of Faith is defined, it becomes obvious that it is not synonymous with the Truth. Yet the people of Faith tend to confuse and confound the notion of Faith with the idea of Truth. **Therefore, Faith is defined as a firm belief in something for which there is no proof. The key phrase here is "for which there is no proof". How can anybody have a firm belief in something for which there is no proof? It is only by Faith**. But organized Faith have gone a little further to provide artificial proofs (falsehoods) through their codified opinions by disguising their myths as historical facts, fitting them into pre-established categories.

And, still the struggle between Faith and Truth persists in an indefinite space until the First year of **Nzoputa Uwa**, when a new universal system of thought and behavior was born, coming from the standpoint of Truth. We can now declare unequivocally that the struggle between Faith and Truth can no longer be ignored for it is now a struggle between the Ekwensu people of Faith and the Ekwueme People of Truth. Because the Truth is supreme and eternal, it stands on its own, out of implicit and explicit knowledge, and does not impose itself as something that it is not. But on the contrary, Faith through its conditioning process imposes itself as something that it is not without any regards to the function of conscience.

If we are to delve into the ontology of being, we shall see that there is a little room in the state of being human, an epistemological instinct, that the founders of organized Faith had exploited unduly in order to create the momentum of their creeds. By ignoring the function of conscience, legendary stories and fabulous myths were developed based on the consensus of a codified opinion to erect structures of historicity without facts and were used to dominate human conscience through arbitrary authority. What made this possible can only be explained as either the workings of an undue fear or the self-interest of an organized group to profit by error and injustice in the order of things during the time of **Oge Nzuzu**.

Since the human spirit must occupy space, the realization of the highest potentiality of what it means to be fully human is impossible without the experience of the Truth. In the absence of the Truth, the human spirit can only occupy space as an object to be acted upon, being susceptible to manipulations and opinions of others, being more or less like a robot as affected by the condition of Faith.

In other words, the partiality of the people of Faith in their view of the world must be balanced with the impartiality of the Ekwueme People of Truth in order to stem the tide of Nzuzu with the moral thrust of Nzuko. Let it be known that the Ekwueme People of Truth are diametrically opposed in their worldview, in their world mission and in their epistemological thrust with the condition of belief of the Ekwensu people of Faith. Since the time of **Oge Nzuzu** has ended, the Ekwensu people of Faith ought to convert to EKUMEKU in order to become fully human. Now, it is no longer necessary to go to the sources of the particulars of Faith in the history of the past because we can now go to The Source to gain the ultimate experience. **The Source is the Truth and the Truth alone is supreme and eternal.**

Everyone now has the moral choice either to remain entangled with evil in the particulars of Faith or to overcome evil by doing good, striving with the Ekwueme People of Truth against the condition of Faith. It is no longer possible to use Faith as a substitute for the Truth because the Ekwueme People of Truth have emerged in the forefront of the struggle between Faith and Truth. We are no longer going to allow the Ekwensu people of Faith to disguise their condition of belief as a substitute for the Truth.

Without any doubt, there is only One Creator of the universe, but the people of Faith have created images of the human mind to substitute for the Truth. Yet the Truth of the One Creator of the universe exists in the wholeness of eternity as the manifest proof that we know as the Hidden One Creator of the universe, the only One worthy of worship. Wherefore, we must be aware and must not be forgetful that the time of **Nzoputa Uwa** has come for the redemption of all humanity from the life of living in agreement with Nsi. THE CREATOR IS ONE. THE ONE IS AMUN AND THE DIVINE PLAN IS EKUMEKU. There is no other Creator of the universe but AMUN in whom we trust. OTUA-KA-ODI!

CHAPTER SEVEN
NOTES

1A. Quoted in Yosef A.A. Ben-Jochannan, *Africa Mother of Western Civilization,* Baltimore, Maryland: Black Classic Press, 1988, p.29.

IB. Molefi Kete Asante, *Afrocentricity*, Trenton, New Jersey: Africa World Press, Inc., 1988, p. 104

1. John Henrik Clarke, *African World Revolution,* Trenton, New Jersey: Africa World Press, 1991, p. 45.
2. Bernard Makhosezwe Magubane, *The ties that Bind,* Trenton, New Jersey: Africa World Press, 1989, p. 106.
3. Molefi Kete Asante, *Afrocentricity,* Trenton, New Jersey: Africa World Press, Inc., 1088, p. 104.
4. The primary object that inspired the development of the theory White Magic is two-fold. One is that the word "racism" is not only narrow and limited in explaining the political, cultural, economic, psychological, intellectual, material and spiritual conditions of Africans over the past two thousand years, but also that the term "racism" with its ambiguities has tended to confuse and reduce the enormity of the African experience in the last two thousand years to a confining and vague term. Secondly, the introduction of the concept, White Magic, is intended to serve as another framework for understanding, conceptualizing and delineating of the African-European intercourse that began in 332 B.C.E., after Alexander of Macedonia conquered Kemet. As indicated, there is a strong causal relationship between the contemporary conditions of Africa and the historical facts on the alien disruptive forces in Africa, from the Greek occupation of Kemet to the Roman era, from the Arab Islamic conquests and penetrations to the European and Arab Slave Trades, from the formal colonization of Africa to the present mundane inadequacies of Africa and Africans. Therefore, the theory of White Magic is grounded on the understanding that any person, African and otherwise, who does not take into serious consideration the African–centered perspective is inherently anti-African.
5. Ngugi wa Thiong'o, *Decolonizing the Mind,:* London: James Currey/ Heinemann, 1991, p.3.
6. Quoted in Joseph E. Harris, *Africans And Their History,* New York: Penguin Books USA Inc., 1987, p.21.

7. Edward W. Blyden, *The African Society and Miss Mary H. Kingsley,* London, England: 1901, p.9. He was quoted as saying, in this journal, that "no race, as a race, could make progress except along its own line of development". *The African Society* is a pamphlet founded by Miss Mary H. Kingsley. She was a consistent admirer, friend, and colleague of Dr. Edward W. Blyden (see her book: *Travels in West Africa (*London, 1897). The description of her ideas by P. Olisanwuche Esedebe, Pan *Africanism: The Idea and Movement, 1776-1963* (Washington D.C.: Howards University Press, 1982, p. 58, gives a clear picture of her understanding of the African dilemma. Thus, he wrote about his impression of Miss Mary H. Kingsley: "To her the African was a different kind of being from the white men; his intelligence might even be found to be superior to theirs (whitemen). But it was a different kind of intelligence incapable of moving along European lines of thought.. Because of this difference it was wrong to regard the African society as childish groping towards the European model".
8. Molefi Kete Asante, *Afrocentricity,* Trenton, New Jersey: Africa World Press, Inc., 1988, p. 106.
9. Chancellor Williams, *The Destruction of Black Civilization,* Chicago, Illinois: Third Worlds Press, 1976, p. 59.
10. Quoted in Maulana Karenga *Selections From the Husia,* Los Angeles: The University of Sankore Press, 1984, p.41. I am following in the foorsteps of the African thinkers like Cheikh Anta Diop, Yosef A.A. Ben Jochannan, Jacob Carruthers, Maulana Karenga, Molefi Kete Asante, Ra Un Nefer Amen and others in calling for the realization of the spirit of our ancient spiritual tradition of MAAT without aping the past through the Almighty Spirit of EKUMEKU. It is relevant to note that this concept of MAAT also exists in traditional African communities but under different names. For instance in Igbo land, it is called OFO. It is the symbol of truth, righteousness, justice, harmony, reciprocity, etc., in the traditional Igbo culture.
11. Na'im Akbar, *Visions for Black Men,* Nashville, Tennessee: Winston-Derek Publishers Inc., 1991, p. 16-17.
12. Gerald Massey, *Gerald Massey's Lectures,* Brooklyn, New York: A&B Books Publishers 1992, p. 71.

13. *THE HOLY ANKHUWA: Abstracts, Vols. 1-3.* See also George G.M James, *Stolen legacy,* Newport News, Virginia: United Brothers Communications Systems.1989, p. 105.
14. IBid, *The Holy Ankhuwa: Abstracts, Vols. 1-3.*
15. It is important to emphasize that most African languages do not have a name for "religion", as the term has come to be used. In the Igbo Language, for example, the closest name for religion is *Igo Muo,* which can be rendered in English language as Spirituality.
16. Nnamdi Azikiwe, *Renascent Africa.* London: Frank Cass and Company Limited reprint 1968, p. 195.
17. Richard King, *African Origin of Biological Psychiatry,* Germantown, T.N Seymour-Smith, Inc., 1990, pp. 27-28.
18. Carol Barnes, *Melanin: The Chemical Key To Black Greatness,* Houston, Texas: C.B. Publishers, 1988, p. 19.
19. Richard King, *African Origin of Biological Psychiatry,* Germantown, TN: Seymour-Smith, Inc., 1990, pp. 13-43.
20. Dr Richard King a prominent psychiatrist has been one of the reputable scholars who has expounded on the properties of melanin and its importance/implications to human existence.

SELECT BIBLIOGRAPHY

Achebe, Chinua, *Things Fall Apart (*New York: Ballantine Books Edition, 1983).

Achebe, Chinua, *Hopes and Impediments* (New York: Double day, 1989).

Addai-Sebo, A., and Wong A. (eds.), *Our Story: A Handbook of African History and Contemporary Issues (*London: Hansib Printing Ltd., 1988).

Afrika, Llaila O., *African Holistic Health* (Silver Spring, Maryland: Adesugun, Johnson, and Koran Publishers, 1983).

Akbar Na'im, *Visions for Black Men, (*Nashville, Tennessee: Winston-Derek Publishers Inc., 1991).

Amen, Ra Un Nefer, *Metu Neter, Vol. 1* (Bronx, NY: Khamit Corp., Publishers, 1990).

Ampim, Manu, *Critical Issues in the Current Africentric Movement, Egypt As A Black Civilization: The Counter School* (Oakland, CA: 1992).

Appleman, Philip (ed), *Darwin: A Norton Critical Edition (*New York: W.W. Norton & Company Inc.1979).

Armah, Ayi Kwei, *Two Thousand Seasons* (London: Heinemann, 1973).

Asante, Molefi Kete, *Afrocentricity (*Trenton, New Jersey: Africa World Press, Inc., 1989).

Asante, Molefi Kete, *Kemet, Afrocentricity and Knowledge (*Trenton, New Jersey: Africa World Press, Inc., 1990).

Asante, Molefi Kete and Asante, Kariamu Welsh (eds.), *African Culture: The Rhythms of Unity* (Trenton, New Jersey: Africa World Press, Inc., 1990).

Ayittey, George B.N., *Indigenous African Institutions* (New York: Translational Publishers, Inc., 1991).

Azikiwe, Nnamdi, *Renascent Africa* (London: Frank Cass and Company Limited, Reprint 1968).

Azikiwe, Nnamdi, *My Odyssey: An Autobiography* (New York: Prawger Publishers, 1970).

Banton, Micheal, *West African City: A Study of Tribal Life in Freetown* (London: Oxford University Press, 1957).

Barnes, Carol, *Melanin: The Chemical Key To Black Greatness* (Houston, Texas: C.B. Publishers, 1988).

Beaud Michel, *A History of Capitalism 1500-1980* (New York: Monthly Review Press, 1983).

Ben-Jochannan, Yosef, *Africa: Mother of Western Civilization* (Baltimore, MD: Black Classic Press, 1988).

Ben- Jochannan, Yosef, *Black Man of the Nile and his Family* (Baltimore, MD: Black Classic Press, 1989).

Ben- Jochannan, Yosef, *Africa Origins of the Major "Western Religions"* (Baltimore, MD: Black Classic Press, 1991).

Bennett, Lerone, Jr., *The Challenge of Blackness* (Chicago: Johnson Publishing Company, Inc., 1972).

Bennett, Lerone, Jr., *Before the Mayflower:* A History of Black America (Chicago: Johnson Publishing Company, Inc., 6th Ed.1987).

Bernal, Martin, Black Athena, *Vol 1: The Fabrication of Ancient Greece 1785-1985* (New Brunswick: Rutgers University Press, 1987).

Bohannan, Paul, *Africa & Africans* (Garden City, New York: The Natural History Press, 1964).

Bradley, Micheal, *The Iceman Inheritance: Prehistoric Sources of Western Man's Racism, Sexism and Aggression (*New York, N.Y.: Kayode Publications Ltd., 1991).

Braithwaite, Edward R., *To Sir, With Love (*New Jersey: Prentice-Hall Inc., 1959).

Braithwaite, Edward, *The Development of Creole Society in Jamaica,* 1770-1820 (Oxford: Clarendon Press, 1971).

Budge, E.A. Wallis, *The Egyptian Book of the Dead* (New York: Dover Publications, Inc., 1967).

Budge, E.A. Wallis, *The Egyptian Magic* (New York: Dover Publications, Inc., 1071).

Budge, E.A. Wallis, *Osiris & The Egyptian Resurrection I* (New York: Dover Publications, Inc., 1973).

Cabral, Amilcar, *Return to the Source: Selected Speeches (*New York: Monthly Review Press, 1973).

Carruthers, Jacob H., *Essays in Ancient Egyptian Studies* (Los Angeles, California: University of Sankore Press, 1992).

Cary, Joyce, *Britain and West Africa* (London: Longman, Green and Co. Ltd., Revised Edition, 1947).

Chinweizu, *The West and the Rest of Us: White Predators, Black Slavers and the African Elite* (New York: Random House, 1975).

Chinweizu et al., *Towards The Decolonization of African Literature* (Washington, D.C.: Howard University Press, 1983).

Churchward, Albert, *Signs and Symbols of Primordial Man* (Westport, Connecticut: Greenwood Press, 1978*).*

Clarke, John Henrik (ed.), *Marcus Garvey and the Vision of Africa (*New York: Vintage Books, 1974).

Clarke, John Henrik, *Africans at the Crossroads: Notes for an African World Revolution* (Trenton New Jersey: Africa World Press, Inc., 1991).

Cleaver, Eldridge, *Soul on Ice (New* York: Bantam Doubleday Dell Publishing Group, Inc., 1992).

Cohen, Chapman, *Christianity, Slavery and Labour* (London: Pioneer Press, 1931).

Coleman, James S., *Nigeria: Background to Nationalism* (Berkeley and Los Angeles: University of California Press 1965).

Crooks, J.J., *A History of the Colony of Sierra Leone Western Africa* (London: Frank Cass, Reprint 1972).

Cruse, Harold, *The Crisis of the Negro Intellectual: A Historical Analysis of the Failure of Black Leadership* (New York: Quill, Williams Morrow and Company, Inc., 1984).

Cruse, Harold, *Plural but Equal: A Critical Study of Blacks and Minorities and America's Plural Society* (New York: Quill, Williams Morrow and Company, Inc., 1987).

Curtin, Philip D., *The Image of Africa* (Madison: The University of Wisconsin Press, 1964).

Dates, Jannete L. and Barlow, William, *Split Image: African Americans in the Mass Media (*Washington D.C.: Howard University Press, 1990).

Davidson, Basil, *The Africans Slave Trade* (Boston: Atlantic-Little Brown Co., 1961)

Davidson, Basil, *The Black Man's Burden* (New York: Times Books, 1992).

Davis, John A. (ed), *Africa: Seen by American Negro Scholars* (New York; Presence Africaine, 1958).

Dike, k. Onwuka, *Trade and Politics in the Niger Delta, 1830-1885* (London: Oxford University Press, 1956).

Diop, Cheikh Anta, *The African Origin of Civilization: Myth or Reality?* (Brooklyn, New York: Lawrence Hill Books, 1974).

Diop, Cheikh Anta, *Civilization or Barbarism: An Authentic Anthropology* (Brooklyn, New York: Lawrence Hill Books, 1991).

Diop, Cheikh Anta, *The Cultural Unity of Black Africa* (London: Karnak House, 1989).

Dobzhansky, Theodosius, *Genetic Diversity and Human Equality* (New York: Basic Books Inc., 1973).

Drake, St. Clair, *Black Folk Here and There Vols I & II* (Los Angeles: Center for Afro-Americans Studies University of California, 1987, 1990).

Du Bois, W.E.B., *Black Folk: Then and Now* (New York: H. Holt, 1939).

Du Bois, W.E.B., *The World and Africa* (New York: International Publishers Co. Inc., 1965).

Dudley, Dean, *History of the First Council of Nice* (Chesapeake, Virginia: ECA Associates, 1990).

Dunston, Alfred G. Jr., *The Black in the Old Testament and its World* (Trenton, New Jersey: Africa World Press, Inc., 1992).

Easwaran, Eknath, *Ganhi the Man* (Berkeley, California: The Blue Mountain Center of Meditation Inc., 1972).

Egudu, N. Romanus, *African Poetry of the Living Dead: Igbo Masquerade Poetry* (Lewiston, New York: The Edwin Mellen Press, 1992).

Ekwe-Ekwe, Herbert, *The Biafran War: Nigeria and the Aftermath* (Lewiston, New York: The Edwin Mellen Press, 1990).

Epps, Archie, *Malcolm X Speeches at Harvard* (New York); Paragon House, 1991).

Esedebe, P. Olisanwuche, *Pan-Africanism: The Idea and Movement 1776-1963* (Washington D.C.: Howard University Press, 1982).

Fairchild, Hoxie Neale, *The Noble Savage* (New York: Russell & Russell, 1961).

Fanon, Frantz, *Black Skin, White Masks (*New York: Grove Press Inc., 1967).

Ferkiss, Victor C., *Africa's Search For Identity* (New York: George Braziller Inc., 1966).

Finley, M.I., *Ancient Slavery and Modern Ideology* (New York: The Viking Press, 1980).

Frankfort, Henri, *Ancient Egyptian Religion* (New York: Harper & Row, Publishers, 1948).

Franffort, Henri et al., *The Intellectual Adventure of Ancient Man* (Chicago: The University of Chicago Press, 1977).

Frazier E. Franklin, *Black Bourgeoisie* (New York: Collier Books, 1962).

Freud, Sigmund, *Moses and Monotheism* (New York: Vintage Books, 1967).

Frucht, Richard (ed.), *Black Society in the New World* (New York: Random House, Inc., 1971).

Fyfe, Christopher, *Africanus Horton: West African Scientist and Patriot, 1835-1883* (New York: Oxford University Press, 1972)

Gate, Henry Louis, Jr. (ed.), *The Classic Slave Narratives* (New York: Penguin Books USA Inc., 1987).

Gilbert, Felix, *The End of the European Era, 1890 to the present* (New York: W.W. Norton & Company, Inc., Third Edition 1970).

Griaule, Marcel, *Conversations with Ogotemmeli: An Introduction to Dogon Religious Ideas* (London: Oxford University Press, 1965).

Harris J.R. (ed.), *The Legacy of EGYPT* (Oxford: Clarendon Press, Second Edition 1971).

Harris Joseph E., *Africans and their History* (New York: Penguin Books USA Inc. (Mentor), Revised Edition, 1987).

Hayford J.E. Casely, *Ethiopia unbound* (London: Frank Cass and Company Limited, Second Edition, 1969).

Herskovits Melville J., *The Myth of the Negro Past* (Boston: Beacon Press, Reprint 1990).

Horton, J. Africanus B., *West African Countries and Peoples, British and Native* (Nendeln, Switzerland: Kraus Reprint, 1970).

Jackson, John G. *Man, God, and Civilization* (Secaucus, New Jersey: Citadel Press, 1972).

Jahn Jaheinz, *Muntu: African Culture and the Western World* (New York: Grove Press, Inc., 1990).

James, George G.M., *Stolen Legacy* (Newport News, Virginia: United Brothers Communications System, 1989).

July Robert W., *The Origins of Modern African Thought* (New York: Frederick A. Praeger, Publishers, 1967).

Kamalu, Chukwunyere, *Foundations of African Thought* (London: Karnak House, 1990).

Karenga, Maulana, *Selections From the Husia: Sacred Wisdom of Ancient Egypt* (Los Angeles:The University of Sankore Press, 1986).

Karenga, Maulana, *The Book of Coming Forth By Day* (Los Angeles California: The University of Sankore Press, 1990).

Katz, Williams L., *Breaking The Chains* (New York: Atheneum, 1990).

Kilson, Martin L. and Rotberg, Robert I. (eds), *The African Diaspora: Interpretive Essays* (Cambridge, Massachusetts: Harvard University Press, 1976).

King, Richard, *African Origin of Biological Psychiatry* (Germantown, T.N: Seymour-Smith., 1990).

Kovel, Joel, *White Racism: A psychohistory* (New York: Vintage Books, 1971).

Lamb, David, *The Africans* (New York: Vintage Books, 1987).

Levi-Strauss, Claude, *The Savage Mind* (Chicago: University of Chicago Press, 1966*)*.

Lewis Rupert, *Marcus Garvey: Anti-colonial champion* (Trenton, New Jersey: Africa World Press, 1988).

Lichtheim, Mirian, *Ancient Egyptian Literature Vol I: The Old and Middle Kingdoms* (Berkeley: University of California Press, 1975).

Lincoln, C. Eric *Race, Religion and the Continuous American Dilemma* (New York: Hill and Wang, 1984).

Lynch, Hollis R., Edward Wilmot Blyden: *Pan-Negro Patriot, 1832-1912* (London: Oxford University Press, 1970).

Madhubuti, Haki R., Black Men: *Obsolete, Single, Dangerous? (Chicago: Third World Press, 1990)*

Maduno, Chukwudi Okeke, *Nnamdi Azikiwe: The Vision of the New Africa*, (Oba: Ekumeku Communication Systems, 2018).

Maduno, Chukwudi Okeke, *Ohacracy: The Undercurrent of Africa-Centered Nationalism,* (Atlanta: Ekumeku Communication Systems, 1995).

Magubane, Bernard Makhosezwe, *The Ties That Blind: African American Consciousness of Africa* (Trenton, New Jersey: Africa World Press, Inc., 1989.

Marable, Manning, *How Capitalism Underdeveloped Black America* (Boston, Ma: South End Press, Inc., 1983).

Martin, Tony, *Race First: The Ideological and Organizational Struggles of Marcus Garvey and the Universal Negro Improvement Association* (Dover, Massachusetts: The Majority Press, 1989).

Marx Karl, *Capital: A Critique of Political Economy Vols II & III* (Moscow: Progress Publishers, 1971).

Massey, Gerald, *The Historical Jesus and the Mythical Christ* (Edmond, WA: Sure Fire Press, 1990).

Massey, Gerald, *Gnostic And Historic Christianity* (Edmond, WA: Sure Fire Press, 1985).

Massey Gerald, *Gerald Massey's Lectures* (New York: A & B Books Publishers, reprint 1992)

Massey Gerald, *Ancient Egypt Light of the Worlds, Vols. I &II (*Baltimore: Black Classic Press, reprint1992*)*.

Mazrui, Ali A. *The Africans: A Triple Heritage (*London: BBC Publications, 1986).

Mazrui, Ali A. *The African Condition (London: Cambridge University Press, 1980)*.

Mbiti, John S., *Concepts of God in Africa* (New York: Praeger Publishers, 1970).

Mbiti, John S., *African Religions and Philosophy* (Oxford: Heinemann International, Second Edition 1990).

McCarthy, Micheal, *Dark Continent: Africa as seen by Americans* (Westport, Connecticut: Greenwood Press, 1983).

Mendelsohn, Jack, *God, Allah and Ju Ju: Religion in Africa* Today (New York: Thomas Nelson & Sons, 1962).

Moody, Anne, *Coming of Age in Mississippi* (New York: Dell Publishing Co. Inc. 1968).

Mudimbe, V.Y., *The Invention of Africa: Gnosis, Philosophy, and the order of knowledge* (Indianapolis, Indiana: Indiana University Press, 1988).

Murray, Margeret A., *The Splendor that was EGYPT* (New York: Frederick a. Praeger Publishers, 1964).

Newby, I.A., *Jim Crow's Defence: Anti-Negro Thought in America 1900-1930* (Westport, Connecticut: Greenwood Press, Publishers, 1980).

Ngugi, wa Thiong'o, *Decolonism the Mind: The Politics of Language in African Literature* (London: James Currey/ Heinemann, 1991)

Ngugi, wa Thiong'o, *Devil On the Cross* (London: Heinemann Educational Books Ltd, 1982).

Njaka, Elechukwu Nnadibuagha, *Igbo Political Culture* (Evanston: Northwestern University Press, 1974).

Nkrumah, Kwame, *Africa Must Unite* (London: Panaf Books Ltd., 1980).

Nobles, Wade W., *African Psychology: Toward its Reclamation, Reascension & Revitalization* (Oakland California: A Black Family Institute Publication, 1986).

Obenga, Theophile, *Ancient Egypt & Black Africa* (London: Karnak House, 1992).

Ojo-Ade, Femi, *On Black Culture* (Ile-Ife, Nigeria: Obafemi Awolowo University Press Ltd., 1989).

Panikkar, K. Madhu, *The Serpent and the Crescent: A History of the Negro Empires of Western Africa* (Bombay, India: Asia Publishing House, 1963).

Patai, Raphael, *The Arab Mind* (New York: Charles Scribner's Sona, 1973).

P'Bitek, Okot, *African Religions in European Scholarship* (Chesapeake, Virginia: ECA Associates, 1990).

Richards, Dona Marimba, *Let the Circle Be Unbroken: The Implications of African Spirituality in the Diaspora* (Trenton, New Jersey: The Red Sea Press, 1989).

Rodney, Walter, *How Europe Underdeveloped Africa* (Washington D.C.: Howard University Press, Revised Edition 1982).

Rodney Walter, *The Grounding with My Brothers* (Chicago: Research Associates School Times, 1990).

Rotberg, Robert I. (ed.), *Africa and its Explorers* (Cambridge, Massachusetts: Harvard University Press, 1973).

Silberman, Charles E. *Crisis in Black and White* (New York: Vintage Books, 1964).

Thorpe, Earl E., *The Central Theme of Black History* (Durham, North Carolina: Seeman Printery, 1969.

Van Sertima, Ivan (ed.), *Egypt Revisited* (New Brunswick: Journal of African civilizations, Transactions, Publishers 1991).

Van Sertima, Ivan (ed.), *The Golden of the Moor* (New Brunswick: Journal of African Civilizations, Transactions Publishers 1992).

Volney, C.F., *The Ruins, or Meditation on the Revolutions of Empires: and the Law of Nature* (Baltimore, MD: Black Classic Press, Reprint 1991).

Weisbord Robert G., *Ebony Kinship: Africa. Africans, and the Afro-American* (Wesport Connecticut: Greenwood Press, Inc., 1974).

Welsing, Frances Cress, *The Isis Papers: The Keys To the Colors* (Chicago: Third World Press, 1991).

Williams, Chancellor, *The Destruction of Black Civilization: Great Issues of a Race from 4500B.C. TO 2000A.D.* (Chicago, Illinois: Third World Press, Revised Edition, 1976).

Williams, Eric, *Capitalism and Slavery* (London: Andre' Deutsh Limited, 1964).

Windsor, Rudolph R., *From Babylon to Timbuktu: A History of the Ancient Black Races Including The Black Hebrews* (Smithtown, New York; Exposition Press, Inc., Fifth Edition 1981).

Woodson, Carter G., *The Mis-Education of the Negro* (Hampton, Virginia: U.B &U.S Communications Systems, INC., 1992).

Wright, Richard, *Black Power* (Westport, Connecticut: Greenwood Press Publishers, 1976)

.Wulf, Sachs, *Black Anger* (Westport, Connecticut: Greenwood Press, 1968).

APPENDIX

My brothers and sisters in EKUMEKU, there are some Black groups who due to the ignorance of history are glorifying the Moors beyond proportion. Let it be known that the enslavement of Africans, the so-called slave trade, the Afrikan Maafa could not have occurred without the disruptive impact of the defeated Moors who were fleeing from Spain. After their defeat and surrender in Spain, the Moors came into West Africa and began the war that would later be called the "slave trade" or the **Afrikan Maafa**. According to **"WHITE MAGIC,"** by Chukwudi Okeke Maduno, "The final defeat of the Moors in their last stronghold in Granada, during the late fifteenth century (C.E.) was the dawn of a different epoch of human existence. It ended the era of Muslim pre-eminence and ushered in what many would call the Age of mindless euphemism".

There is no good reason for the contemporary glorification of the Moors, by some Black groups, who by all historical evidence were the people who made it possible inside Africa for the so-called slave trade after they have been defeated in Spain. We must never identify with the so-called Moors whose conception of world history was distorted, bearing the imprint of calamity and negative conception of blackness. We are the Kemites and our Kemetic World Identity speaks louder than any other voice.

There are now people making noise all over the place claiming that they are Moors without knowing that our ancestors were enslaved because the Moors once defeated in Spain infiltrated Timbuktu, destroyed Sankore University, kidnapped Ahmed Baba, the renown scholar, among others, destroyed or carried away precious manuscripts of great learning, and began a war of tremendous proportion in West Africa. The Moors lost out in Spain, even though they were blacks, because they did not understand the ideology behind the skin color contraption of the religions of ISFET.

Those who do not know their history are a people doomed for they cannot understand the reasons why things are the way they are. They are the **Akwunakwunas** who are very ignorant of EKUMEKU and have refused to accept the actual facts of history. When the Moors were defeated in Spain, if they had come to West Africa and become a positive force, the world would have been a different reality today. **But instead, the Moors came to West Africa to loot and destroy and thereby started the war that would later be known in history as the slave trade. The history of the Moors in West Africa ought to be exposed so that those who are now claiming to be Moors will be aware of the historical facts.**

We are not Moors; instead, we are the Kemites and our Kemetic World Identity speaks for itself. **Let it be known that we the Kemites are the Black people of the world and we must never be confused with the so-called Moors. We the Kemites are the devoted followers of the Divine Plan of AMUN in whom we trust who follow in the footsteps of the Chosen One of Nzoputa Uwa.** No doubt, the marginal groups who call themselves, Moors, should be taught the correct version of the African history. If they have the mental discipline, they should listen to the great voice of our historian, **John Henrik Clarke.** Otherwise, history may repeat itself again; but this time in another context.

What we know as the slave trade would have been an impossibility without the Moors who were expelled from Spain and coming into West Africa infiltrated and destroyed the process of development making West Africa ungovernable and vulnerable to the dictates of outsiders. Defeated and forced by the millions to seek refuge in Africa, the Moors went into rampage in West Africa, creating anarchy and disorder which inevitably destroyed the patterns of development among the people. **We do not deny that the Moors achieved greatness in Europe, especially in Spain. But we must be aware that their fall impacted negatively on West Africa, which gave birth to the so-called slave trade**. What the Moors did in West Africa would have been justifiable if they had done it in Spain or even in other European nations. But to the contrary, they had to come to West Africa to revenge their defeat on fellow Blacks. There is no logic to what the Moors did in West Africa and the Kemites would never honor them as true ancestors. All the sufferings of our people during the Middle Passage and in the Americas would seem to have been in vain if we are apt to forget the past without learning any lesson from it.

If the New Moors have surrendered like the Old Moors, let them know that we are very proud to be black. But we must not allow their surrender to affect us this time. We have learnt our lesson from the past. We know that they have surrendered that is why they say that they are not black. So, we are Black because we will never surrender to become anything other than being positively Black. Let them be white for that is what they have surrendered to. But we will never treat them as our equals. We shall be their teachers and we shall teach them the Truth of Positive Blackness.

Since they say that they are not black, we must disregard them. But if they insist on being anti-Black, there will be no mercy this time. The Old Moors surrendered in Spain, we had pity on them. Now the New Moors have surrendered to the skin color contraption of the religions of ISFET, we have now learnt our lesson from the past. We shall have no mercy for anti-Black *Akwunakwunas.* **They hate being black and that is their deepest problem. But we are profoundly proud to be black. Therefore, we are not the same with them. They cannot be one of us, for they hate themselves for being black and we love ourselves for being Black. You see what I mean?** They are full of double talk and contradictions. Pay no attention to what they say for they want to get away from being black. We Black people have a Motherland. They do not have a motherland for they have rejected the mother that gave birth to them.

Listen to what they say. One day, they are this. Another day, they are that. Today, they are Asiatic; Tomorrow, they will be Native American; next Tomorrow, you may hear them say that they are African but not black. They are indeed confused. They want to eat their cake and still have it. Is it possible? You don't want to be black. Yet you want to claim the **"Introduction To Black Studies",** by Maulana Karenga as your own. Why not write your own book since you hate to be black? Why not write a book called **"Introduction to Akwunakwuna Studies"?** And, we shall read it as a comic book from another planet. A word is enough for the wise.

The Kemites know who is who: Those who are consistent and those who are inconsistent. Those who will betray their mother or brother or father for personal gain. By declaring that they are not black, the New Moors have become homeless and landless on this planet. That is why, they want to go to another planet with a space ship or craft. But they cannot even manufacture a bicycle. It is hilarious like a .... Truth alone is supreme and eternal and EKUMEKU is the whole Truth of everlasting life.

OBAMA is a Black man, a proud African American man. Yet he became the president without denying who he is. And then, you see people who cannot even be in a position to polish Obama's shoe saying that they hate being black. **TUFIAKWA!**

Listen to my words, if you hate being black get away from my sight. I don't want to have anything to do with you. Anyone who hates his mother or father is not worth my precious time. Stay away from me and do not come close to me. I don't want to hear anything from you. I love being Black because I love my mother and father. **I am a Kemite for life!** OTUA-KA-ODI!

OTHER BOOKS BY THE AUTHOR

OHACRACY: The Undercurrent of Africa-centered Nationalism

NNAMDI AZIKIWE: The Vision of the New Africa

THE HOLY ANKHUWA: Abstracts, Vol. 1

NZOPUTA UWA: The Holy Ankhuwa Abstracts, Vol. 2

NKUZIMATISM: The Holy Ankhuwa Abstracts ,Vol. 3

Free your mind from the bondage and slavery of the world of Ekwensu. Seek ye the Truth: Contact and Like our Facebook Page: The EKUMEKU Universal Foundation or nzoputa.uwa@gmail.com.

www.ingramcontent.com/pod-product-compliance
Lightning Source LLC
Chambersburg PA
CBHW072112270326
41931CB00010B/1528

* 9 7 8 0 9 6 4 4 5 9 6 0 1 *